I DIE IN A GOOD CAUSE

THOMAS ASHE: A BIOGRAPHY

SEÁN Ó LÚING

MERCIER PRESS

IRISH PUBLISHER – IRISH STORY

Do Ghearóid agus Róisín

MERCIER PRESS

Cork

www.mercierpress.ie

© The estate of Seán Ó Lúing, 2017
© Introduction: J. J. Lee

ISBN: 978 1 78117 505 7

An Roinn Ealaíon, Oidhreachta,
Gnóthaí Réigiúnacha, Tuaithe agus Gaeltachta

Department of Arts, Heritage,
Regional, Rural and Gaeltacht Affairs

Published with the assistance of the Department of Arts, Heritage,
Regional, Rural and Gaeltacht Affairs

10 9 8 7 6 5 4 3 2 1

A CIP record for this title is available from the British Library

CONTENTS

FOREWORD

Our father, Seán Ó Lúing, was born in Ballyferriter, West Kerry, on 16 May 1917, only a few months before the death of Thomas Ashe on 25 September of that year. From an early age, he was aware of the legacy of Thomas Ashe, having first heard of him from his grandfather, Daniel Manning, who travelled to Dublin to attend his funeral, and whose son Patrick was in Jacob's Factory during the Easter Rising.

In Seán's poem 'I gCuimhne Thomáis Ághas' in *Bánta Dhún Urlann*, published in 1975, he wrote:

> Fadó riamh, nuair bhí Clochar agus Riasc ar an imeall ba shia dem aithne,
> Chuala tuairisc Thomáis Ághas á lua ar bhéal mo sheanathar …

> Long ago, when Clochar and Riasc were the farthest border of my acquaintance,
> I heard the story of Thomas Ashe from my grandfather's lips …

After attending St Brendan's Seminary in Killarney from 1929 to 1934, Seán studied Latin, modern Irish and archaeology at University College Dublin, graduating in 1938. He taught for some years in Portarlington. Later, while teaching history in the University Tutorial Institute (Darragh's College) in Dublin, he developed his interest in modern Irish history. He joined the Translation Section of the Houses of the Oireachtas in 1943. He researched regularly in the National Library, happily adjacent, and published his first book, *Art Ó Gríofa*, a biography of Arthur Griffith, in 1953.

His first published essay on Thomas Ashe, 'Tomás Ághas', appeared in the Irish-language periodical *Feasta* in September 1961. His lecture of 25 September 1967, at an event commemorating the fiftieth anniversary of Ashe's death, was published as 'Léacht Chuimhneacháin: Tomás Ághas' in the November 1967 issue of *Feasta*. An article, 'Thomas Ashe', appeared in the *Capuchin Annual* (1967), which noted that 'he is at present working on a full length life of Thomas Ashe'.

I Die in a Good Cause was published in May 1970. In the Acknowledgement, he wrote that 'my gratitude goes first and foremost to his sister Nora Ashe. Without her help it is the plain truth to say that this book could not have been written.' Sadly, Nora Ashe died on 20 January 1970, before the book was published. The author recalled, however (in an interview in 1994 with his former colleague Áine Ní Chonghaile), 'do léigh sí é mar chlóscríbhinn agus bhí sí sásta leis'. ['She read the typescript and she was happy with it.']

He had known Nora Ashe for a long time, and in a short memoir (in the National Library collections: MS 42,176/1) he recalled many visits to 156 Rathgar Road, where she spent her years of retirement with her companion Mrs Agnes Fitzgibbon of Sligo:

I had known Nóra Ághas since I was a student at St. Brendan's Seminary, Killarney, abt. 1932, having been introduced to her by my uncle Father James Manning (St Augustine's Parish Des Moines) who was a great friend of hers. I afterwards used to visit her at her home in Clontarf … but visited her most frequently when she retired to Rathgar Road.

She was one of the best conversationalists I ever met, and her range of knowledge was wide and varied. She was an excellent teacher and when in Rathgar Road would give lessons in Irish, gratis, so eager was she to give instruction in the language, which was the primary love of her life … She knew practically everyone who had been in the national movement, and could be as sharp in her criticism as she could be sincere in her praise. She was proud of the Ashe family tradition and would enumerate the parts of Ireland where they had settled, from Antrim to Cork …

She was at home in any company, a good mixer and talker, with great human sympathy.

Her brother Gregory was also of great help – 'Agus ar ndóigh, fuaireas an-chuid eolais ó dheartháir Thomáis Ághas, Griaire,' he told Áine Ní Chonghaile. ['And of course, I got a lot of information from Thomas Ashe's brother Gregory.']

I Die in a Good Cause is dedicated 'Do Ghearóid agus Róisín'. In 1970, the year of its first publication, we were entering our teens. On several occasions we accompanied our parents to meet Miss Ashe and Mrs Fitzgibbon in the high-ceilinged drawing room in Rathgar. We recall our father's frequent visits to the National Library, and research notes, in his strong clear handwriting, covering the dining-room table at home.

He was a loyal and conscientious correspondent, and for over fifty years wrote regularly to his brother Paddy in Kerry and to his friends in England, the O'Briens, with whom he had stayed in Portarlington. He also corresponded regularly with a number of greatly valued friends in Germany, including his fellow translators Heinrich Sasse and John Marin. As he said, 'Ní thogann sé ach cúig nóiméad cárta poist a scríobh.' ['It takes only five minutes to write a postcard.']

He enjoyed researching and writing, and though happy in company was equally happy to find companionship in books. One evening, when we were both occupied, we asked him if he minded being on his own. 'Ach ní bheidh mé im'aonair,' he replied. 'Nach féidir liom an tráthnóna a chaitheamh i gcuideachta Catullus, nó Hóiméir?' [But I won't be on my own – can't I spend the evening in the company of Catullus, or Homer?]

Dad met his future wife, Marie Sloane from Wexford, when they were working in Leinster House. They married in 1949. Theirs was an exceptionally happy marriage. Our mother quietly supported our father in every way, and her death in 1988 was a source of great sorrow to him. Eventually, he returned to his studies and writing, and these, along with his many interests, including sport, music, film, and travel, sustained him, as did the support of his family and friends.

It is strange to think that our father was born one hundred years ago, for he never seemed old to us. He was a loving husband and father, and a courteous, considerate and gentle man. He had a profound religious faith, and enjoyed life. We often recall his advice to us – 'Bainigí taitneamh as an saol!'

Gearóid Ó Lúing
Róisín Ní Lúing

INTRODUCTION

The tragic and avoidable death of Tom Ashe at the age of thirty-two on 25 September 1917, from botched forced feeding while on hunger strike in Mountjoy prison, not only removed him from the centre stage of Irish life, but in large measure from the national historical memory, at least outside his native Kerry and the area around Lusk in North Dublin where he was a school principal before the 1916 Rising. It is hard not to believe that had he survived his name would now feature far more prominently, given the central role he would likely have played in the War of Independence, perhaps indeed in the Civil War (although who can tell if there would have been one – or at least the one that occurred – had he lived) and possibly even in government. Yet, if cut off, like Michael Collins, far before his potential prime, Ashe remains one of the most remarkable personalities in Irish history, as is abundantly clear from Seán Ó Lúing's biography of nearly fifty years ago, now happily reissued.

Ashe and Collins had much in common, however different the routes by which they reached Easter Week. They got on well, and it was their co-operation – even with Ashe in an English jail – that largely ensured Sinn Féin ran a candidate in the important 1917 Longford by-election, despite the hesitation of the more cautious de Valera.

It is nevertheless quite possible that Ashe would have been a member of de Valera's Sinn Féin cabinet, perhaps indeed of the Treaty negotiating team, for in some ways, and despite his regard for Collins, he was temperamentally and culturally closer to de Valera.

Lacking something of Collins's eventual elasticity, he might then have been a crucial vote against acceptance of the Treaty terms as they stood, and we would know whether Lloyd George was bluffing or not in his threat of immediate and terrible war had the Treaty delegation refused to sign unanimously on the dotted line.

This, of course, is all speculative. Who can know how he might have revised his own views during the War of Independence? He was president of the Supreme Council of the IRB at the time of his death; how may his attitude have changed – or not – during the subsequent struggle? That one can speculate endlessly about the myriad 'what-ifs' itself testifies to his stature. His vision of an independent Ireland, as far as one can tell, was generally tolerant and inclusive towards the unionist population, and smacked remarkably little of localism by the standards of the time, perhaps even of today. He was a native Irish speaker, with a wide range of cultural interests, and it would have been intriguing to see what his attitude towards the blinkered policies for reviving the language as a vernacular might have been.

However problematical it must always be to speculate on the possible futures of lives prematurely terminated, it can certainly be surmised that, like some of the 1916 leaders, he had much more to offer at the time of his tragic death than he had already achieved. What can be said without exaggeration is that his personality remains among the most attractive, and his record among the most impressive, of any fighter for an independent Irish state and a distinctive Irish culture. This timely reprint of an important work on so distinctive a figure deserves to be warmly welcomed, both for itself and for the stimulus it promises to provide for further meditation on issues of enduring importance.

Professor J. J. Lee

1

ANCESTRY

It is Oireachtas week in Galway, 1913. The capital of Connaught is gay and full of colour in the July sunshine. The narrow streets are busy with movement, for the city is thronged with visitors. Most of them have come for the annual Ard-Fheis of the Gaelic League, at which there would be a stocktaking of past progress and a programme laid down for future action. Youth predominates. There is animated conversation, joyous greeting, keen rivalry. In the distance is heard the rousing skirl of the war pipes, well suited to this historic environment. The music comes nearer, echoing through old byways and arches of the Spanish-Norman-Gaelic city. The kilted pipers emerge from Shop Street, swing past Lynch's Castle, march up Williamsgate Street. The crowds part before them as they come into full view, their standard floating in the breeze, a great black raven on a cream-coloured background. There is a martial rhythm in their movement as they advance towards Eyre Square to the throbbing beat of the drums and the pulsating rhythm of the pipes. Amongst that fine body of kilted players their leader is conspicuous. Striding at their head, six feet in height, well formed, well knit, with blue eyes and classical features topped by a shock of auburn wavy hair, he looks every inch a patrician. The onlookers murmur appraisingly. His name is caught. Thomas Ashe, leader of the Black Raven Pipe Band of Lusk, County Dublin. Yes, he is prominent in the Gaelic League.

The music pauses. There is a sharp word of command, the players stand easy, dismiss and mix with the crowds. Friends press around Thomas Ashe. Some are gay, blithe, exuberant; some grave and serious; they are all young. Seán Mac Diarmada, The O'Rahilly, Seán T. O'Kelly, Éamonn Ceannt, Piaras Béaslaí, George Nichols and many others are there. What time holds for them nobody knows. They are met only for the business in hand.

Later, at a public meeting in Eyre Square, Thomas Ashe addresses the crowd. His fine voice carries full across the square, his earnest manner wins approval and applause. Calm and dignified (his description by his colleague Éamonn Ceannt), Thomas Ashe means what he says.

Four years go by. The scene changes to Dublin, on a mild Sunday afternoon in September 1917. A hearse bears the body of Thomas Ashe through the central streets of the city to Glasnevin cemetery. Dense crowds pack the route. There is deep silence as the cortege passes. The coffin is draped in the colours of the Irish Republic. All Ireland is represented. Church and civic dignitaries follow in procession. Trade, craft and cultural organisations, Volunteers and Citizen Army men, men from forgotten Dublin streets and from remote country parishes accompany their dead comrade to the graveside. A group of schoolchildren carries a banner with the words: 'In Memory of Thomas Ashe who died for Ireland'. Men in khaki look on, wondering, puzzled. Everything is orderly, peaceful, disciplined. The quiet, the silence, the vast throngs, the loving homage are impressive and strangely disturbing. This is a nation in obvious revolt.

Dead at thirty-two, Thomas Ashe was laid to rest in Glasnevin.

His end was unexpected, poignant, tragic. It stirred Ireland more profoundly, according to observers of long experience, than the executions of the previous year or than any event since the hanging of Allen, Larkin and O'Brien at Salford jail in 1867.

Who was this man whose death so deeply moved and influenced Ireland? Who were his forebears and what were his origins? What were the influences that moulded him into the resolute, stubborn, uncompromising man whose spirit refused to bend or break? What did he believe and do that brought him to his death?

Thomas Ashe was born in the townland and parish of Kinard, near Dingle, in the Corkaguiney peninsula. This region, at the southwest extremity of Ireland, reaches out into the Atlantic Ocean, a mountainous, cliff-bound, rugged rib of country, forty miles from Tralee in the east to Dunquin in the west. Towards the east is the lofty fortress of Caherconree, further west the dominating pile of Mount Brandon, the one dedicated to pagan tradition, the other hallowed by the Christian, symbolic of the diverse wealth of legend, romance and history comprised within the borders of this half-isolated promontory. On the flank of Slieve Mish was buried Scotia, the Milesian queen, so legend says, after some great battle of prehistory. At its western tip, challenging the fury of the Atlantic, is Sybil Head, named after Sybil Lynch, betrothed lady of Pierce Ferriter, poet and chieftain. Here she was drowned by the rising tide while battle was joined for her cause and a minor Troy was enacted on Ballysibele Strand. Her gallant suitor fought Cromwell and was hanged by the Puritan soldiery at Killarney, but his stately poems are recited in his native territory to this day.

Five miles off Sybil Head are the Ferriter Islands, now the

Blaskets, once occupied by people, inhabited today only by rabbits and sea fowl. From the foot of Brandon Mountain in the sixth century Saint Brendan set out in a frail bark and explored new lands across the Atlantic in a journey that has ever since puzzled and fascinated. To confirm legend, the peninsula is richly endowed with antiquarian remains, Christian and pre-Christian. There are cairns, souterrains, megaliths, dolmens, cahers, ancient oratories, cells, termons, castles and churches by the dozen. The pages of the excellent *Journal of the Royal Society of Antiquaries of Ireland* bear witness to the wealth of interest which archaeologists have found in this remote segment of Ireland. The savage legions of the Tudor monarchs left their mark on this territory so that not the lowing of a cow nor the voice of a human being was heard throughout its extent to the farthest verge of Dunquin, a fate it shared with the rest of Munster. Within the memory of living people the majority of its inhabitants spoke or understood Irish, and the Gaelic ethos retained its vigorous and expressive being. How expressive and vigorous it could be we can infer from the autobiography of Tomás Ó Crohan, who recorded the life of his beloved Blaskets in prose powerful and gaunt as the crags that surrounded his home.

The land has given its characteristics to the people who live on it. They are a rugged, intelligent, sturdy and versatile race. Between the mountains are sheltered valleys where the land is surprisingly good and fertile. There is much bog, which gives fuel for a pleasant fire. There are mountain lakes, of unfathomable depth, teeming with silver trout. Along the coast, where the cliffs do not intervene, tracts of fertile land slope towards the sea. The people till the land, save the peat from the bogs and fish the sea in craft that make life a gamble. The Atlantic has claimed an impressive toll. There was much congestion and much, far too much, emigration. Corkaguiney is a pattern of small fields and villages, clusters of houses nestling in valleys or perched on hillsides, cruachs and lofty passes, lonely cottages sheltering coyly in remote coums. In Thomas Ashe's boyhood the people lived on holdings of ten or twenty to fifty acres of mixed-quality soil, part hill, part bog, part arable. Possessions were modest, ranging from one to a dozen cows, some sheep, a goat or two to ward off animal disease, a pony, mule, horse or donkey and a collie dog. Twenty cows was affluence. Every cow had a name, so had every field. Not everyone had a plough. Mowing machines, by McCormack of Chicago as like as not, were owned by the select few. There was neighbourly cooperation and cohesion. There were patriarchal family loyalties. There was courtesy to the stranger and an extraordinary interest in his business. In field and fair snatches of old sagas became mixed with talk of the price of cattle or the prowess of O'Brien and Parnell. Speech might be salty and down-to-earth or exquisite with subtle sophistications, but unfailingly rich in phrase, proverb, turn and idiom. A good speaker was much appreciated, a keen discussion loved. Here was a Gaelic Arcadia. The soul of this country was born into Thomas Ashe.

The Ashe (originally D'Esse) family came from France at the time of the Norman conquest and settled in Devon, from where they crossed over to Ireland, various individuals or families probably at various times. MacLysaght in his *Irish Families* (p. 288) tells us that the Ashes were domiciled in Kildare and Meath since the fourteenth century and are recorded in the sixteenth century as among the leading gentry there. Branches dispersed to various parts of Ireland and are found in Limerick, Cavan, Louth, Derry and Antrim. It is not improbable that the Captain Thomas Ash who defended Derry for King William in 1689 came from the same roots as Commandant Thomas Ashe, who occupied North County Dublin at Easter 1916 for the Irish Republic. One of the family mottoes was 'Fight'. Fight they did, for whatever cause their convictions upheld. The motto, however, by which the family is particularly identified, *Non nobis sed omnibus* – Not for ourselves but for all – is nowhere made more manifest than in the life and death of Thomas Ashe of Kinard.

Tradition has it that the Ashes of West Kerry came from Kildare, where, in a time of turmoil, a stubborn Ashe, loyal to his conscience, was hanged for being a rebel, and other members of the family, refusing to renounce their Catholic faith, had their lands confiscated and were forced to leave. Moving south, as did many other midland families in similar circumstances, they settled at Murreagh near the shores of Smerwick harbour in the extreme west of Dingle peninsula, not far from the ancient oratory of Gallarus. A country of surpassing beauty, it was not without its memories. Looking across the harbour they could see Fort del Oro, where Walter Raleigh dishonoured his pledge to eight hundred Spanish prisoners-of-war, a grim reminder to the recent outlaws of Kildare. Already in the midlands the Ashes may have come under the influence of Gaelic Ireland and the separate identity associated with it. Be that as it may, they thoroughly assimilated with their West Kerry background and absorbed, if indeed they did not already possess, the civilization and culture of their Gaelic milieu. Cherishing its literary heritage, scholars of the family copied the poems and histories of Ireland in manuscript, since print and all forms of Irish development were curbed or denied. In 1762–63,

Séamus Ás copied in the town of Dingle the entire text of Geof-frey Keating's *History of Ireland*, along with genealogical tracts and poems, and his manuscript, with its fine print-like penmanship, may be seen in the O'Curry Library of University College Dublin.

From Murreagh came the founder of the Ashe family of Kinard, which is some three miles to the east of Dingle town. He was Séamus Ághas (James Ashe), who came to Kinard and married Mary, daughter of Big John Griffin. Big John had the standing of a local chieftain. A man of substance, he owned all the townland of Kinard and part of the neighbouring townland of Tobar. He had another business besides, which was profitable, al-though not without its hazards. He was a smuggler. On the coast of Kerry this occupation was not unusual, and because of its defi-ance of an unloved government it had an honourable status. Those engaged in it called it 'free trade'. False chimneys, built craftily into gable ends, became secret caches of wines, brandies and silks from Europe. Revenue men, or sea-fencers as they were called, were nobody's friends. Well-to-do men smuggled, like Robert Hickson, last man to hold the official post of Sovereign of Dingle. It is more than probable that some at least of the local magistrates and officials closed their eyes to the business. They, being human, were no enemies to good rum and brandy, nor to a well-flavoured tobacco, tax free. Wares like these were brought ashore at the cove of Trá Bheag by Big John's boats, which went out the bay to meet the ships from Spain and France. Big John Griffin, so described on his headstone, lies in Kinard cemetery.

Five sons and five daughters were born to James Ashe and Mary Griffin. The sons succeeded to Big John Griffin's patrimony and settled in Kinard and the neighbouring parish of Minard. The eldest son, John, married Hanora Connor from The Bridge, Lispole. She was the daughter of a local distiller, quite a personality, who had concocted a tasty brew which the drinkers of the place called 'Toddy'. John Ashe and Hanora Connor had three sons and three daughters. The sons, Jim, Matthew and John, all settled in Kinard townland. John (Jack) married twice, firstly Siobhán Kavanagh from Rinn Bhuí, Lispole and secondly a Miss Herlihy. He had one son and one daughter of the first marriage. The son, Gregory, succeeded to his father's place in Kinard townland. He married Ellen Hanafin, daughter of Patrick Hanafin of the neighbouring townland Tobar. Gregory Ashe and Ellen Hanafin had ten children, one of whom was Thomas Ashe, destined to become commandant of the Fifth Battalion, Dublin Brigade, victor at Ashbourne in 1916, harbinger of a resurgent Ireland and, finally, the victim of ill-treatment in Mountjoy jail which resulted in his death in September 1917.

2

FAMILY AND ENVIRONMENT

The children born to Gregory Ashe and Ellen Hanafin were, in order of seniority, Siobhán, Seán, Séamus, Pádraig (who died at the age of one), Máire, Nora, Thomas, a second Pádraig, Gregory and Michael.

It was a rapidly changing country into which Thomas, the seventh of the family, was born, on 12 January 1885. The nation was in angry revolt against the feudal land system. For Thomas's father, preoccupied with drawing from the land sustenance for his growing family, the great question of the day had more than a passing interest. Revolution was in full swing throughout Ireland and politics were aggressive and exciting. Side by side with the movement for the recovery of the land, the agitation for Home Rule flourished. Charles Stewart Parnell, Michael Davitt and William O'Brien were at the helm, and the movement, magnificently led, was getting results. Across the Atlantic came funds, supplies and other invaluable support from John Devoy and Patrick Ford. From America too came small bands of intrepid, formidable men who pelted London and Glasgow with dynamite bombs. They, the advance guard of Irish revolution, included one Henry Hammond Wilson, sentenced in 1883 to penal servitude for life. His real name was Thomas J. Clarke. He was already a generation old at Thomas Ashe's birth. A generation more and their paths would converge dramatically. The Ireland into which

Thomas Ashe was born was articulate, resourceful and determined. Men took an eager interest in politics. His father, Gregory Ashe, was no exception.

Gregory Ashe was a man of unusual talent and character. It must have been a man of marked qualities who impressed his son Thomas and all his family so profoundly. His truth, faith and idealism became their standard. Scholarly and versatile, fond of music and literature, bilingual with the easy proficiency of naturally acquired speech, his fluent Irish had a strong literary flavour. His daughter Nora describes him with affection:

> It was our father who influenced not only Tomás, but every one of us. He was constantly teaching us, impressing on us the value of learning and was himself a man who had read and absorbed widely and had a fine appreciation of literature. Learning from him came easily and naturally. When working together out in the fields he would recite history and legend to us. He impressed on us a strong historical sense. He was constantly talking of Irish history, referring to it, relating it to us in its many different aspects, social, national, political and local, and he imparted to us his own deep convictions of what was right and wrong in the story of Ireland, of what it was necessary yet to do and to strive for. Yes, our father was the real influence on Tomás and on all of us.

Gregory Ashe worked hard on his land, late and early, and devoted himself to bringing up his family. He cultivated, too, the gifts of his finely endowed mind. His memory was a treasure house in which he accumulated immense reserves of Irish story, poetry and legend. He loved Irish poetry and could recite all 'Laoi Oisín ar Thír na nÓg' and many other long poems, both Irish and English, by heart. Poetry and song were inseparable from life, hard though life sometimes was on the land. The workmen sang in the fields, or drawing home the turf, or coming from the fair. Thomas's younger brother, Gregory, remembers how profound their father's influence was:

> My father impressed Tomás immensely. He transmitted [to] him a great store of seanchas, legends and songs. My father was a very good singer. Some nights he would begin to sing at seven o'clock and the company of neighbours, seated around, would sing each in his turn and so the night passed until ten o'clock. Tomás himself had a very fine voice.

It was a time when people made their own amusement. The fireside gathering was an old-established institution of social life, happy, relaxed and companionable. It was a forum of opinion, a mart of ideas, a theatre and a symposium, where thought and discussion were free. Gregory Ashe's hearthstone was a favourite rendezvous. The neighbours would gather for the evening's talk, cares were put by, songs were sung and parish or national affairs scrutinised in fine and searching detail. The children would sit about listening, becoming unconsciously merged in the strange alchemy that is the soul of a nation. A well-remembered neighbour was Tomás Ó Sé, a regular visitor to the Ashe household. Gently caressing young Thomas's shock of fair curls he used to say: '*Aha! déanfaidh sé sin fear maith fós.*' A fact remembered, too, was that when asked as a little boy what he would like to be when he grew up, Thomas would reply that he wanted to be a soldier.

Certain experiences, commonplace enough in the times, made

an impact on Thomas Ashe's mind. In the 1890s keeping the bailiffs from the door was more than a figure of speech. It was a stark and serious problem facing many a tenant. On one occasion the vigilance of Thomas helped to baffle the unwelcome intruders. His brother Gregory told the present writer:

> I remember well one of the things that influenced Tomás. It happened just as I was beginning school at the age of five-and-a-half. Tomás, then about twelve, saw a posse of four or five bailiffs coming towards Jackie Herlihy's house to seize his cattle for arrears of rent. The bailiffs in error took the wrong route and Tomás, seeing their intention, raced ahead and warned Jackie Herlihy's son of their approach. The result was that when they arrived there was not a cow or a calf to be seen in the place and the bailiffs retired in discomfiture.

That was one of the things which set Thomas Ashe thinking. He abhorred the social injustice that made the weak the prey of the strong and secured for the strong the reinforcement of the law. In the context of Dublin's labour revolt in 1913 Thomas Ashe found it easy to support Jim Larkin in his campaign for the working man.

Thomas went to school at Ardamore National School, Lispole, where his teachers were John Hickson and Michael O'Connor. Both men were accomplished Irish scholars. John Hickson's scholarship was especially distinguished and his rich fund of racy sayings and idioms was much admired by lovers of fine speech. Kinard parish was bilingual. English and Irish were used by most people with the same easy competence and the two ways of speech gave an edge to the intellect. There were great Irish speakers in the Ashe clan. Amongst the four Ashe families of Kinard townland

Irish was the language of daily life. Gregory's kinsman Séamus Ashe was particularly noted for his correct and graceful use of language.

Thomas Ashe learned well from his brilliant schoolteachers. He was an attentive pupil and learning came easily. The textbooks included Geoffrey Keating's *Introduction to the History of Ireland* and Rev. Patrick Dinneen's *Cormac Ua Conaill*. He practically learned these two books off by heart. Ardamore National School was a small building but the attendance in Thomas Ashe's time was fairly large, sometimes numbering 350. They could not all be accommodated in the building at the same time and even in winter some of the classes had to be held in the open air. Thomas Ashe had a retentive memory, which he used to great advantage. A favourite subject of his was Irish history. So was the poetry of Ireland whether in Irish or in English. Mr O'Connor regularly assigned the task of reading for the class to Thomas as best fitted for it by his ability and flair for leadership. Having passed successfully through the various classes, Thomas, in 1900, was appointed a monitor. A monitor's term ran for five years. At the examination held at the end of the third year he won the premier Reid Prize and repeated the success at the end of the fifth year. That same year he was appointed assistant organiser under the Gaelic League for the period Easter to September.

The Gaelic League, founded in 1893 by a group of scholars which included Douglas Hyde and Eoin MacNeill, created a new, sparkling and vital intellectual dimension with immense and far-reaching effects. The destiny of the Gael was suggested in striking terms by Patrick Pearse, in October 1897, as 'more glorious than that of Rome, more glorious than that of Britain … to become the saviour of idealism in modern intellectual and social life, the regenerator and rejuvenator of the literature of the world, the instructor of the nations, the preacher of the gospel of nature-worship, hero-worship, God-worship.' By any measure these were lofty standards to set, but they indicate the way in which the Gaelic League acted on the rare and sensitive mind of Pearse. The Gaelic League attracted minds of the most various range and calibre. Pearse's lofty concepts were balanced by the sentiments of Arthur Griffith who, a few years later, stated acidly that if the Gael had a mission it was to make a man of himself. He, too, voiced with vigorous logic the call of a Gaelic, self-reliant Ireland. The most brilliant and intelligent minds in Ireland were attracted to the Gaelic League and it encouraged the best in them. Thomas Ashe, like Pearse, was profoundly inspired by it. Like Pearse he was an idealist. Allied to his idealism were other qualities of mind, realistic, practical and positive, that kept his feet planted firmly on the ground.

He did his Gaelic League work in the evenings and at week-ends. It was concerned with organising language classes and visiting the schools to encourage the inclusion of the Irish language in the programmes. In this he had considerable success, especially in and around Lispole. A solid foundation for his work had in fact been already laid in the Lispole district through the hard work and patriotism of John Hickson, Michael O'Connor and their assistants, who had been teaching the language since about 1890. As a result of their efforts a good number in Lispole had some reading and writing knowledge well before the Gaelic League began organising in the district. At the Oireachtas of the Gaelic League held in June 1899, John Hickson won the William O'Brien Cup for having secured, the year before, the largest number of passes in Irish, sixty-one, among pupils attending the National Schools.

A Feis, the first of many, was held in Dingle in September 1903, at which Canon O'Leary, PP, and Thomas O'Donnell, MP, delivered opening speeches. The literary competitions included reading, writing, recitation and storytelling. There were also singing and dancing competitions. The feiseanna became centres of pageantry, entertainment and competition which gave a great impetus in the district to the cause of the Gaelic League. Thomas Ashe took an active part in organising these feiseanna. He also submitted entries for the written competitions and won prizes for the best collections of proverbs, recitations, Fenian tales and folk tales. About this time he wrote a little Irish play, *An Puncán* (The Yank), a comedy on the popular theme of the returned American. With the aid of local colleagues, who were his fellow workers in the Gaelic League, he produced the play in connection with the Dingle Feis. Dr O'Connell, a solicitor who was an enthusiastic supporter of the Gaelic League, was so impressed by it that he took the entire cast to Tralee, where they gave an open-air performance at the Feis. The setting was in the town park where unusual lighting effects were provided by a plentiful display of torchlights. There was a good audience, due to a novel and effective advertisement. On their way to the park, Ashe with the whole cast marched through the streets of Tralee carrying the costumes and stage properties, led by Brian O'Donovan of Carbery playing the bagpipes. The crowds followed.

In the early years of the century, under the impact of the Irish renaissance, thought, ambition and resolve took on heroic forms. The inspiration communicated itself to Thomas Ashe's receptive mind. Under its stimulus he read every available printed text in Irish literature and his studies ranged over the allied fields of folklore, history, hagiography and Brehon Laws. Irish literature had an unending fascination for him. Much of his education in this was necessarily oral, because of the dearth of printed texts.

But a great body of literature was accessible by way of oral recitation and there were many traditional storytellers in Kinard and Lispole, with prodigious memories, who could go over any particular tale, time and again, as accurately as a printed text, without deviating a syllable. Such popular Fenian tales as were in print were avidly read by Ashe, some in Irish, some in English, like *The Pursuit of Diarmuid and Gráinne, Cath Chnoc an Áir* and others. Stories of the Red Branch Knights were less well-known in West Kerry, but when a few became available in print, like *Cathair Conroí* and *The Death of Conor Mac Nessa*, Ashe procured and read them. The collection and comparison of folktales was another interesting pursuit. Dramatic recitations and duologues were a favourite literary form in the country. Ashe collected them also, revelling in their gorgeous language and imagery, committing passages and phrases to heart, memorising apt quotations for future reference. He assimilated eagerly, widely, diversely. He used to love to sit with other boys listening to a celebrated local seanachaí who combined the twin crafts of stonemason and thatcher with the ancient art of storytelling. The seanachaí found them an appreciative audience but he appeared to address himself particularly to Thomas Ashe, whom he found the most responsive of all his youthful circle. Ashe did not attend university but had an excellent substitute in the colourful, diverse environment of his native district.

Ashe acquired an extensive knowledge of Irish poetry, espe-

cially the chief Munster poets, Eoghan Rua Ó Súilleabháin, Pierce
Ferriter, Aogán Ó Rathaile. Some of their verse he learned from
his father, more from O'Daly's *Poets and Poetry of Munster*, a copy
of which was in the house. From his father he also picked up the
airs to most of these songs. His excellent ear for music was a great
help. His favourite Irish novelists were Charles Kickham and
James Murphy.

When not studying Irish literature, his reading centred on
history, biography and memoirs, Irish, American and European.
He liked reading about the achievements of great military leaders.
Amongst these Napoleon was his favourite. With soldier thoughts
anticipating the future, Ashe in his early years gave much thought
to the methods by which Irish terrain might best be used for
tactics of defence and attack. He read a great deal about the
American Civil War and its generals, of whom he chiefly admired
Stonewall Jackson. Amongst Irish military leaders he considered
Owen Roe O'Neill to be the greatest tactician and probably more
than a match for Cromwell; he would speculate on what would be
the outcome of an encounter between them. His heart went out to
those who fought heroically in lonely causes or against desperate
odds, and he had particular affection for Peter O'Neill Crowley,
Michael Dwyer, Robert Emmet and Pierce Ferriter. The inspiration of the times conjured the years away and brought these men
close to him. Greatest of all Irishmen for Thomas was Theobald
Wolfe Tone, font and source of the republican idea, the architect
and designer of the ideal of a united, cohesive, egalitarian Irish
Republic. Tone's democratic message to the men of no property to
become the advance guard of Irish freedom appealed immensely
to Thomas Ashe's heart.

As the Ashe boys grew up, each one had to give a hand with the work of the farm. The strenuous physical labour, inseparable from farming life, was accepted by Thomas and the rest of the family as all in the day's routine. His muscles and fibres became toughened, steeled and inured to hardship. Before going to school in the morning he helped to feed the farm animals. Nobody can idle on a farm. There was the seasonal round of turf, hay and corn saving, the occasional early morning journey to Dingle fair, the digging and pitting of the potatoes, the thatching of the farm buildings. Hard, healthy work it was, chiefly outdoor and nearly all done by hand. It hardened and developed Ashe's physique so that by the time he reached sixteen he had acquired a man's strength and height and the capacity for any manly task. He attributed his robust health to a diet in which fresh milk largely figured. It was only when he went to college that he drank tea regularly.

Football was his favourite pastime. There was little or no hurling played in West Kerry at that time. When, in later years, Ashe saw hurling played by experts and acquired some practice at the game himself, it became his choice in preference to all other field games. He considered it far and away more skilled and spectacular than football and a better medium for physical development and stamina. He enjoyed all games of strength and agility, like weight throwing, putting the shot, long and high jump, swimming and rowing. He liked wrestling, not the all-in kind, but a more subtle variety popular in country districts in which the protagonists clinch around waist and shoulders and try to throw each other. In this contest any participant who is not doughty and tough is liable to have his stomach well squeezed and it is no occupation for weaklings. Ashe excelled at it. Although a fine oarsman he preferred sailing. While his youthful companions trimmed the craft he would take the helm. Eager and venturesome, he revelled in the strong breezes blowing across Dingle Bay and recoiled from no hazard. The boys' elders would watch palpitating from the heights overlooking the bay. All the boys could swim well and feared no danger but at times they gave some anxious moments to their seniors, who had a keener awareness of the sudden perils of the sea.

Another recreation to which Ashe was attracted at an early age was fowling. Myriads of wildfowl inhabited the bogs, marshes and mountains around Lispole, and the sportsman could ask for no more ideal situation. With practice he became an accurate shooter and could bring down woodcock and snipe, the latter an extremely elusive quarry, with almost professional skill. He loved the day-long tramps over moorland and heather, taking in his stride hedges, ditches and streams. Keeping up with him on these excursions was an endurance test. Apart from his exhilaration in open-air exercise, he had a conscious motive in taking these long, arduous cross-country tramps. They were part of a soldier's training and he saw himself in the role of a soldier of Ireland some day.

3

IN DE LA SALLE

Having completed his term as monitor, Ashe entered De La Salle Training College, Newtown, County Waterford, to become a national teacher. He commenced his two-year course in 1905, at the age of twenty. What we can glean concerning him from the college register is spare and succinct. The details are:

No. 1079 Ashe, Thomas. County: Kerry. Position in School: Monitor. Date of Birth, 1884 [Error for 1885]. At the end of his first year he passed the examination in First Division. He passed his final examination in Second Division. He obtained his Christian Doctrine Diploma with second class honours and qualified in Vocal Music, Plain Chant and Irish. He obtained a College Diploma with Honours and later, after the usual probationary period, the Teaching Diploma of the National Board of Education.

As it happened, an illness on the day of his final examination affected him to such an extent that he could not complete some of the papers. So it turned out that a normally assured First Division result became a Second Division one.

A very close friend, Michael Sheehan of Annascaul, who was with him in De La Salle College, looks back with fond remembrance on the days they spent in college together. He gave the writer the following recollections of his comrade:

Tomás and I were together in De La Salle Training College in 1906. We started a Gaelic League class in college with the approval of the authorities and Tomás taught it. Tomás was very interested in the Fenian period of Irish history and was a member of the Irish Republican Brotherhood. He was also a strong supporter of Sinn Féin and would refuse in the shops to accept articles not of Irish manufacture, even to so small an item as a box of matches. He was a grand athletic type and fond of walking. I remember a fine Saturday afternoon in June that we walked the seven miles from college to Tramore, drank a bottle of ale and walked back. Gay and bright of heart, he loved to sing his favourite songs, *Aililiú na Gamhna* and *The Kerry Dances*. He was a good footballer and played hurling too. He smoked a turned-down pipe but was a very light smoker. A great companion of his and mine was Henry Good, who used chaff us both about the odd little Dingle train which ran its leisurely way at the back of our houses at home. Good used tell a story for the amusement of our fellow students about how the engine-driver, when he saw a woman walking on the tracks with a basket of eggs on her head, offered her a lift which she politely declined, saying she was in a hurry! Tomás and I always kept in touch up to the very last. He wrote me from Lewes prison and I also have a letter he sent me from Mountjoy jail and which may well be the last one he ever wrote. The portrait of Tomás which hangs in the Teachers' Club, 36 Parnell Square, is not a good likeness. It makes him too thin. He was a big well-knit man. I was with him one day when he weighed himself at Limerick Junction and he tipped fourteen stone. At De La Salle he took part in our debating society discussions and was a very competent speaker. All the Ashe family were practical and industrious. After qualifying he taught in Minard for a while along with John Kavanagh. I was at Tomás's funeral. I came up from Craanford near Gorey, where I was teaching. The funeral was immense, but it was a sad, sad day.

At De La Salle his qualities of leadership and all-round competence were recognised by his professors, and Brother Brendan took a special interest in him. He became the obvious choice to put in charge of the senior Irish language class. Those who were Ashe's students in the Irish class partook of his idealism and supported the language movement in the different schools throughout Ireland where they taught afterwards. In the study hall of De La Salle College there is a photograph of the 1905–07 group of students in which Ashe is seated on the right of Brother Maximus, FSC, Prefect of Studies. Since this is the position in all such photographs of the chairman or head of the students, elected by the students themselves, it is probable that Ashe in his final year occupied that position.

De La Salle College was well equipped for athletics of all kinds. Ashe excelled at field sports, and though new to hurling, took to it with such eagerness as to consider it the greatest of all team games.

'He was a very fine-looking man, with a mop of fair hair: moustaches were fashionable then and he was just beginning to grow one. We were good friends, Tom and I, and he was a grand companion.' So recollects Andrew Keaveney, NT, of Loughglynn, County Roscommon, who studied with him in De La Salle. Mr Keaveney has a photograph of the 1907 college football team showing Ashe as a fair-haired young man with a moustache. Ashe was a good average footballer, although not up to traditional Kerry-team standard. He played left full-back and opponents found that getting a score off him was not easy. He could take and give hard knocks as a normal part of the day's sport. Once a team from outside the city played De La Salle. Whatever the quality of its football, the visiting team was not noted for gentleness, and included an exceptionally robust player who threw his weight around dangerously. Provoked by his behaviour, Ashe manoeuvred a well-timed collision with him at the end line, when the referee's attention was elsewhere, and for the rest of the game that player was more pacific. 'Tom was a very determined man on the football field and feared nothing.'

His fine voice was heard regularly in the Saturday-night concerts. Mr Keaveney was captivated with the catchy air of a certain song of Ashe's, 'Máire an Chúil Bhuí', about which he made many enquiries afterwards but failed to trace. Although Ashe was a good student he was not by any means a hard worker at his studies. Generous of his time with others, said Mr Keaveney:

> He never minded giving an hour of his time at night to any students who wanted to learn Irish from him. We had an Irish class. There were 75 in our year altogether and of these 25 or 26 were in Tomás's Irish class. There was a certificate examination for these at the end of the year and 23 out of the 25 were successful. Tom was in his glory when he was teaching a bit of Irish. He loved it, as he loved everything Irish. He loved to relate traditional stories and sagas about Fionn Mac Cumhaill and the Fianna. There was another thing about Tomás I found admirable – he had no use for countyism or provincialism in any shape or form.

Thomas Ashe, in an article which he contributed to the first number of *Irisleabhar De La Salle* in 1911, wrote appreciatively about the profound influence of the college on its students in the nationalist sense, and praised the encouragement given to Irish ideals by the president and staff. The article is entitled 'De La Salle agus Éire Ghaelach'.

De La Salle and Gaelic Ireland! … looking back on the two years which I spent there, it is difficult for me not to visualise an Irish Ireland, strong and robust, every place you turn your eyes. From morn till eve, and from Saturday to Saturday – at work, at prayer, at play – Róisín Dubh was appearing before us, faintly enough indeed at times, but at other times in full spirit and energy, calling and beckoning to us …

He regretted that the taboos of the Board of Education, which were designed to deny the existence of an Irish heritage, did not permit the college to teach Irish history or even a subject so close to the experience of a country teacher as agriculture.

On qualifying as a national teacher he got a post quite near his home, in Minard Castle National School. The Department of Education records tell us that he took up duty there as assistant teacher on 15 July 1907 and served until 6 March 1908.

Minard Castle School dates from 1873.[1] Nearby was a coast-guard station and the school was located there, not far from the edge of the sea, for the convenience of the officials' children amongst others. Ashe's principal was John Kavanagh. John's son Michael, who has recently (1966) retired as principal of the same school, recalls that he was taught by Ashe, as a child, for six months or so, though his recollection is necessarily obscured with the years:

I barely remember being in his class, for I was very young, and he probably only taught me singing. He was very mild and nice and fond of telling stories to keep the children in good humour. He used to cycle from his home to the school and back daily. He was great friends with my father. I remember himself and Pádraig Ashe coming one time with shotguns to go fowling and they called on my father and spent the evening singing. Tomás was ultra-patriotic. He was a good swimmer and would sometimes go for a swim in the sea before school in the mornings.

During his period of teaching in Minard he took a leading part in the organisation of the Lispole football team. Insisting on regularity of practice and team discipline, he helped to bring the parish fifteen to many successes in the county GAA competitions. Out of rivalry on the football field he made better acquaintance with Austin Stack, which ripened into mutual respect and friendship. He continued his studies in the oral Irish literature of the district, in the gracious company of seanachaí and storyteller. As evidence of his interest in local history we find his name, during his teaching days in Minard, in the list of subscribers to Foley's *History of County Kerry*.

His stay in Minard was short. Seeking to improve his prospects, he applied, probably in February 1908, for a vacancy as principal in Corduff National School in the parish of Lusk, County Dublin. He was presently notified by the Rev. Manager, Father Byrne, that he was successful. Brief as it is, Ashe's letter of acknowledgement is remarkable as a signpost to his life's great adventure. It gives some idea of the determination and spirit with which he approached his 'first real individual trial':

Lispole
Tralee
March 7th 1908

Dear Rev. Father

I am very thankful to you for appointing me principal of Corduff School, and for your very kind offer of paying my expenses to Lusk.

I shall not be able to take up work until the end of this week, as I am only just recovering from a slight cold. Besides with regard to clothes, etc., I will have some delay. I intend leaving here if possible on Thursday next and I hope that you will kindly give me permission to remain so long.

I am not one bit afraid of the average of Corduff School and I already entertain a feeling that I shall be successful there. My only hesitation in accepting the position rested in the fact that I pondered deeply on my first leap into life. I regard this as my first real individual trial for I have been at home during all my past life.

I am dear Rev. Father
Yours very respectfully
Thomas Ashe

Rev. Father Byrne PP.

He took up duty at Corduff National School on 16 March 1908, and there he taught, with one intermission during which he was in the United States, until 19 April 1916, a period of some eight years. For Thomas Ashe they were intense, creative, golden years.

4

THE TEACHER

The village of Corduff consists of a series of modest little cottages scattered at some length on each side of the main Dublin–Belfast road, a dozen or so miles north of Dublin city. Travelling through the place at modern speeds, its existence can easily escape notice. It is located in the parish of Lusk, Barony of Balrothery East and County of Dublin. The school, a one-storey structure of conventional design, stands a little in off the main road. In recent years an entrance hall has been added and it has been divided into two classrooms where originally there was only one; otherwise the building, which dates from 1908, is much the same as when Thomas Ashe entered it to teach the children of Corduff. A plaque has been erected to his memory in one of the classrooms by his comrades and supporters of Lusk. It was unveiled on 18 September 1967 and in its exquisite workmanship it finely betokens their loyalty and appreciation.

His personality blended quite naturally with his new community. Centre of the district was the village of Lusk, two miles away off the Dublin–Belfast road, remote, rural and somnolent in the heart of North Dublin County. Its houses clustered around the green, which gave it an open spacious appearance. It had churches, post office, police barracks and library. When Ashe first arrived the teacher's house attached to Corduff School was not ready and he boarded in Lusk in the house of Mrs Bridget Hurley, whose son Charles is at present the courteous and obliging secretary of the Black Raven Pipe Band. The district lies in the ancient territory of Moynalty, *Magh nEalta*, the Plain of the Birds, which extends throughout North County Dublin, a lush, rolling champaign which was cleared of its forests in ancient times and gave rich pasturage to herds of cattle. The wealthy soil was coveted by many invaders. Vikings and Normans arrived, first to plunder, then to remain, and the name Fingal, which derives from their settlement, means the community of foreigners. Surnames and placenames of Danish and Norman origin are common. Romance, of old and historic flavour, has added its quota of enchantment to the place. At Turvey Castle, no great distance from Corduff, Hugh O'Neill, greatest of Irish rebels, kept tryst with Mabel Bagenal. In the shadowy times of prehistory it figures in ancient Irish epic literature. The warrior Cúchulainn strode its plain. Thomas Ashe found himself in territory which differed nothing in its primal associations and character from his native West Kerry. Legend and saga gave them a common denominator. He felt at home.

A few days' journey around Fingal, even at the present day, brings us close to Thomas Ashe's actual experiences in this attractive community. To go and see where he lived, walk the roads and byways and paths he trod, enter the little houses of the district where he was welcomed, respected and loved, and where every memento of him is treasured and cherished, is to understand what he meant to it. Those whom he taught at school, or their children, or their neighbours, bear living testimony to the way in which Ashe became identified with the district and of the impact which his personality made on it.

Thomas J. Brangan, whose people suffered eviction during

the land wars of the last century, and farms now at Gormanston, County Meath, was taught in Corduff School by Thomas Ashe. He can talk about his teacher as if it were only yesterday, so warm and vivid are his classroom memories. In the six years during which Ashe taught him he got one solitary slap, which was for fighting, during the girls' sewing class, with Paddy Carton for possession of a blotting paper. 'Tom Ashe did not believe in the rod. He was the most outstanding teacher I ever met. He had such a way of putting things that you took them in without any feeling of having them forced on you.' He remembers with appreciation his teacher's aptitude for drawing and sketching and how enjoyable a subject it became under his tuition. Ashe drew sketches of some of the children in class and Tom Brangan had a book containing a number of these but regrettably this prized possession disappeared. Mr Brangan recalls:

Tom Ashe commanded the respect of the pupils and of the people around to such an extent that I never heard him called by his first name. His assistant was Miss Monks, and while Father Murphy, the curate from Lusk, would address her 'Good morning Mary,' to Thomas Ashe it was always, respectfully, 'Good morning Mr Ashe.' He would get the morning paper regularly and read the headings near the window. He had wonderful class control, easy and natural. There were about 32 pupils, boys and girls mixed, in the school. There was one large classroom. School began at 9.30 a.m. and ended at 3 p.m. with a break at midday.

Ashe was idolised by his pupils. When he returned from America in the autumn of 1914, after an absence of seven or eight months, the schoolchildren went wild with delight. He would sometimes take some of the smaller children on his knee while he gave the bigger ones some task of reading or recitation; for variety he would at times give each a trick to perform, like the novel one of jumping a stick held in both hands.

He taught us all the Fenian and rebel songs and ballads which of course were not on the programme. First he would note down the airs for us in tonic solfa. Then he would teach us the words, songs like *Who Fears to Speak of '98*, *Boolavogue* and *The Castle of Dromore*. He altered the wording at the end of *The Castle of Dromore* to suit his own preference as he did not care for the original words.

At any Thomas Ashe commemoration held in Corduff one can make the acquaintance of a gracious lady in a wheelchair. She is Miss Kate Kelly, of Corduff village, a pupil of Ashe's who remembers him with more than ordinary gratitude:

I can read and write [she says] thanks to Mr Ashe. I can take the day's papers up to bed with me and read them every night. I had been struck with polio and had come home from the Children's Hospital, Temple Street, incurable, and it wasn't planned to send me to school. I was at the door of our house with my mother, sitting in a little chair, when Mr Ashe came over to my mother and said it would be a pity if I grew up and went through the world unable to read or write and he asked that I be sent up to the school to learn. He took my younger sister into school with me for company. He had a little chair and put me sitting in it and used put me over near the fire at lunch hour. He was a grand teacher and not cross except when it was absolutely necessary and was very easy and lenient with the girls. We had mixed classes.

Miss Kelly attended school until her Confirmation. Besides her memories of Ashe she has in her keeping ribbons off the wreaths on his grave the day he was buried. A bit worn and frayed with time now, they are treasured with none the less reverence.

Tom Ashe was also a great science teacher [she recalls]. He made himself well acquainted with Fingal history; he went out to Grace Dieu to investigate the remains of the nuns' convent there, learned all about it, and taught it to us at school. He went to Ballyboughal to see where the Wexford men of '98 made their last stand. He visited all places of note in Fingal and was wonderful at teaching us the history relating to them. He walked a great deal; he said walking was good for one.

Kate Kelly is one of a nationalist family, all of whom, influenced by their mother, gave their support to Ashe and his ideals. Her two brothers Richard and Thomas were in the Irish Volunteers and fought in the Rising. Richard lives in Rogerstown, near Lusk. He was a pupil of Ashe's in Corduff for a few years. What he remembers particularly are the geography lessons. Maps of the countries of the world hung on the walls and would figure in the geography discussions. The display included a map of England, about which Ashe would humorously remark: 'Never mind it, boys, it will disappear one of these days.'

He was a great leader, and put spirit into us, too [says Richard Kelly]. He told us a yarn at school about the Boer War in order to impress on us that the British Empire, then regarded as invincible, was not so in fact. A new rapid firing gun of Maxim pattern was trained by a British unit on a hillside populated with grazing goats. They fired it continuously for hours, at the end of which it was found that all the goats were alive and two of them had kids.

Richard Kelly remembered some distinguished visitors who came to see Ashe at Corduff School, names that interest us for the way they link up with the activities in which he was involved. They included Claude Chavasse, a notable personality in the Irish language movement, and Señor William Bulfin, a former editor of the Buenos Aires *Southern Cross* and leading figure of Sinn Féin, designated by his friend Arthur Griffith to grace the presidency of the movement had he lived. Thomas Ashe advised his pupils to obtain and read Señor Bulfin's fine travel book *Rambles in Éirinn*. Francis J. Biggar, the Belfast solicitor who was an encyclopaedia of antiquarian knowledge, came to see Ashe at Corduff School, and so did Roger Casement, humanitarian and patriot, who admired Ashe's capacities as a language worker, community leader and Volunteer organiser.

William O'Brien, now retired from teaching and living in Donabate, knew Ashe well, having walked the plains, paths and byroads of North County Dublin many a time in his company. He remembers him as being passionately interested in the singing of Irish songs and the recital of Irish folktales and stories. 'He had an intense and detailed knowledge of Irish history.' At a meeting of the friends of Thomas Ashe, organised one time in Lusk by Joe Kelly, Mr O'Brien described him as 'a lover of folklore and Irish history', a tribute from a man who is himself an authority on Fingal's legends and associations. Inspectors, whose names have suitably passed into oblivion, were jealous of Ashe's exact and detailed historical knowledge.

Tom Ashe had great influence in Fingal with the young people, boys, youths and young men. He was a fine athlete. He put up the ball alley in Lusk. He founded the Pipers' Band. No, he had no difficulties whatever [said Mr O'Brien] in organising or leading them. The people here are easily led if they take to their leader. They are not showy or demonstrative people in Fingal but they are responsive to a leader they can take to. They took to Tom Ashe.

Ashe joined the Dublin city branch of the Irish National Teachers' Association (INTO). Inspectors did not like him. The senior inspector of National Schools probed Mr O'Brien one day trying to find out about Ashe's political activities but he came to the wrong man. The senior inspector muttered in disapproval of Mr Ashe's Gaelic League projects. The inspectors generally did not favour the teaching of Irish at that time, thought Captain Richard Coleman's sister Anna. It was her strong impression that they rather disapproved of it and that it did the teacher who taught it no good officially. Ashe ignored the taboos.

The present caretaker (1963) of the school, Mrs Annie Finnegan, who occupies a little cottage nearby, relates that her husband, a pupil of Ashe, had no words of praise too high for his excellence as a teacher. Very talented and clever he was, and great at drawing pictures. He set up his easel on the other side of the road and painted a picture of her cottage. Many a time in the evenings, when his day's work was over, he would come and sit in the cottage for a chat.

Some few dozen yards down the road towards Dublin from Ashe's school the Sheridans live in a little stone cottage. He was, said Mrs Sheridan, 'a good teacher but not a cross teacher', and what better answer is known to a schoolchild's prayer? Her own mother idolised him: 'He used to come down to our house for a night's talk and have a cup of tea. She bought a special cup for him, which she called his moustache cup, to suit his moustache, and he used to make fun of her about it.'

Her husband, James Sheridan, played with Ashe on the Lusk football team in many a hard-fought game of the Fingal League. A fine midfielder, scientific without being robust, is Sheridan's summing up of Ashe as a player. His outdoor interests were numerous. For his sporting excursions he had a splendid red setter which he brought from Kerry. He hurled, produced plays and acted in them, held Irish classes in Lusk Library on Tuesday nights and Irish dancing classes on Fridays. Mr Sheridan has a postcard of the Pipers' Band on Lusk green, which is one of the earliest existing pictures of the band.

> He'd walk anywhere. He used walk from here to Dublin. He was very partial to the yellow meal bread which is made in Kerry from fine Indian meal and would bring cakes of it back to Dublin. He enjoyed a drink of buttermilk and would, just as in Kerry, love to call into farmers' houses and have a drink of it.

In the hall of Joe Carton's cottage, near Hanna's Avenue, Corduff, there hangs an oil painting of the Cartons' house, done in moments of leisure by Ashe. He lived in the two-storey residence attached to the school. His housekeeper was Mrs Thornton, who looked after his needs carefully, kept the house trim and tidy, clipped the hedges and sometimes talked absentmindedly to herself. During Ashe's occupation of it, the house became a noted centre of discussion. Friends and neighbours frequented it and, as views on many things differed, there was keen and at times high argument. A wag chalked 'Liberty Hall' on the door. Music and song enlivened the evenings. Late-night teas and impromptu meals were prepared with cheerful bustle.

Although Ashe was a great teacher, as his pupils bear witness, and would, had he taken a prudent line, have qualified for the rank of inspector, he was not the sort of man to suppress his opinions for the sake of entering the good graces of those who possessed the authority to make him one. Walter Starkie, the Chief Inspector, when visiting Corduff School after Ashe's prowess in 1916 had brought fame on it, observed that 'Mr Ashe was a better soldier than he was a teacher.' Starkie, solid imperialist that he was, had a vision jaundiced by his disapproval of Ashe's act of rebellion against the British Empire.

Ashe's assistant teacher in Corduff for seven years was pretty, petite Mary Monks. Few people knew him as well as she did. Yet there were times when she found him a man of contrasts, even mystery. That, in effect, is what she expresses to him in a letter she wrote to him on 5 May 1917. How was she to know that he was involved in secret plans of revolution which from his gay exterior nobody would have guessed? Here is what she tells him:

> I think I really did know you – and that is saying a big lot – and what very few around here can say. Of course I had seven years to study you and sure I'd be very dull entirely if I didn't make something of you in that time. Still, I think you were different every day.

Miss Monks, who lives now (1963) in retirement in a Dublin suburb, kindly gave the writer the following recollection of her colleague:

Looking back over the years when as a very young teacher I first met Tom Ashe, I find that memory centres around three outstanding traits of character which were his – an intense love of children, of music, and of country. It is hard to say which came first. He really loved children and actually played with them on many occasions. If he were compelled to punish one of them he was sad and worried for the day. He arrived at school each morning humming a traditional Irish air and during recreation or even during a short interval would sing for me, in his beautiful tenor voice, one of the hundreds of songs which he knew. He tried to instil into his pupils his own characteristics. History lessons were all about Ireland – he always used the blackboard to illustrate historical facts. The opposing armies were drawn up, moved around and blotted out as they were defeated – the children sat in rapt attention and the timetable was forgotten for the time being. Admittedly the favourite parts of Irish history were where the English were defeated – at this the children applauded; again we were all brought through the long centuries of persecution and told of the wrongs inflicted on Ireland by England. When a drill lesson would follow one of those sadder history lessons, there would be flag signalling, etc.; he would say, 'Stand erect, hold up your head, remember you are Irish soldiers and may have a chance to fight for Ireland one day.' He would come to me then and say, 'I hope I will get that privilege myself – to fight and die for Ireland.' … His activities for Ireland and everything Irish did not end in the schoolroom. He started the Black Raven Pipers' Band in the parish of Lusk, encouraged Irish games, chiefly hurling, started dramatic classes, organised concerts, feiseanna, and formed Irish language classes in many parishes. He had untiring energy. Anything and everything was done to arouse the national spirit, to make the children and people he came in contact with proud of their country, their language, their ancient culture, and above all to make them realise that they were Irish first and last and all the time. He was also a poet, dropping into rhyme on the slightest provocation – sad, joyous, or comic situations called forth the poet in him. In his letters and communications he frequently broke into poetry.

Thomas Ashe wrought many changes in Fingal. He roused to action the latent qualities of its fine people. Week in, week out, he taught in his school at Corduff and those who came to know him could not doubt that he was working for Ireland all the time. Personally he was the most courteous and chivalrous of men. 'He was gentle and kind, and hated to see pain occasioned,' writes Colonel J. V. Lawless.[1] His cousin Mrs Sheila Gunning was struck by the sincerity of his nature and compared him with his friend Seán Mac Diarmada, whom she also knew well.

> Tom Ashe [she said] had a terrific love of Ireland but he was not bitter against England. Tomás just wanted freedom for Ireland. There was no hate or bitterness in his nature; he wasn't like that. Tom wouldn't say a wrong word about anyone.

Ashe aimed his protest at the national and political wrong of centuries. This protest was not a negative attitude; it was positive and constructive. He taught his pupils the love of their land, of its rich heritage of literature, language, song, music and saga, of its quiet byways and dramatic battlefields, of its long quest for freedom, of the extraordinary humanity and inspiration of its experiences and of its future hopes and ideals. The men and women of Fingal, who as children attended Ashe's school, remember him with pride. They are not affluent, but their minds and memories have become enriched by contact with him in a way which they would not exchange for all the wealth of the world.

5

THE COMMUNITY LEADER

Paddy Doyle of Ballaly, Lusk, remembers the first day Ashe came on the hurling field. In Lusk they called him Big Tom. Six feet one inch he stood. He played hurling and football and was a good sportsman. 'He was hefty and strong, with a pair of legs as thick as my body.'

When Ashe came to Lusk, there had been such an accumulation of disappointment at the failure of successive national leaders that the urge to follow a good man did not appear at once. 'We did not run after Tom Ashe at once,' said Paddy Doyle. 'We let him do the running. It was only after his death that we realised what a man we had lost. Big Tom Ashe was a shrewd man. He picked his men well and made few mistakes.'

Paddy Doyle is a born Dubliner. He saw the light of day in 1893 in Great Brunswick (now Pearse) Street, in the neighbourhood of an immense gasometer which put a smell on the air all round and affected Paddy's health so that he had to move at the age of three to his uncle's at Lusk. Paddy Doyle's people came from Wexford. They fought in the Rising of 1798 and his great-grandfather was one of the detachment of Wexford men who, scorning to surrender, moved north through Leinster and made a last stand at Ballyboughal in Fingal, where they were surrounded and butchered by superior forces, all but three who escaped. Paddy's great-grandfather was one. Two of the escapees died and

Paddy's ancestor survived. 'Tom Ashe knew my history and ante-cedents when he swore me into the IRB,' said Paddy. 'Our IRB circle in Lusk consisted of Tom Ashe, Joe Kelly, Bill Morgan, Dan Brophy, Charlie Weston and myself. We held meetings but not too often for fear of attracting attention.'

Lusk was always a very Gaelic place. The early influence of the Gaelic League in Fingal had resulted in the establishment of the Naomh MacCullen Hurling Club in the parish. In the course of visits to Dublin members of the club were so impressed with the pageantry and performance of the Armagh Pipers' Band that they formed the idea of organising a band of their own. It was not until the arrival of Tom Ashe that the idea was translated into practical terms. He obtained a pair of bagpipes from Paddy White, a long-distance runner, and set about learning to play them, receiving his first lessons from Patrick Archer, author of 'The Yeos were in Dunshaughlin', a great personality, scholar and poet of Fingal.

The enterprise grew up around Thomas Ashe. John Rooney, of Raheny House, Lusk, helped, collections to promote it were held, more sets of pipes were bought and costumes designed during the winter of 1910 out of materials procured by Francis Joseph Biggar of Belfast. Also of value during the formative period of the band was the advice of Denis McCullough who was an enthusiast for the *píb mhór*. During 1911 and 1912 the band progressed. In 1913 it won the Championship of Ireland at the Gaelic League Oireachtas in Galway and in 1914, while Ashe was in the United States, it competed with magnificent success in Killarney. Many of its members fought in the 1916 Rising. One of them was Paddy Doyle, who, as a founder member of the band, knows its history. He recalls:

I was with Tom Ashe in the first photo ever taken of the band. That was on St. Patrick's Day 1910, in the old Church yard here in Lusk. The first members were: Tom Ashe, John Rooney, Paddy Doyle, Richard McArdle, Frank Morgan, Joe Clarke, John Clarke, James Sheridan and Matt McGann. That was the first band that ever set foot in Lusk. I was the drummer. It was a Rush man, Davy Langan, who taught me drumming. Pipe-Major Andrews of Dublin taught us piping. We had no difficulties in collecting money for the band. We organised aeraíochts and tournaments. Denis McCullough and F. J. Biggar helped. It was Biggar who presented the first flag to the Black Raven Band.

The Black Raven design derived by tradition from a Danish standard captured at Clontarf. The Lusk Pipers' Band, with its great Viking-pattern standard floating in the breeze, brought colour and romance to many a North County hosting and the best-played pipe music in all Ireland. A favourite picture of Thomas Ashe shows him in kilts, striding at its head, a lithe and magnificent figure, his patrician countenance topped by a shock of fair curly hair, a model of masculine physique, the kind a Praxiteles might love to mould. In any company he caught the eye.

Ashe's early experience as an actor, writer and producer now proved to be of practical value in providing recreation of its own for his community. He organised plays and produced them in the library at Lusk. The dramatic society staged *The Boys of Wexford, The Resurrection of Dinny O'Dowd, The Rising of the Moon* (in which Ashe played the part of the big constabulary sergeant and acted it finely), *The Workhouse Ward* and *The Leadin' Road to Donegal*. Ashe was in charge of everything: producing, managing and directing. A versatile man, he was good at anything.

Paddy Doyle affirms that the coming of Thomas Ashe changed Lusk. Before he came it was a dull, dead place. His coming seemed to resurrect it. Once he got the band started, and the Gaelic League going, everything changed under his influence. He made a new town out of Lusk. He put a lot of work into feiseanna and aeraíochtaí.

John Devine of Lusk first met Ashe about 1910 when the Black Raven Pipe Band was founded.

> We were delighted with Tom Ashe [said John]. He was dreadful straightforward. If he was your friend, he was your friend. If not you had to stand up in argument against him. He played hurling and football for the Lusk team. Then he formed the band. Concerts and tournaments were organised and a collection was made throughout the parish to finance it, to buy pipes and costumes. We formed a Pipers' Club, and Mr Andrews, an expert piper from Dublin, instructed the men in playing. In 1913 we won the championship of Ireland at the Galway Oireachtas.

Ashe was a powerful footballer. No one, said John Devine, could take a ball off him, with the size of him. In play he was a determined man who went for the ball and nothing else. He played midfield. 'We were just the same as brothers with Tom Ashe. Loyalty was intense in the Gaelic League and Volunteers and we would think nothing of going to one another's aid. We were all one.' He organised a number of feiseanna, said William O'Brien, two at least in Swords, and practically ran them himself. He did immense work in organising feiseanna, recalled Anna Coleman, and acted as secretary, treasurer or in any other capacity required. Ashe was a man for getting things done. The Rooneys of Lusk were the same and assisted every Irish enterprise with great spirit. John J. Rooney helped to organise the band. He owned land and gave the hurling and football teams one of his fields to play in, telling a grump who objected, 'That's their field now.'

As for concerts and singing, John Devine believes there was no end to the songs Thomas Ashe had. He was listened to with such attention when he sang that you could hear a pin drop. 'He loved a good yarn and he got plenty of them, I'm telling you, from all the hard chaws around Lusk. It didn't matter what sort a man was, drunk or sober, Tom Ashe mixed with them all and he knew a lot of hard chaws. We used to hold our céilís in the library in Lusk. At céilís, if there was anyone shy of asking the girls out, he insisted that you take a partner. He was great for organising.'

Hard chaws and characters enough there were whose company Ashe enjoyed, the 'Gutler' Kavanagh and the 'Ginner' Carton, for instance, the latter of whom, a noted wit, put to rout his opponent in a battle of words one day with the sally, 'Ye'r so mean ye could hide behind a fishin' rod.'

Ashe was a frequent visitor at the home in Swords of the Colemans, one of the leading nationalist families of North Dublin. There were eleven of them, four girls and seven boys, including Ashe's colleague, Captain Richard Coleman, who died in Usk prison on 9 December 1918 at the age of twenty-nine. 'I often made the tea for Tomás,' recalled Anna Coleman:

> He was companionable and a very good mixer and was greatly admired wherever he went. Of course girls admired him but he didn't bother much with girls. I always liked Tom Ashe. He was a nice, good-looking fellow and a very nice singer. He taught Irish language

songs to the local people in the Gaelic League. He was often in our house in Swords. He used to come wearing his kilts and looked very well. He told me he didn't like wearing kilts. He had lovely fair curls which waved in the breeze. One girl in Lusk told me she was in love with him but that he never noticed her at all.

There was a Fingal girl whose name was associated with Thomas Ashe and with whom he was very friendly. She was Elizabeth Dempsey, who lived close to the site of the old convent of Grace Dieu near Ballyboughal. She was a lovely girl, but delicate, and died young, some years before 1916. Elizabeth Dempsey may be the girl mentioned in a reminiscence given the writer by Anne McAllister of Turvey, Donabate, who remembers Ashe when he first came to Corduff to teach. She was with a group of other girls, all under twenty, when they met him after school hours. To Anne McAllister he looked twenty-two, intensely intelligent and artistic, with a sympathetic friendly nature. In their company that day, she recalls, was 'an exceedingly pretty girl' whose name became linked with Ashe 'though I do not believe either of them ever contemplated marriage', and who later died. Afterwards Ashe became friendly with Anne McAllister's younger sister Nellie, who had returned from school in Girvan, Scotland. Quite naturally girls liked him, and in relaxed moments he was happy in their society. Piaras Béaslaí told me that during Galway Oireachtas week in 1913 Ashe and Sive Trench, a girl of striking beauty, were seen so often in each other's company that people thought their companionship might become a steady one. Ashe was friendly with many girls. But his national work made great claims on his attention and perhaps, with the deprivation of liberty it entailed, did not permit him to commit his heart decisively to any girl. To enquiries I made I received different answers and the question is briefly discussed in the last chapter.

There are men in Fingal whose loyalty and devotion to the memory of Thomas Ashe remain undiminished with the passing years. So vividly does he come to life in their conversation that one would think it was only a few days ago he stood in their midst. Speaking to Paddy Doyle it is easy to see that his association with Ashe was so integral and sincere a part of his experience that he never got over Ashe's death. For him Ashe had no peer, and he speaks for many when he says:

> Tom Ashe would get the people of Fingal to do anything. The youth of Fingal would follow him anywhere. He was a good teacher. What Tom Ashe would tell you you'd never forget. He knew everything about Fingal, its history and associations. He'd sit down and talk to a stranger and find out all about a place. They were all the same to him, no matter whether they were high or low, he talked and mixed with everybody.

Would he recommend Thomas Ashe as an example for Irishmen to follow? In Paddy Doyle's answer there are no reservations. He is well in his seventies now, but the ancestral years of 1798–99 are warm in his blood, and his reply is typical of what you may hear from the men of Lusk who placed their faith in Thomas Ashe:

> I would recommend him as an example for Irishmen to follow. Anyone that was for him would never do wrong and he would never lead you to do anything wrong. Everything Tom Ashe did, no

matter what it was, he had a motive for. Yes, Lusk contributed a great number of good men to the Rising of 1916 and we can thank Tom Ashe for it; it was all his doing. It is my belief the British picked him up in 1917 as he was the most dangerous opponent there was to her rule. They were out to capture him and put him away. I had no hopes of ever again meeting anyone as good as him.

In a letter (printed in Chapter 15) Thomas Ashe states that the parish priest of Lusk (Father Byrne) used to call him a modernist and an anticleric. This is interesting, but it means no more than that Ashe would not brook any interference from clergymen in his politics. Father Byrne was a strong Irish Party man and would have liked the whole parish of Lusk to agree with his views. In the years before 1916 a vigorous political clash took place in the parish between Irish Party interests, championed by Father Byrne, and the independent nationalist group which was largely represented in the Gaelic League and the hurling club. In actual fact it affected the band and the hurling club and there were resignations. In the words of a witness, 'there was hell in the parish for years'. It was in these circumstances that Thomas Ashe became in the parish priest's fertile imagination 'a modernist and an anticleric'.

6

THOUGHTS OF AN IDEALIST

There is good land in Fingal. The broad acres roll and undulate horizonwards to make a picture splendid to the eye and guarantee a bountiful harvest to those who use them well. In Ashe's day, as now, there were many fine farms and substantial houses. Farm labourers were fairly numerous. It was they who did most of the hard work in drawing the wealth from the soil and for this they were miserably rewarded and badly looked after. In terms of simple humanity these farm labourers made rural Ireland a rich, diversified and interesting place. With their numbers, their variety, their vitality, their wit and country wisdom, they gave life, colour and character to the countryside they occupied. They were gay, free and uninhibited, with a great love of music, dancing, roving and adventure. The crossroads rang with the laughter of young men and women. They were able to live, and lived, on little, and how near some or any of them might have been at times to starvation was a secret withheld from the world by their fierce pride. Those of them who married and raised families did so on means so slender that it may well mystify the economists how they managed to remain alive at all. Since the Great Famine of 1847 their numbers, though large, kept decreasing. Their plight and position had aroused the concern, in their time, of reformers like Michael Davitt and Dr Thomas Nulty, but their problem remained without solution. Their plight and problem was viewed by

Thomas Ashe as one of the grave social questions of Ireland and one cognate with problems that existed elsewhere in the world. We may be sure that he saw in them also, as did his beloved Kickham, the raw material of national insurrection, 'the rough and ready roving boys, like Rory of the Hill'. They were the rural counterpart of what might be witnessed in the slums of Dublin and other cities, a large population of underpaid and impoverished working men, who received but a fragment of the wealth which they produced.

Thomas Ashe gave a great deal of thought to the farm labourer's lot. How was he, a producer of the land's wealth but no owner of the soil, to receive a just return for his labour on a permanent and satisfactory basis? Pondering on this issue, as well as on the general features and character of the countryside in which he taught school, Thomas Ashe cast his ideas into the form of a novel, which he wrote while a prisoner in Lewes jail, from the thoughts, impressions and experiences that had accumulated in his mind during his eight years in Corduff. It runs to eleven chapters, written some in pencil, some in ink. He never had the opportunity to finish it or even give it a title.

It is a novel of country life and derives its style and method to some extent from Ashe's study of Charles Kickham, one of his favourite authors. The central character is Fergus O'Farrell, the youngest son of a strong farmer of Clare and a graduate in arts and agriculture, who becomes the owner by purchase of Moyroe farm, in the parish of Moynalty, near to Dublin city but yet too far from it 'for expeditious cart work'. Tensions develop between O'Farrell, who is an idealist, and Captain Mason, a neighbouring squire, who is a martinet towards his workmen. There is fluent, easy, natural dialogue and the novel is full of the ways of the country, as they were and as Thomas would like them to be. Music and song and country pastimes figure in it largely and there is a passage describing the hounds in full chase after the hare, which is obviously from a familiar experience of Thomas's active outdoor life. O'Farrell is friendly with another neighbour, Robert McCormack, who, although sympathetic, finds some of O'Farrell's ideas unusual and disturbing. The following passages from the manuscript will indicate the approach of Fergus O'Farrell towards many things that agitated the world at that time, as well as the ideals which he sought. We may take it that his approach and his ideals represent accurately enough those of the author. Here O'Farrell discusses them with Robert McCormack:

'There are six houses in my native county to every one you see here,' said Fergus. 'There is no more beautiful sight in Ireland than a countryside of white snug farm houses. You can see them in many parts of Ireland, and I much prefer to see them any day than the most lovely scene in Killarney or Wicklow.'

'I agree with you,' said Robert. 'Around the sea coast of Ireland you have a little of the population left, even there only a little. But in many of our inland counties we are desolate. And we are becoming more desolate every day. It is sad to think of it.'

They spent the next half hour not only thinking of it, but discussing it very seriously. They touched on land and land laws, on farms and factories, on labour and labourers, on capital and capitalism, in fact they touched on most Irish problems of the day and Robert finished by stating that the solving of not a single one of these problems rested with Irishmen.

'I don't agree with you in that,' said Fergus.

'What then do you hold concerning them?' asked Robert, rather surprised.

'I hold,' said Fergus very seriously, 'that not a single one of these problems will be solved by methods applied so far and I further hold that the solution of them all rests with ourselves.'

'You surprise me,' said Robert.

'I have spent a good deal of time in thinking over these very problems,' said Fergus, 'and in many cases my conclusions are not complete and in nearly all cases they are untried. But I mean to test them,' he said firmly ...

For some time past Fergus had two ideals before him which he was anxious to see materialised; one was to work a farm of land in the most up-to-date methods or even to foresee and anticipate methods if possible; the other was to pay his workmen the full value of their labour ...

[In the district] They [the farming community] lived rather luxuriously, they were lavish of time, and their richly furnished and comfortable-looking residences showed all the appearance of strong bank accounts. Such bank accounts are, save in exceptional cases, the result of industry. But here Fergus halted. The farms were not being half-worked, not even quarter-worked. This of course prevented the farmers ever learning anything of the organisation and economy of labour. And Fergus peering through the glitter and glare about him saw at last what he had failed to see on first casual observation, that there was very little work given in the district. That caused a curtailment of results and that this lessened the bank accounts. Yet the apparent comfort was real, as the land, being naturally rich, would have kept the farmers in plenty with even the minimum of tillage. And Fergus sighed heavily for the lot of the farm labourer.

A first draft of Chapter III contains the following passage:

The labour world had been very uneasy for some time. A living wage was claimed in nearly all trades. Already it had been granted in many instances, and Fergus thought that the immunity enjoyed by farmers in the past from attacks by organised labour would not extend very far into the future … Fergus believed that justice was not done the farm labourers and as far as he thought his duty lay, he intended doing it …

The custom of profit sharing, such as was used by the fishing crews on the south and west coasts, was naturally a familiar one to Ashe and appeared to him to suggest a principle by which the farm labourers might receive a fair return for their work on the land. In the following excerpt from the novel this idea is proposed by his hero in conversation with Robert McCormack. There can be little doubt that it represents in principle Thomas's own solution for the complex problem involved.

'What are all the strikes you read of nowadays but complaints?' said Fergus. 'The labourers of Europe have complained, so have those of America and Australia. England is a hotbed of strikes for some time and even Ireland has already commenced in her cities.'

'You take a very gloomy view of matters …'

'Nothing gloomy whatever about it,' answered Fergus. 'I see in it all simply a natural growth, a natural outcome of conditions that have existed for some time, and that are ripening every other day. … First of all I hold they (the farm labourers) are entitled to better wages on moral grounds. They do practically all the labour on our farms, which is another way of saying that they are responsible for most of the income got from the sale of all farm produce. Therefore they have a right to a decent part of that income …'

'Let me give you a few particular instances,' said Fergus, 'and I'll make my meaning clear to you. The fishermen in the west coast of Ireland have a peculiar custom in their division of the week's profits. One man owns the boat, nets, sails and provides the food and all other necessaries. These are all said to belong to the boat. The owner, who is practically always skipper, and his assistants, form the crew … The proceeds of a week's work are divided between the crew and the boat – half going to each. An equal division is made of one of the halves among all the crew. Nobody ever grumbles against that arrangement, and I think we should take a leaf from that system and build up our payments for work done in some such way.'

'You mean that we should halve our profits with the workmen,' said Robert.

'No … but I say we should divide our profits on some such principle. At present we pay a man twelve or fourteen shillings a week without knowing why,' remarked Fergus.

It was no casual accident, but a kinship of mind towards the pressing social problems of the time, that led to the close friendship between Ashe and Sean O'Casey the playwright. The hard and sometimes harsh lot of the rural worker, of which Thomas was keenly aware, and the grave injustices borne by the slum-ridden workers of Dublin, which made O'Casey wince with anger, gave these two men of widely different origins an affinity and common cause which drew them together and which they would discuss, with Mícheál Ó Foghludha or Tom Johnson or some other companion, in the course of long walks by Dublin's quaysides. 'Tomás thought the world of him,' Nora Ághas told the writer. Sean O'Casey shared his Irish ideals with Ashe. His tributes to the dead leader in *The Sacrifice of Thomas Ashe* and in the magnificent

Inishfallen Fare Thee Well are touching and tender evocations of a lost comrade. There is no truth in the preposterous legends that make an atheist of Sean O'Casey. That he was a man of profound, if unconventional, religious convictions, who cared deeply for his fellow men who were ill-used, ill-housed, unemployed, badly off and victimised, is the memory retained of him by Nora Ághas, Thomas Ashe's sister, who knew him well through his friendship with her brother.

It is clear from Ashe's writings, as quoted, that he held the concept of an Irish society in which a just return for an honest day's work would be the acknowledged norm. He was a fair-minded man to whom underprivilege was an evil to be eradicated. The march of time, if not of progress, has practically made academic the problem which concerned him. That the farm labourers have almost melted off the face of the land and have, in their generations, become absorbed into the demography of Kilburn and the Black Country does not, however, absolve modern Ireland from the blame of having done too little to halt their disappearance.

7

HOLIDAYS AND
A KERRY JOURNAL

The road to Ashe's birthplace branches off the Tralee–Dingle highway and winds over Abhainn an Londraigh up to Kinard village, which is perched on a lofty shoulder of hill. Above the village are the crags of Carraig an Mhionnáin where he would recline at ease and sketch the trawlers fishing offshore, or cast his eyes over the magnificent land and sea prospect that stretches away to the west. He could see, map-like, the smugglers' cove of Trá Bheag, the harbours of Dingle and Ventry with their magic hinterland of little fields, valleys, villages, and heather-cropped foothills backed by the great mole of Brandon Mountain. Immediately below him lay a fascinating bowl-shaped valley, patterned with all the colours of nature and encircled by great hills.

Thomas Ashe, on a summer's evening, would stand on lofty Carraig hill and fill the valley below with the rousing music of the war pipes. At other times, in more reflective mood, he would let his eyes rove happily over the richly quilted panorama, the golden patches of corn, the little fields tufted with haycocks, the men shouting at the horses and calling to the dogs. In a long letter, which practically takes the form of a journal, written in 1913, he describes the well-loved home scene to his brother Gregory, who in far away Boston was eager to hear every scrap which would bring him the flavour of his native parish. Ashe writes:

I am lying up here on the top of the Carraig. There is a nice breeze of *gaothanoir* blowing. I came up specially to paint a picture of the landscape to the west but owing to the heavy haze that is over the land I think I won't mind this evening ... I can see just as far as Ventry to the west and the sea is as calm as a lake. The trawlers are all going in after spending the day over near Inch, and I can see Mick Hanafin fishing bass down at the Carraig ... From where I am I can see all the neighbours working all round in the fields. Our people are below in the long Gort a'Sgeiche; they have all the rest cut down. Flahive is finishing his last field, the near *Seantóir*, and Matt has all cut down and all hands are working at the new house these days. They are finishing one chimney today and they'll have the whole building done this week.

It is a rural canvas, splashed with local idiom and colour, that Ashe paints. His writing is peppered with Irish phrases. He delights in the idiosyncrasies of Tomáisín Bán, who every day asks him for tobacco and is every day refused by Ashe for the sheer delight of hearing his torrent of curses, 'which would make your hair stand', or of Dónall Michíl who has been persuaded by wags that Ashe is married to a sister of Earnán de Blaghd's and offers the remark that '*nuair a théann siad san as baile ní bhíonn aon chiall acu*'. Two local characters, whose descriptions of girls 'would make the County Kerry laugh', travel by donkey and cart to Annascaul sports, lose a lynch pin on the way, and for good measure steal a round half-dozen from other unfortunates to make sure one fits for them. Another, upset by a volley of banter as he stands on a ladder at haymaking, falls and breaks two ribs, after which he relates his misfortune to Father Casey in fascinating dialect.

Ashe took special pleasure in the company of Séamus Griffin. Griffin was a tidy husbandman whose haystack was always a model of neatness. One evening a savage Atlantic gale lashed the heights of Kinard and drove every creature, human and animal, to the refuge of the nearest shelter. Séamus Griffin, uneasy about his bay and corn stacks, got up to secure them with stays. Neighbours tried to dissuade him from going out on such a night. 'Why worry?' said they, 'God will look after your crops and care for them.' 'It's all right to talk,' said Griffin, nothing reassured, 'and it's all right for God. He can sit in his parlour, eating meat and cabbage.' This was his idea of heaven, and the philosophy of it appealed immensely to Ashe. So did the quip about another local, no genius at letters, whose talents at the alphabet were summed up by his sarcastic neighbour as *D'aithneodh sé O* (he would recognise O).

Earnán de Blaghd, afterwards Minister for Finance in Cosgrave's government, was at that time, the summer of 1913, living in Gregory Ashe's house in Kinard, where he had come, having resigned from a post with the *North Down Herald*, to perfect his knowledge of Irish. He became as one of the household, doing his part of the farm work and sharing in all the tasks and chores common to life on the land. It was hard but healthy work and Earnán de Blaghd's stamina improved along with his Irish. Thomas Ashe writes to Gregory:

> Earnán is nearly killed from working. He speaks no English and I have to laugh when I hear him saying *Gortabhaile* and all the other names of the fields. He's a very nice fellow and is a capital scholar and knows everything.

Earnán de Blaghd in his description of 'The Old Time Farm' in the April 1914 issue of *Irish Freedom* described the features of older life and methods which in his time still survived in Kinard:

> Twenty yards from where I write, lives a man who ground corn with a quern every winter until old age incapacitated him two or three years ago. I see men go to Mass every Sunday wearing linen shirts, for which they grew and dressed the flax, only sending it a little way from their own houses to be woven. In nearly every house about me the women spin wool, and for all I know there may be places where they still spin flax. An odd quern, I am sure, is still in use.

Thomas Ashe's brother, John, married and took over the working of the family farm in Kinard. John's son, Tomás, now of Ballsbridge, Dublin, kindly furnished me with his childhood memories of his uncle:

> I remember Tomás well. We, as children, looked forward with the greatest delight to the times he would come home to us on holidays. He loved children, all children, but naturally he had a special grá for us. My mother loved Tomás. He used bring the pipes with him and go up on the Carraig, overlooking our home, and take us along with him and play the pipes there. To hear the music filling the whole parish would lift up your heart. Though there might be people in the house, Tomás would become altogether absorbed in his conversation with the children. I remember when he came home after his release from prison in 1917. His stay was very short. He went back to Dingle but had to leave almost at once to take part in the Clare election campaign.

Thomas Ashe's sister Mary was married in Dingle to Michael

Devane and the ties of family called him on many a visit to that sociable and pleasant little town. He found kindred spirits there who joined him in his earnest desire for an Ireland that would have her own special identity of language, custom and heritage. Dingle was a town with a proud past, though fallen on lesser days than when it was the resort of Spanish merchants and mariners, and its position as trading centre of the West Kerry Gaeltacht gave it a Gaelic flavour which could be best appreciated on fair and market days.

Ashe invariably brought his war pipes with him to enliven its ancient streets and draw echoes from the surrounding hills. He writes to Gregory:

> We had great times in Dingle this year with the Irish folk. I had the pipes there every night and we had many a march round the town. On the last night of the break-up we marched round the town at two o'clock and they all singing behind me. I played 'A Nation Once Again', 'Who Fears to Speak of '98', 'God Save Ireland' and 'The Wearin' of the Green'. They sang them all and we woke up the whole town.

New and vehement strains of nationality, deriving from old, heroic sources and introduced mainly through the influence of the Gaelic League, were acting like a tonic to renew the life force of the nation, and large segments of Ireland's youth were responding to their appeal. They produced impulses which no restricted form of Home Rule was likely to satisfy. The Gaelic League had banished nineteenth-century parliamentary traditions to limbo. Local and sporadic hints of rebellion were coming into evidence. When a brisk and impromptu rebel demonstration took place at Inch, under the inspiration of a group of young Dingle nationalists, Thomas Ashe indicated its significance to Gregory by describing some of these boys as *all right*. It was an old Fenian echo. The words were commonly used between the initiated to show that the person so described was a member of the Irish Republican Brotherhood (IRB). This was the organisation founded in 1858 to which James Stephens, Thomas Clarke Luby, O'Donovan Rossa and many other famous Irish leaders belonged and of which, at that very time, Thomas Ashe was a member, as were his colleagues Seán Mac Diarmada, Tom Clarke, Patrick Pearse, Éamonn Ceannt and many others. It appears from this too, that a body of the organisation existed in the Dingle district. Its object was the achievement of an independent Irish Republic. It was an object which occupied much of Thomas Ashe's thoughts.

Ashe was in his full health and vigour and the prospects of youth in that glorious time were full of promise. Life teemed with adventure. He tramped the hills, gun in hand, with his favourite red setter. He swam in the sea every day. He drew landscapes and portraits in oils and pencil. He loved country life, and its attractions figure constantly in his thoughts and writings. He writes of the Kinard pastoral:

> The whole country has a look of peace and quiet, and it would delight one to hear the children playing down in Kinard. I always like to hear the laughter of children, and I can hear them now plainly down near Matt's new house.

His excellence at the pipes was appreciated by a music-loving people and made him a favourite wherever he went. Sometimes men cried at some memory or emotion awakened by old strains, as his neighbour, Séamus Thomáis, did on hearing 'Maidin Cheoidh'. He sang songs, with the flair for singing that was in his blood. "Twas in the breed, you know, the singing was in his breed,' was the way it was put to the writer (in 1966) by eighty-or-so-years-old John Matt Ashe, of Minard East, who travelled much of the world and never saw, in his life and wanderings, a finer looking man than Thomas Ashe, 'and I have seen them in all colours, white and black and yellow'.

On Sunday afternoons and evenings the young people of Kinard, as everywhere in the west and south of Ireland, enjoyed themselves at dancing, mainly the attractive figure dances known as sets, which have done so much to make Irish airs familiar. Every parish had its quota of accomplished melodeon players for these occasions, and the dances took place in the open air in fine weather, preferably at a crossroads. 'Yesterday,' writes Ashe, 'I went to the dance at Doonshean Point. We had a big crowd and we were dancing sets until quite late. I enjoyed it very much.' It is not strange that girls found Ashe an extraordinarily attractive man. His fine physique and handsome features were enhanced by his friendly and pleasant manner. The distinguished Irish writer Pádraig Ó Siochfhradha (An Seabhac) described to me a Gaelic League outing to Dunquin organised by Ashe and Fionán Mac Coluim. It was a great success, but very noteworthy was the fact that Ashe became the centre of feminine attentions while Fionán Mac Coluim, for all the notice that was taken of him from first to last, might as well not have existed. This may have been the occasion recalled to the writer by Father Maurice Boland, Ventry,

County Kerry, now of Waterville, Maine, USA, who accompanied Ashe and the students of Dingle Irish College on an excursion around Slea Head in the sunny summer of 1913:

We started from Dingle about twelve noon. There were no buses or autos in those days. There were about 35 jaunting cars and on the way west through Ventry many boys and girls with bikes joined the parade. There were students from Cork, Limerick and Tipperary who wanted to enjoy the beauties of Slea Head. Our first stop was at Dunquin National School, where after a picnic lunch we danced sets, reels and polkas. It was a merry throng and the dancers raised clouds of dust. After that we had songs and recitations. Tomás Ághas was a good singer and dancer. His first song was an Irish one I had never heard before and his second was 'A Nation Once Again' into which he put great feeling. Thomas Ashe had character written on his face. He was thoughtful and considerate of everyone and a real gentleman.

8

THE GAELIC LEAGUE

We give here an extract from a letter of Patrick Pearse in *Sinn Féin*, 18 November 1911:

> At the May meeting of the Coiste Gnótha, during the course of a discussion on the position of Irish in the primary schools, Mr Thomas Ashe suggested that it might be worthwhile to consider the feasibility of establishing under Gaelic League auspices and in or near an Irish speaking district a training college for primary teachers, which should be frankly Irish in standpoint and which should specialise in the training of teachers to handle Irish education in the Gaeltacht. The suggestion was received with unanimous approbation. We all felt that in the midst of a babel of Talk a man had stood up and proposed a Deed. The proposal, be it noted, was not to ask the National Board to do anything: it was a proposal to do something ourselves.

It is unnecessary to go into the controversy which followed this proposal or to deal with its fortunes, except to say that it received the approval of the Bishop of Galway, in whose diocese it was intended to locate the college, and was promised consideration by Dr Starkie of the Board of Education. Pearse approved of it strongly and we quote from him to show how well he thought of Thomas Ashe. The proposal indicates Ashe's flair for initiative and self-reliance.

In forwarding the work of the Gaelic League, Thomas Ashe

showed no hint of personal preferences or fads. He was completely indifferent about regional dialects and took no part or interest in the futile controversies that raged on the subject. What he considered of pressing importance was that the language should advance in strength, no matter in what dialect. Dr Seán P. MacEnrí has described him as 'a liberal-minded Munsterman' free from narrow provincialism.[1]

Like all earnest language workers he was profoundly disturbed by the revelations of the 1911 census. This showed a considerable decrease in the number of Irish speakers over the previous ten years. In the examination of conscience which followed this disclosure a strong reaction set in amongst the younger members of the Coiste Gnótha against the policy pursued by the League within more recent years. An Irish article in *Sinn Féin* entitled 'Staid Chonnartha na Gaedhilge' makes a reference to the left wing (*An Foirsciathán Clé*) of the Executive Body of the Gaelic League and stated that the infusion of new blood was imperative.[2] Critics of the Coiste Gnótha accused that body of being too cautious, inoffensive and cajoling in its approaches to the government. They stated that up to 1906 the Coiste Gnótha had been aggressive and direct in its policy towards the Balfour government and while so had been a potent and respected force in Irish affairs but that, in 1906, when the Liberal government took office under Campbell-Bannerman, the Coiste Gnótha altered its fighting policy to one of diplomacy and negotiation. The sincerity of those at the head of the Gaelic League was no asset when it came to playing the game of diplomacy with government departments. They were out-manoeuvred, gulled and chloroformed with promises which were not kept, as for instance that a second language would be made compulsory in the training colleges in 1911. The strength focused behind the Gaelic League was partly dissipated until from being a significant force it declined in strength and status. This, in substance, was what its critics accused.

The shock of the 1911 census, which showed that the efforts of the Gaelic League had failed to arrest the decline in the number of Irish speakers, caused demands within the Executive Body of the League for a more decisive and forward policy. These demands came from a group of young men who, in the controversies of the time, were called the left wing.

The Gaelic League was professedly a non-political body. In the Coiste Gnótha, which numbered fifty persons, there were people of differing political complexions. Some supported John Redmond and his nationalist party, others reflected AOH [Ancient Order of Hibernians] views, others were moderate and conservative; there were individualists of strong national calibre like The O'Rahilly, and a youthful, active and progressive group of left-wing nationalists, republicans by preference and tradition. Over them all presided Douglas Hyde, of no declared conviction in politics but in his earlier years, as author of *Smuainte Bróin* and correspondent of O'Donovan Rossa, a fervent nationalist, now grown more cautious, mellow and conservative, holding responsibility for a great national movement composed of diverse elements, a diplomat of rare skill who tried to hold left, right and centre in equipoise and co-operation for the furtherance of his beloved Irish language, a man held in immense respect throughout Ireland.

Included in the activist left wing were Frank Fahy, the brothers Risteárd and Mícheál Ó Foghludha, Diarmuid Crowley, Seán Mac Diarmada, Seán T. O'Kelly, Pádraic Ó Máille, Éamonn Ceannt,

The O'Rahilly and Thomas Ashe. Most of these men, Thomas Ashe included, were members of the IRB. They formed the most active and earnest element in the Coiste Gnótha. In their resolve to show no deference to the departmental forces which hampered the language movement and to brook no official opposition to its advance, they incurred the resentment of an influential right-wing conservative group in the Coiste Gnótha which had much influence with Dr Hyde. Piaras Béaslaí, a well-informed authority on the period, tells us that one of the most prominent of this group or clique to oppose the left wing was Dr Agnes O'Farrelly, who was in politics a supporter of John Redmond. Although Dr O'Farrelly did on occasion support and acclaim Thomas Ashe in certain points (*Táimse le Tomás* she would say) she was an opponent of the more aggressive and uncompromising policy which he represented on the Coiste Gnótha. In later years she was appointed to the Chair of Modern Irish Poetry in University College Dublin.

The tensions between the two rival elements within the Executive Body kept mounting until a near crisis developed in 1913. The differences between them followed the classic pattern of revolutionary left and conservative right and in the years between 1911 and 1915 the views of Thomas Ashe and the left wing as to the proper and urgent functions of the Gaelic League gradually gained supremacy.

Early in 1913 there was difference of opinion on a proposal made by The O'Rahilly, and supported by Thomas Ashe and Eoin MacNeill, that Sir Edward Carson, William O'Brien, Arthur Griffith and John Redmond, the acknowledged leaders of Irish opinion, ought to be asked to sign the annual appeal for funds

by the Gaelic League as evidence that the whole Irish people, ir-
respective of politics, were united in support of the language. Dr
Hyde objected to the inclusion of Carson's name and the proposal
was finally dropped because only Griffith and O'Brien signified
their willingness to sign.

The tensions between the groups developed in part over their
different attitudes to the Insurance Act, recently passed into law,
which declined to recognise the existence of an Irish language. On
a wider basis they differed in their attitudes towards the education authorities, who denied any proper status to the language in
the educational system. The Coiste Gnótha passed a resolution
calling for adequate provision for the language in the schools. In
pursuance of this, the left wing insisted on a more aggressive and
energetic policy for the League and for the fulfilment by appro-
priate steps of the Coiste Gnótha resolution. This line of action
was opposed by the conservative wing of the Coiste Gnótha and
deprecated by Dr Hyde.

Finally the controversy overflowed into the press and a brisk
public correspondence ensued. *The Freeman's Journal* of July 1913
covers in detail the public aspects of the discussion (3, 4, 7, 8,
9, 12 and 14 July 1913). In a long article, prominently headed
'Gaelic League Irreconcilables', Dr Hyde claimed that the progress of the League up to the present time was accomplished by
'sweet reasonableness, mutual forbearance and good feeling on all
sides'.[3] In an exchange of correspondence with Arthur Griffith,
who espoused the left wing, Dr Hyde expressed his policy as one
of 'sanity and reasonableness and making friends all round, and
getting the whole country, priests and people, Parliamentarians,
Sinn Féiners, O'Brienites and Unionists, to bring pressure to bear

upon big and vital issues, especially upon our Education Boards, so as to accomplish Irish-Ireland changes according as we are ripe for them'. Hyde considered that ten years of this policy should see them 'well-advanced towards an Irish-Ireland'.[4]

Men like Thomas Ashe and Éamonn Ceannt, who represented the activist left wing, saw the policy pursued by Dr Hyde in a different light. To them it savoured too much of behind-the-scenes diplomacy and backstairs negotiation, especially with the Liberal government with which Redmond was aligned, and with the all-powerful Parliamentary Party. Unlike Dr Hyde, they were not particular about whom they might offend by plain speaking. There are times when one is tempted to believe, like a certain confidant of Sean O'Casey's, that Dr Hyde would have liked to see a large sprinkling around him in the Coiste Gnótha of dukes, baronets and earls. Developing further the left-wing point of view, Éamonn Ceannt stated that the Gaelic League had three policies to choose from: the parliamentarian or deputation-cum-negotiation method, the Sinn Féin or self-reliance method, and the physical force method. At present, he went on, certain people wanted to restrict the League to the use of the parliamentarian method. This attempt would have to be resisted at all costs. Ceannt equated Dr Hyde's policy of sanity and commonsense with the parliamentarian method and considered it as the one least likely to succeed in dealing with the Irish people. It was the business of the Gaelic League to fight every force in Ireland which opposed the language. 'If peaceful methods fail, then let there be war.' The League would respect no politicians who publicly opposed its advance or privately pulled strings against it. No single weapon could be discarded, whether it be branded Sinn Féin, physical force or parliamentarianism. It was open to the League to use all three or any one of them with reference to nobody except those in control of the organisation.[5]

Some months earlier Ceannt, in reference to the non-political banner of the Gaelic League, conceded that the device was good policy in the past but he declined to be committed to it in future. 'Irish must be made a political fact.'[6]

These were views which Thomas Ashe would applaud and with which he was in full agreement. Both Ashe and Ceannt would likewise be in accord with the national teachings propounded by Arthur Griffith in the columns of *Sinn Féin* while rejecting his dual monarchy concept and his anti-Larkin attitude.

It may be doubted if the step taken by Dr Hyde in July 1913, of publicly denouncing six members of the Coiste Gnótha, was in accord with his policy of sanity and commonsense. He accused them of obstructing his efforts at conciliation and of antagonising moderate supporters of the language. Amongst those denounced by Dr Hyde were Thomas Ashe, Diarmuid Crowley, Frank Fahy and Mícheál Ó Foghludha. The right wing was supposed to have inspired this action of Dr Hyde. Simultaneously a legion of rumours, suspected to be of right-wing origin, was set in circulation, to the effect that an opprobrious and sinister conspiracy was on foot to unseat Dr Hyde from the presidency of the Gaelic League. The right-wing coterie, which leaned heavily on the immense popularity of Dr Hyde, used the supposed threat to his presidency as a stick to beat the left wing.

Thomas Ashe contributed two letters to the public controversy which followed. The first, which is of considerable length, appears in *The Freeman's Journal* of 7 July 1913. It reads in part:

A Chara,

I much regret being obliged to enter into anything of the nature of a public controversy with Dr Hyde, for whom I entertain, in common I believe with all Gaelic Leaguers, feelings of the highest esteem. But in his speech on Thursday night he singled out myself and others and accused us of refusing to 'play fair' in a way which, he says, 'disgusts all reasonable people.' That is very unusual language coming from An Craoibhín Aoibhinn regarding anybody, much less regarding members of the Coiste Gnótha ... and I simply want now to show that in one particular educational matter there is no justification for it ...

Tomás Ághas
Member of the Coiste Gnótha

Cor Dubh, Lusca
5 July 1913.

Protagonists from both sides joined in the subsequent controversy, in defence and in criticism of Thomas Ashe who in this correspondence was obviously recognised as the left-wing leader. Supporting him were, amongst others, Alderman Peadar Macken and P. S. Ua Dubhghaill, a later lord mayor of Dublin, the latter of whom asked whether certain jottings in *An Claidheamh Soluis* were samples of Dr Hyde's 'sanity and commonsense', while his critics included S. Mac Coillte and Uaithne Ó Lochlainn of Castlebellingham, a member of the Coiste Gnótha.[7] Ashe replied, very briefly, to his critics, pointing out that his views had been upheld by the Education Committee of the Gaelic League and by the Coiste Gnótha, unanimously in both cases.[8]

In *Sinn Féin* Arthur Griffith entered the discussion on behalf of the left wing with a vigour which showed the esteem in which he held Thomas Ashe and his colleagues. In an open letter to

Dr Hyde he deprecated his association 'with a resolution calling for the resignation of some of your colleagues whose sincerity is as transparent as your own, and whose offence is their perhaps caustic criticism, not of you personally, but of those within the League to whose timid and whiggish counsels you have latterly succumbed'.[9] In an exchange of correspondence with Dr Hyde, Griffith, himself no competent Irish scholar, gave support to the language movement in terms that deserve the widest recognition. It was his reasoned conviction that without the language there would never be seen again on this planet an independent Irish nation or indeed an Irish nation of any kind. It was his conviction, too, that Dr Hyde was the fittest man in the ranks of Irish Ireland to stand at the head of the Gaelic League, but with equal firmness he asserted that the men whom Dr Hyde had been misled into condemning were the best working elements in the League.[10] These colleagues of his Dr Hyde had denounced as mutineers, representing them to the public as a minority and pointing to six of them as ripe for execution. He appealed to Dr Hyde to assert his presidency and to discard the coterie with whom he had unfortunately associated himself.[11]

Two other noted personalities who entered the controversy were Patrick Pearse and P. S. O'Hegarty from whom contributions appeared in the August 1913 issue of *Irish Freedom*. Pearse, in an article headed 'From a Hermitage' and signed P. H. P., took Dr Hyde's side unreservedly:

I love and honour Douglas Hyde above all the men who are leading us Irish today … O ye of little sense, know ye not when ye have got a good captain for a good cause.

while O'Hegarty, who signed himself 'Sarsfield', charged An Craoibhín in the strongest terms with having:

> … thrown all the weight of his personal influence, and his long and strenuous service to the language, into the scale on the side of the reactionaries in the League and, not content with that, he threatens to resign if he does not get the aforesaid heads (of his critics) upon a charger.

In Coiste Gnótha sessions Thomas Ashe was sensible, businesslike and, when necessary, very forthright. To say that he did not suffer fools gladly would be putting it in a way which might be an injustice to his innate sense of courtesy. His purpose, as stated in his own forceful words, was 'to remodel the Gaelic League to get it to preach strong, sterling nationality, and to rid it of some of the old women, and of some of the fossils that control it at present … to preach such teachings as will make the Gaelic League a resourceful novitiate, so to speak, for societies who want freedom and who mean to get it by the only means that men worthy of freedom ever thought of attaining such.'[12]

Corresponding to these views of Thomas Ashe is the import of a passage in an open letter in Irish from Éamonn Ceannt to Dr Hyde:

> *Tá cuid againn a's ní shasódh aon ní sinn ach clann Sheáin Bhuí do ruaigeadh as Éirinn. Ceapamuid gur maith an t-arm chum na hoibre sin an Ghaeilg.*[13]

The writer is indebted to the well-known Irish author Pádraic Óg Ó Conaire for the following description of Thomas Ashe:

I knew Thomas Ashe fairly well as I often met him at the Gaelic League Ard-Fheis and at Oireachtas functions. He was a man you could not help but notice, a man whom it was a privilege to know personally. He was tall, straight, loose-limbed, athletic, with auburn wavy hair, rather fair-complexioned. I would say he was close to six feet in height, always well-dressed, in appearance a perfect aristocrat. He usually wore tweeds, which accentuated his fine physique. He wore a moustache as was the custom of the times. Usually a serious man, he could at times laugh heartily. He reminded one of Michael Collins, only Collins had a more hearty and cheery temperament. As far as I can remember he was not very talkative. Even at a dance or social gathering you would think his mind was occupied by things far away. He would listen patiently to a discussion but if he thought anything irrelevant was brought up he would say so bluntly. I do not think he would put up too gladly with fools.

As far as I know, it was Tomás who founded the Black Raven Pipe Band of Lusk. I can still recall their great floating banner with its raven design. Of that fine company of pipers none was more impressive than he, as he marched at their head in kilts, a dress which well became him because of his form and physique, and it is not everyone it so becomes. He was a great long distance walker and came on foot many a time to Coiste Gnótha meetings at 25 Parnell Square, and because of the fondness for talk and argument displayed by some of the members you may be sure that Tomás at times wished he was back at his lodgings, that is if he remained till the end at all.

His colleague on the Coiste Gnótha, Professor Liam Ó Briain, told the writer in conversation that Ashe, 'a Viking chief in appearance', spoke at meetings only as much as was necessary and related to the business on hand. 'He was very close to the great men of the national movement, Tom Clarke and Seán Mac Diarmada.'

Left wing, right wing, all were agreed that there was no other president for the Gaelic League but Dr Hyde. The presidency was not the question in issue, but an all-out attempt was made by the moderates to make it appear that it was, and a campaign was launched to create a climate of opinion against the offending left wing in which, at the forthcoming Ard-Fheis in Galway city, they would be ousted from the Coiste Gnótha so as to leave the government of the League in charge of the reactionary and Whig-ridden right wing.

There was another powerful but not obvious factor to be reckoned with. The IRB, of which Ashe was a member, in pursuance of its policy of permeating key nationalist organisations and securing a controlling influence within them, now rallied its forces to support the left wing. The right wing gathered its forces to crush out the alleged disturbers, making skilful use of Dr Hyde's popularity. They had no real conception of the cohesion, firmness and solidarity of the republican forces which composed the left.

The plan of campaign was to reduce the personnel of the Coiste Gnótha from fifty to twenty-five and this proposal was put by Dr Agnes O'Farrelly to the assembled delegates in Galway. Thomas Ashe's amendment that the number be reduced to thirty-five was lost by seventy-three to forty-two but it was evident that the meeting was much impressed by his earnest demeanour and sincerity. A compromise was suggested in an amendment by Éamon de Valera, Professor of Mathematics at Carysfort Training College, that the number be reduced to thirty and this was agreed. De Valera's main interest at the time was centred in the language movement (he was principal of Tawin Summer School, County Galway) and he took no part in public affairs, being in politics, if anything, a supporter of the Irish Party's Home Rule policy. Dr Hyde, who had been threatening resignation and made some tactical disappearances at the inception of the Ard-Fheis, reappeared dramatically and was proposed for the presidency by The O'Rahilly, a left-wing member. The proposal was seconded by another left-wing man, Éamonn Ceannt, in striking contrast to the accusations that the leftists had sought to displace him. Dr Hyde was re-elected amidst the applause of a united Ard-Fheis, and in a conciliatory speech of acceptance he did much to smooth the troubled waters. In the elections to the Coiste Gnótha Thomas Ashe was re-elected with a substantial vote, a personal triumph achieved under the handicap of being pointed at by Dr Hyde as a disturber of the peace.

The left wing was not wiped out, as its detractors had hoped. On the contrary, it was returned with a representation which made its strength on the Executive Body secure. Elected along with Ashe were Ceannt, The O'Rahilly, Seán T. O'Kelly and Diarmuid Lynch. At the Ard-Fheis much colour was given to the proceedings by a display of bands, prominent amongst which was Thomas Ashe's own Black Raven Pipe Band from Lusk.

At a public meeting in Eyre Square he was one of the chief speakers, his fine address and presence being marked with the calmness and dignity which were noted in his personality by Ceannt. There were serious meetings held in deep secrecy, as at Pádraic Ó Máille's, which Ashe attended. To balance them were social gatherings which made the evenings pleasant and interesting, at one of which, Piaras Béaslaí in his valuable record tells us, Ashe played bridge with Seán Mac Diarmada, Mícheál Ó Foghludha and himself, at the Imperial Hotel, until four o'clock in the morning.[14]

Writing to his brother Gregory, who was in Boston, Ashe described pithily the conflict within the Coiste Gnótha and its outcome. He related that they had a great row in the Gaelic League, that five of them were named as disturbers of the peace and that Dr Hyde exhorted the Gaelic League to throw them out at the Ard-Fheis elections. There was a public correspondence in which Dr Hyde made a fool of himself. Ashe believed Dr Hyde had been urged on by the Coiste Gnótha conservatives. Out of the five persons named only himself had been re-elected, although he was supposed to be their leader. He was confident they would all have been re-elected had the Coiste Gnótha not been reduced from fifty to thirty. Nineteen out of that thirty were left-wing supporters. Every one of those who had attacked him failed to secure re-election. They were completely beaten and the Gaelic League would be kept straight for another while. Had the left wing been defeated, the League, he thought, would have become an adjunct of Redmond's party before Christmas. But they would be purchased by no upholder of empire.

In the outcome everything worked smoothly again, for the time being at least, and Ashe, writing from Corduff on 14 November 1913, tells Gregory that things are calm and quiet:

The Gaelic League is working away as usual. We have no more rows at headquarters but there will be none either as our party have a complete majority. We have played a very clever game with the Insurance Commissioners. We want cards in Irish, and Irish an equal place with English, in the working of the Act. They refuse and threaten to summon and fine us. Well this is what we have done. We have printed a card in Irish ourselves and on to this we'll affix their stamps. The stamps are the whole thing. As long as we buy them they can't fine us. And if they accept our card we have them beaten. There will be fun if they summon us still. Dr Hyde agreed to this, but it was only when he saw that we were all against him. He believes we shouldn't spend any of the Gaelic League money in contesting things in the courts.

The year 1913 had been an important and significant one for the Gaelic League. It marked the end of the temporary depression through which it had been passing and the definite establishment of left-wing supremacy in the governing body. It was a step further towards committing the Gaelic League to the separatist idea. In 1914 the republican group increased its strength on the Executive Body and at the 1915 Ard-Fheis, which was held in the Foresters' Hall, Dundalk, a climax occurred. A resolution was submitted to it in the following terms:

> The Gaelic League shall be strictly non-political and non-sectarian, and shall devote itself to realising the ideal of a Gaelic-speaking and free Irish nation, free from all subjection to foreign influences.[15]

There was some discussion about the political implications of this resolution, and it was obvious enough that it was displeasing to Dr Hyde, but in the end it was carried unanimously. In the elections to the Coiste Gnótha Thomas Ashe was re-elected, along with a very strong left-wing and IRB representation. This was the result which really disturbed Dr Hyde. He wrote to the general secretary to say that pressure of work was telling on his health and he could not remain president of the League any longer.[16] He was succeeded, after an interval, by Eoin MacNeill.

9

A JOURNEY TO AMERICA

The Executive Body of the Gaelic League now showed the esteem in which it held Thomas Ashe by selecting him, along with Diarmuid Lynch, to go to the United States on a fundraising mission on behalf of the Gaelic League, which was hampered in its work by lack of money. Diarmuid Lynch had considerable previous experience of America, where he had been a leader in the Irish language movement and, although not a Clan na Gael man, had been in close touch with John Devoy and other leaders of Irish-America.

They left for the States early in 1914. The Department of Education records show a break in Ashe's teaching service in Corduff dating from 31 January 1914 to 3 October the same year and this period coincides roughly with his absence in America.

It was a new experience for Ashe, although his brother Gregory and numerous relatives lived in America. However, he did not use the occasion to explore the amenities of the country but literally slaved night and day at the task on hand, for the next seven months, chiefly in New York and the New England states.

In New York City the headquarters of the Gaelic League of Ireland was located at 624 Madison Avenue and its cable address, appropriately enough, was 'Blaskets, New York', a reminder that a favourite local saying on the West Kerry coast was 'Next parish, America.' While in New York it became Ashe's headquarters. Here he would put in a full day's work from ten in the morning until twelve midnight. His area of work lay mainly in the eastern states. His diary, with brief entries, is extant. It includes addresses of relatives, of leaders like Judge Cohalan, and reminders of duties or functions such as a *Céilidh* and *Óráid i nGaedhilg* for certain dates. In America at the same time was Patrick Pearse, collecting funds for his great educational enterprise at St Enda's School. Support for Ashe and Pearse came from the same sources, namely Clan na Gael, Gaelic League and AOH members.

Emigration from Ireland had provided a considerable population of Irish speakers in the United States and an extensive and sympathetic milieu for the ideals of the Gaelic League. Readers of Dr Hyde's interesting and valuable *Mo Thurus go hAmerice* will be aware of the impact of the League on American intellectual life as well as on the Irish race. A great Irish-American political movement had given the lead, at the Philadelphia Convention of 1883, in adopting the study of the Irish language as part of its programme, setting a precedent which it took a long time for any political party in Ireland to follow. John Devoy in the early eighties had recommended the study of the language in his paper *The Irish Nation* and engaged the services of Thomas O'Neill Russell to discuss language problems in the paper. In the presidential election campaign of 1884 the successful candidate, Grover Cleveland, received an Irish address of welcome in New York from his supporters of 'An Páirtí Comhfhlathasach', which was read by the scholarly Captain Thomas D. Norris of Killarney. An address of welcome in Irish was composed and read by O'Donovan Rossa to greet the Sixty-Ninth Regiment home from campaign. The manufacturing cities of New England had a large content of Irish speakers.

In the O'Curry Library in University College Dublin is a collection of Irish manuscripts bequeathed to Dr Douglas Hyde by Patrick Ferriter, an Irish scholar of Ballyferriter, County Kerry, who lived in the United States from 1896 until his death in 1924. Many of these Irish manuscripts were collected by Ferriter in the States. More contain poems and other literature taken down by him from Irish speakers resident in America. It goes to show that it was possible at that time to carry out a great deal of first-hand Irish language research in America. Consequently a large potential of Gaelic League support existed in America.

Ashe's programme of work included the interviewing of prominent Irish leaders to ask them for funds in support of the Gaelic League. He also had to draft and circulate numerous collection cards and appeals. Diarmuid Lynch and himself divided, each taking certain territories. Thomas toured the New England cities, which contained large Irish populations. He organised fund collections in Providence, Worcester, Springfield, Holyoke, Hartford and many other centres which were, and still are, household names in the counties bordering the west and south coast of Ireland. Amongst the American-Irish of New York and New England he came up against some real hard-hitting criticism of the Gaelic League. There was no fight in it, they said, and for some time past it had been altogether without spine or spirit. Ashe's own firm opinion was that if the League at present was blessed with the same energy as it showed ten years previously, his journey to America would have been unnecessary. He also discovered that the Irish in America supported the League because, and only because, they believed a re-Gaelicised Ireland would seek to achieve complete political independence. The figures of the recent census had shown them, however, that the Irish language was not making progress and that seemingly the dawn of freedom was further away than ever. For this reason they were dissatisfied with the Gaelic League. So Ashe reported to Pádraig Ó Dálaigh, General Secretary of the Gaelic League, in a letter of 6 April 1914.

He kept in close and constant touch with his friends in Dublin and with Gaelic League affairs. Every month, at his request, the Coiste Gnótha minutes and *An Claidheamh Soluis*, official organ of the Gaelic League, were mailed to him. He sent a report of his progress to the secretary once a month with a request that it be placed before the Coiste Gnótha. He kept a record of his expenses with meticulous care and submitted it to headquarters in Dublin. He worked to a definite plan. When going to a city he took with him introductions to the leaders of Irish societies in that city and through them secured invitations to speak to the societies on behalf of the Gaelic League. Committees were then selected by the societies to raise funds. Ashe was pleased with his progress in New Haven, where the Irish societies were very patriotic. It was tedious and plodding work, however. It used to take him at least two or three weeks to visit all the societies in a city. Sometimes he worked two or three cities at the same time. He had warm praise for the Irish women and girls of America because of the support and loyalty they gave to Irish national ideals.

In Hartford a suggestion was made to him which, if acted on promptly by his Dublin colleagues, would have made his work easier and the results more satisfactory. Within recent years the development of the movie camera had made possible new and exciting techniques of publicity. The idea was to get films of Irish national interest from Dublin to be shown in the theatres, illustrating such events as Volunteers drilling, football and hurling matches, parades, races, feiseanna and industries. In Dublin Ashe had seen a lot of these in the Rotunda picture house, which he was sure could easily be hired. The American theatre managements were willing to show them in order to attract the Irish public. It would add to the success of the scheme that the theatre managers were very pro-Irish. Thomas proposed to explain the pictures from a Gaelic League standpoint, which was the 'safest, strongest and most impressive standpoint at present'. News of the Volunteers was much sought after by the American-Irish. If he had the films he would find his work much more pleasant and very much quicker, for in one night, in any city, he would attract to the theatre most of the interested Irish population.

A personal canvass was slow and unsatisfactory. When he arrived in Connecticut he spent four days calling on people in the large city of Bridgeport. It took him a solid half-hour to convince each individual that he 'wasn't a fakir'. He had no money to show after his four days' interviewing but all had given promises to send some through the treasurer. He found that the rich people, when they subscribed, liked to do so through the Irish societies so that they might get credit for what they gave. Chief support for the Gaelic League came from Clan na Gael. Clan na Gael, although probably not then the most extensive Irish national organisation in America, was the most advanced and determined. As it was the American counterpart of the IRB, Ashe and Diarmuid Lynch had an immediate affinity with it. Men of influence within it were John T. Keating of Chicago, Joseph McGarrity of Philadelphia, and most celebrated of all, John Devoy of New York, now in his sixty-ninth year, one of the most persistent, dedicated and powerful minds that ever directed a revolutionary movement. Knowing that his personal and public support would carry immense influence in favour of the Gaelic League amongst Irish nationalists, Ashe wrote to him from New Haven on 27 April 1914 urging him strongly to help the Gaelic League in his paper *The Gaelic American*. Ashe told him that the assistance of *The Gaelic American* and of the Irish republican nationalists of America would make their mission a success and strengthen their hands on their return home. He was speaking for Diarmuid Lynch as well when he said they proposed to make the Gaelic League a vehicle of strong, sterling nationality, and rid it of some fossils and others about whom his comment was caustic. To do so effectively they would have to achieve success in their American mission through the help of *The Gaelic American* and what it represented. Ashe went on to state in fairly plain terms what Devoy would appreciate with great satisfaction. He said he and his friends in Ireland would preach in such a way as to make the Gaelic League a resourceful novitiate for societies who wanted freedom and who meant to get it by the only means open to worthy men. This was a clear enough indication that an appeal to physical force was in destiny.

> I appeal to you for aid in your columns [wrote Ashe] not for any personal reason. I am not anxious for any self-advancement, or anything of that kind. If I were I could have attained such from the National Board of Education in the educational world of Ireland long ago, as I was on more than one occasion led to believe that promotion to the Inspectorate of N[ational] Schools was open to me if I desired it. But I have stuck to the ship and I mean to do so. And I believe it will help our command of her, if you in your columns and through the Clan na Gael here, will assist us. Because I, for one, will boldly state before

the Irish people the source and the reason of my success here if such will be the result of my mission.[1]

He found an immense interest taken in the Volunteer movement which was now fast spreading throughout Ireland. Correspondence from Dublin kept him informed of Volunteer developments. Ashe's views about the calibre of the movement in general were not optimistic, though noting that it contained a few good men. He considered the AOH and Irish Party interests to be too strongly represented to give it much backbone and he communicated his doubts to Devoy. He also told Devoy of his efforts to persuade the Gaelic League to make clear its disapproval of the division of Ireland proposed under the Home Rule Bill as well as to take a firm stand on the future status of Irish education. In these matters he was ruled out of order, and the views he expressed about his opponents on the Coiste Gnótha are crisp and pungent. There is a note of grim determination running through his letter to Devoy, which he closes by wishing the Fenian chief long life to work for the complete freedom of Ireland.

During his sojourn in America Ashe met Roger Casement a few times. On his train journey to Norfolk, Virginia, to see Casement, he became aware that he was being shadowed by watchers. Casement was collecting funds for the Volunteers. In retrospect Ashe described Casement and his work:

During my stay in America in 1914, I had the honour of meeting Casement on a few occasions. At the time he was weak and he was frail in health, but his weakness did not prevent him from touring the States in order to raise funds to arm the Volunteers of Ireland. I was present at the Convention of the Ancient Order of Hibernians of Norfolk City, Virginia, when Casement spoke before 4,000 delegates from all parts of the States. He appealed at this time for funds to arm and equip the Volunteers in Ireland, and a resolution was passed by the delegates in answer to his appeal, pledging themselves to raise funds in America, 400,000 dollars for the purpose of arming and equipping the Volunteers ...[2]

Among the American-Irish, events in Ireland were visualised in general terms of Home Rule and the Volunteers. Their impressions of those were not very clear-cut, and of many nuances and distinctions of the Irish scene they had not a notion. It seemed to Ashe that they knew wonderfully little about either Home Rule or the Volunteers but this was a factor which helped his Gaelic League work. Developments in Ireland and the threat of partition were causing him worry. Writing in Irish to Pádraig Ó Dálaigh, on 2 July 1914, he urged that the Coiste Gnótha make a firm stand against the proposed exclusion of part of Ulster from Home Rule:

You ought to pass a resolution against this partition which is being put into operation by the British parliament. All the realistic people here are talking about it and they say the League ought to oppose that partition strongly. You remember how I did my utmost to persuade the Coiste Gnótha to do something about it. Of course you all thought it would be senseless but when I tell you that Judge [Martin] Keogh and Bourke Cochran are going to quarrel with Redmond for permitting that partition you will understand the good you will do the League here if you act even now.

Ashe would permit the Coiste Gnótha to fall down on no job if he could help it. Criticism by The O'Rahilly of the Coiste Gnótha's tardiness in some other matter was reflected in caustic comment by Ashe in the same letter. Referring to Judge Keogh's eagerness to help the Gaelic League in every possible way, he goes on, in vigorous Irish:

> He has two clerks. They are paid by the State. They are half-idle (just as some of you are according to O'Rahilly) … This is a pretty state of affairs The O'Rahilly relates. Some of the League workers will not wake up until the unfortunate League is dead. And anyone who wants work will go some place else where men will be found who are in earnest.
>
> I shall do my best here at any rate. I hope to God that I, and all of us, will succeed. Perhaps the money will put some spirit into you at home.[3]

His correspondence denotes a pragmatic, purposeful mind which had little use for frills. An urgent request for film-reels (which never came), an estimate of what money the different cities will give, an appeal to John Devoy to use his influence in favour of the League, all are put down in plain functional terms, and no punches pulled. They show the purpose of a man who knew where he was going.

There was nothing complex about Thomas Ashe. His American audiences appreciated him, and he spoke to them and gave them the gospel of the Gaelic League in a way they could understand. 'You can trust me as to what I will say,' he wrote to Pádraig Ó Dálaigh (7 July 1914). 'If I didn't preach strong nationality here I might as well go home as with such exciting events in Ireland these Yankees want us to be a little exciting too. Whatever I say or do, is in the interest of the Gaelic League.'

He welcomed the tidings from Dublin that the Coiste Gnótha would engage in no more negotiations, presumably of the diplomatic kind to which he had taken such strong exception. 'NO more negotiations! *Cabhair Dé chugainn sa deireadh.* I was more delighted over the last minutes of the Coiste Gnótha than I have been for a long time. *Is fearr déanaí ná ró-dhéanaí.*' Writing to Stiofán Bairéad on the same date, 7 July 1914, he estimates his collection in various New England cities at $3,480 and hopes to send on £1,000 to meet Oireachtas expenses.

Much as he was taken with America's warmth and hospitality, he did not think he would care to make his home there. So he told his assistant teacher, Mary Monks, when writing. This correspondence will be found in Father Seosamh Ó Muirthile's excellent *Tréithe Thomáis Ághas.* No place outside of Ireland would make him feel the happiness he felt there. How odd, he said, that when he thought of going 'home', the home in his mind was County Dublin. On a splendid sunny American day, his chief thought was that it would be lovely walking down Corduff's new road or tramping across Kerry's mountains. He sings in public for his audiences, Irish songs, but in the seclusion of his room he sings them again with greater pleasure in the old and gentle thoughts of home and people they bring him. Should God grant him happiness, it could only be in Ireland.

In Europe the long smouldering political crisis blazed up unexpectedly with the assassination at Sarajevo of the heir to the Austrian throne and the invasion of Serbia followed by a quick succession of militant events which included the declaration of war by England on Germany and Austria on 3 August 1914. It was the beginning of an immense conflict. The excitement of war communicated itself to neutral America. The interest of the American-Irish in the Gaelic League began to decline and to centre on more warlike things, like the fortunes of the Volunteers. In a letter to Pádraig Ó Dálaigh, dated 3 August 1914, Ashe outlines the effect European events were having on the Gaelic League in America. It will be noted that the letter contains a suggestion that there might be some move towards Irish freedom which would necessitate his return home if possible:

A Phádraig, a chara,

Táim anso i Hartford fé láthair. Bhí Diarmuid [Ó Loinsigh] agus mé féin ag an A.O.H. Convention agus do shocraíodar ar $1000 a thabhairt don gConnradh.

We must I fear suspend operations owing to the present war crisis, and also to the fact that all Irish societies at present are working for the Volunteers. The U.I.L., the Clan na Gael and the A.O.H. are all raising money for the Volunteers and it is only the real Gaelic Leaguers that are helping me at present. Still I have little to complain of so far. But appeals for the Gaelic League will remain unanswered in the near future.

Had you sent me on those films as I asked I could make $500 a week at the very least. Everybody says so. The interest in a militant Ireland would have helped me to raise funds, and I am surprised that I have not received those pictures.

I do not know what may occur in Ireland in the near future. *Má bheidh aon ní ar siúl i dtaobh saoirseachta na tíre sé mo thuairim go mbeidh orm dul abhaile más féidir é.*

Our funds are running short. If the mail service is suspended between here and Ireland you should cable me some money at once.

Ar deineadh aon ní ag an Ard-Fheis i dtaobh na toscaireachta go hAmerica? Cuir scéala chugam.

Mise do chara

Tomás Ághas.

The moment England declared war on Germany John Redmond assured her that she might withdraw her troops from Ireland and leave the country's defence in charge of the Irish and Ulster Volunteers. The implications of this statement were disturbing. Redmond was immediately committing Ireland to the support of England's war in a moral sense and foreseeably in physical terms as well. His policy was backed by the party, which used its entrenched influence to stimulate recruiting for the British Army. His action caused strong resentment amongst the American-Irish. In the letter partly quoted below we are left in no doubt as to Thomas Ashe's reactions to the news from Ireland. The Ashe that writes it is there no gentle and placid man, but a man stirred by anger, as he passionately denounces the compliant and supine spirits that would surrender Ireland's will and merge it with her conqueror's. His correspondent is unknown.

Let us reverse the picture of Emmet on our walls. Let us no longer dream of the Ireland of Brian's days. We blame the Saxons for their slavery in asking the Romans to stay and keep them in shackles. We look with horror on the Negro who asked that he might still be a slave. But no slavish people ever did what we propose doing – defend our land and our people for the tyrant during his difficulties that he may come when they are over and enchain us again. No, no people ever sank to the slavery of the Irish – the fighting Race! ... I feel strongly in this matter.

This letter, from 624 Madison Avenue, was dated 24 August 1914.

Ashe and Lynch were still in America when John Redmond made his speech, on 20 September 1914, at Woodenbridge, County Wicklow, to a parade of Irish Volunteers, exhorting them to prove their gallantry on the field of battle, not in the unlikely event of an invasion of Irish soil, but wherever the firing line extended, 'in defence of right, of freedom and of religion in this war'.[4] It was a sugar-coated request to participate in the war on the British side. Its immediate effect was to divide the Volunteers.

It made impossible the further progress of Thomas Ashe's work in the United States. Diarmuid Lynch remained in America and he returned to Ireland. Gregory Ashe stated to the writer that his brother's American journey was also directly concerned with the collection of funds for arming the Irish Volunteers. Diarmuid Lynch's papers in the National Library (MS 11,123) contain evidence in support of this:

In September Ashe brought £1,000 (I believe that was the amount and in gold). My impression at the time was that it was delivered to Tom Clarke but am not certain.

Passing through Belfast on his way back to Dublin he called into the branch office of the Irish Transport Union to see James Connolly and Cathal O'Shannon. He was extremely angry about the Woodenbridge speech and used robust language about Redmond and his supporters. 'He told us,' writes Cathal O'Shannon, 'that Redmond's action made them bring their mission to an abrupt end because it had so infuriated the Irish in America that they refused to go on donating funds.'[5] He discussed with Connolly and O'Shannon the situation created by the war and the opportunities it would give the separatists. His friends were optimistic and Ashe's good humour was restored. He resumed teaching in Corduff on 3 October.

A month later, on 5 November, he lectured at the Ard-Craobh of the Gaelic League on his experiences in America. In the course of this lecture, which he gave without the aid of notes, he related that the American-Irish were dissatisfied with the recession in recent years of the language movement. For this they blamed the Gaelic League, which was much less virile and vigorous in its fight against anglicisation than it had been some years previously. This opinion, Ashe said, was practically universal amongst the American-Irish. He drew attention to a fighting speech Dr Hyde uttered eight years before in San Francisco, and urged the Gaels of Dublin to review the condition of the Gaelic League and make Irish nationhood its basis as it had been in the beginning of the movement.

10

THE IRISH VOLUNTEERS

In April 1912 a Home Rule Bill for Ireland was introduced by Asquith, the Liberal Prime Minister, and passed successfully through the House of Commons. It was held up by the implacable House of Lords, but certain limitations on their powers ensured that it would automatically pass in the summer of 1914. The bill, which was the result of prolonged exertion, offered Ireland a defective legislature, to which republican reaction, voiced in *Irish Freedom*, was sharp and scathing.[1] An aggressive campaign against its proposed operation was set on foot in England by the Conservatives under Bonar Law and in north-east Ireland mainly by Sir Edward Carson. Although their campaign added up to nothing short of rank treason against the British constitution, not one of them was brought to book. In fact later events went to prove that they were regarded as favourite, and highly favoured, sons. A solemn covenant against Home Rule was signed by 500,000 people. An Ulster Volunteer Force was organised, drilled and armed by Carson and his lieutenants, secure in their assurances of support from the most powerful and influential quarters in England. On the unrealistic parliamentary front it was a misfortune that Prime Minister Asquith and the Irish Party leader Redmond were of a calibre too inferior to meet the crisis. The former lacked the nerve and the will to control the situation, and the latter proved too amenable to pressure.

On 24 September 1913 a provisional government of Ulster was formed to resist Home Rule and was buttressed by the strength of the Ulster Volunteer Force. It was in such circumstances that the Irish Volunteers came into being. The organisation, drilling and arming of the Ulster Volunteer Force set a headline for nationalist Ireland. Alert to all the possibilities involved, the IRB was swift to take advantage of the situation. Numbering about 2,000 men in all at this time, of whom about 700 were located in and around Dublin, it formed a compact and dedicated nucleus of men sworn to the achievement of an Irish Republic. Formerly, under the leadership of James Stephens, it had sought strength in numbers, but, in the circumstances prevailing before 1916, it relied on re-cruiting to its ranks a select body of men chosen for their charac-ter, integrity and intelligence, who in time of crisis would supply leadership. Thomas Ashe was one of these.

Walking back one evening with Eoin MacNeill from Gaelic League headquarters at Parnell Square, Ashe threw out the sug-gestion to his companion that the time was opportune to profit from the North's example and organise a national volunteer force. He pointed out that since the British government had not inter-fered with Carson it could not very well prohibit nationalist Ire-land from doing the same thing. Our authority for the foregoing is a statement made by Ashe to his cousin Pádraig Ághas of Dun Beag, County Clare. The initiative in forming the Irish Volunteers was really taken by the IRB.

As Carson's movement grew in strength throughout the North and made its impact on the rest of Ireland, the IRB laid its plans with foresight and exceptional skill. Earlier in 1913 Bulmer Hobson, acting for the Supreme Council, ordered a secret drill of all the IRB men in Dublin. This was done, and when the Irish Volunteer movement was formed, the majority of the officerships fell to these men because of their experience in drill and military instruction.

On 1 November 1913 an important article, 'The North Began', by Eoin MacNeill appeared in *An Claidheamh Soluis*, the Gaelic League organ, advocating the organisation of an Irish Volunteer Force. As *An Claidheamh Soluis* did not have a large circulation, the article in itself did not attract widespread notice, but it projected the idea of an Irish Volunteer Force into public discussion and provided a cue on which the IRB was enabled to act. Hobson approached The O'Rahilly, a prominent nationalist but not an IRB man, and put the suggestion to him that the time was opportune. The O'Rahilly said he was in favour of the step if only fifty joined. Hobson guaranteed at least five hundred and asked The O'Rahilly to see Eoin MacNeill about the proposition. MacNeill was in full agreement and attended a number of preliminary meetings at Wynn's Hotel, composed mainly of IRB men, for discussions on the proposed movement. A Provisional Committee was formed and the Irish Volunteers were inaugurated in the Rotunda on 25 November 1913. At that first meeting nearly 4,000 men were enrolled. The Provisional Committee included IRB representatives, individual nationalists and supporters of the Irish Party.

It had not been very easy to find Irish Party supporters willing to take their place on the committee and the party as a whole looked with disfavour on the movement. Tribute must be paid to the Sinn Féin, Gaelic League and IRB groups, who acted persistently and perseveringly for their convictions in face of the hostility or opposition of the powerful Irish Party. Eoin MacNeill was chosen chief of staff of the Irish Volunteers and from everybody's point of view no more ideal choice could be found. He was well-known and popular throughout Ireland as vice-president of the Gaelic League and had attained distinction as a scholar in the field of early Irish history and laws. As a moderate in politics his appointment would not arouse concern in conservative or official quarters. The choice suited the republicans perfectly. They were better able to plan for revolution in the security provided by his well-known moderate views, but in choosing him they also made for themselves a difficulty which acted like a boomerang at the critical moment. While these moves were on foot, Ashe, who was fully conversant with what was going on, was writing to Gregory in America:

> They all say here that Home Rule is as dead as a door-nail. Carson has frightened the Government. He's getting fellows to join his army every other day, and we have it on the best authority (our own) that they are continually drilling. If he only gives them the guns some good may come out of it, and good that neither he nor England expects.

This letter is dated at Corduff, 14 November 1913.

The tensions of the Irish scene were increased by a new and stormy element. This was a full-scale revolt of the Dublin working-men who were roused by the cyclonic personality of Jim Larkin to protest against the conditions clamped on them by employers who had sinned to the depths against humanity. Anger, fire and passion were thrown into the scale by Larkin, who was no theorist but a man goaded to fury by the injustices he saw flourishing. To his fire and fury was added the intellectual resource of James Connolly, a wholly different type of man but inspired by the same ideal, the achievement of social justice for all. Thomas Ashe knew both these men, sympathised with them deeply and supported them fully in their battles for the weak and under-privileged. Friendship he had for Larkin but he revered Connolly.

Sean O'Casey, the future dramatist, Ashe and Mícheál Ó Foghludha were constant companions, sharing common interests, ideals and sympathies. Born and reared in poverty, O'Casey's fighting, fiery spirit overcame the harsh limitations of his environment. He learned the Irish language from O'Growney's textbooks and has acknowledged how much he owes to it in helping him write as he did. Like Ashe he learned to play on the war pipes and they both loved Irish music, songs and ballads. They were united in feeling for the wrongs of the Dublin tenement dwellers and the exploited toilers of the city. In the letter to Gregory quoted above, Ashe refers to events connected with the labour revolt:

I suppose you know by this that Jem Larkin was sent to jail. He's out for the last two or three days again. The Government got afraid of a general strike in England which the Englishmen were organising in his favour. So they let him out. He and Jem Connolly are now asking their men to drill like Carson's. If we had them all drilled I know what they'd direct their rifles on very soon. I hope they'll continue drilling. We are all here on Larkin's side. He'll beat hell out of the snobbish, mean, seoinín employers yet, and more power to him.

The Volunteers created a fresh and urgent interest for Ashe. From his boyhood he had ambitions, frankly declared, to be a soldier of

Ireland. In the Irish Volunteers he realised them. His tremendous physical energy found a new outlet in calling the youth of Fingal into the Volunteer ranks, drilling them, teaching them military routine and discipline, shaping them into an army the purpose of which he determined should be the winning of Irish freedom. The founding and organisation of the Volunteers in Fingal engaged his attention until he was selected by the Gaelic League, early in 1914, to go with Diarmuid Lynch to the United States, on the fundraising mission described in the previous chapter. While he was in America the Volunteer movement was split in two by the divisive action of John Redmond.

Redmond had looked with alarm on the rapid expansion of the Volunteers, which by May 1914 numbered about 75,000. At that stage he made a public demand that twenty-five nominees of his own be placed on the Executive Committee. The original committee gave way to this demand by a majority decision arrived at in an atmosphere of sharp disagreement. Thomas Ashe, in America, was against giving any accommodation to Redmond. Following Redmond's quasi-control of the movement there was an immense accession of his followers to Volunteer ranks. Ashe expressed strong doubts of their value and feared the genuine men would be swamped by the huge influx of United Irish Leaguers and Hibernians.

By September 1914 the number of Volunteers had risen to 180,000, though a great number of these was merely nominal. Then Redmond's Woodenbridge speech, on 20 September 1914, divided the movement into those who followed himself and those who did not. In this respect at least matters were fully clarified. Those who followed Redmond were called Irish National

Volunteers. They were in the vast majority but it nullified their effectiveness that they had no national objective in view. Without this they lacked cohesion and earnestness. Their strength declined and large numbers were later absorbed in Redmond's recruiting drive for England. Those remaining loyal to the original concept of the Volunteers, of giving their services to Ireland within her shores, numbered about 11,000 and retained the title of Irish Volunteers. Small though their number was, they were under the virtual command of men who had a clear objective, an Irish Republic, and were determined to achieve it. In Lusk a meeting of the local Volunteers was held in the library and the position discussed. Ashe, who had recently returned from America, was there. The meeting ended in a definite division. Ashe walked out and a crowd followed him.

On 25 October 1914, five weeks after the split caused by the Woodenbridge speech, the Irish Volunteers held their first convention at the Abbey Theatre, Dublin, and elected an Executive Committee. Eoin MacNeill remained chief of staff. Unknown to him a majority on the Executive Committee were members of the IRB, who had planned, shortly after the outbreak of the European conflict, to rise in arms before it ended.

Although his interests branched in many directions, including the short-lived Irish Neutrality League, under the auspices of which he gave a lecture, Ashe's attention from this point on centred mainly in building up the Volunteers.[2] There was first-rate fighting material in Fingal and a body of men collected around him who derived confidence from his leadership and gave him unswerving loyalty and assent. Young, idealistic and earnest, they shared his ideals and interest in Irish music, language and athletics. Realising that at no distant time they would have to face the supreme test of battle, most likely against heavy odds, Ashe brought them to military exercises and manoeuvres as often as possible to make them familiar with the terrain and prepare them physically and mentally for battle. We quote from one of the best-informed authorities of the period, Piaras Béaslaí:

> Early in November, 1914, just after the Volunteer Convention in the Abbey Theatre, Tom Ashe, who was then a National Teacher at Lusk, and already the leading spirit of the Fifth, or Fingal, Battalion of the Volunteers, issued a challenge to the First and Second Battalions to march out to the Swords area and make a joint attack on a position prepared by him and occupied by his men at Broadmeadows, near Swords. The challenge was accepted and Sunday, November 8, was fixed as the day for the fight, which we came to call 'The Battle of Broadmeadows.'[3]

Captain Robert Monteith, whose competence was widely recognised, acted as umpire. Ned Daly commanded the First Battalion and Tom Markham the Second. Thomas Ashe, Piaras Béaslaí tells us, though not yet elected a commandant, was accepted by all the defenders as the man to command them. The First and Second Battalions marched to Swords. Scouts reported that the 'enemy,' under Ashe, held a strong position on the other side of the river at Broadmeadows. The ensuing engagement was a useful and instinctive manoeuvre, one of many from which the Volunteers drew lessons of resource and initiative which they put to good use. Ashe kept his men up to standard by drill, route marches, military exercises, hardening them physically and making them familiar with every road and contour of Fingal by frequent manoeuvres.

Although faced with multiple difficulties in obtaining arms, he armed his men as well as possible under the circumstances. The provision of arms, ammunition and proper equipment was one of the chief handicaps with which the Volunteers had to contend. The supplies landed at Howth and Kilcoole fell far short of their actual needs. There were frequent appeals made by Volunteer headquarters to company officers, whose responsibility it was to see that their men were armed, like the following, which appeared in the *Irish Volunteer* of April 1915:

> A five pound note will give a Volunteer a sufficiently good gun and a sufficient stock of ammunition. He is not asked to pay the five pound note down at once. He can pay it at a shilling a week, at sixpence a week … Our movement lacks reality until it is armed.

The Fingal Volunteers, responding to this advice, contributed sixpence a week and, although there was a major disaster in store in the loss of the expected arms ship, every man of the battalion had a firearm of some sort for the Easter Rising.

Accounts differing about the exact time of Ashe's appointment as commandant have been given by various people. The point is academic. There is common agreement that the best man was given command and the position may be summed up in the words of Paddy Doyle: 'I can't say exactly, but Tom Ashe was a good military leader, no matter when he was made commandant, and the men would follow him any place.'

Jack Devine agrees: 'There is no mistake about it but that Tom Ashe was the man for the job; the men were devoted to him.'

We follow here the account of Piaras Béaslaí, who writes:

In the beginning of 1915 Battalion staffs were formed; on January 30, 1915, a meeting of the Captains of the First Battalion elected Ned Daly, brother-in-law of Tom Clarke, as Commandant; and, at a subsequent meeting on February 10, I was elected Vice-Commandant. About the same time Tomás Ághas was elected Commandant of the Fifth Battalion, which at that time consisted of the Volunteer Companies in North County Dublin – the bodies known in 1921 as the 'Fingal Brigade.'

Ashe usually spent his Saturdays in Dublin, sometimes walking into the city from Corduff, and at the Tyrone Restaurant in Cathedral Street would meet, amongst others, Seán Mac Diarmada and Piaras Béaslaí who like himself were IRB members. Joseph Plunkett had asked Béaslaí to draft and submit military plans for his particular area and to tell other officers who might have plans and suggestions to submit them. Béaslaí goes on to say:

On Saturday, January 30, the day of the election of Ned Daly as Commandant, but prior to the meeting, I met Tomás, and, remembering Plunkett's request, I asked him if he had any plans for operations in his area.

He answered with enthusiasm that he had. He said he had made a special study of the military possibilities of that part of Fingal where he held his command. He promised to commit his plans to writing, and made an appointment to meet me again in a fortnight's time, and submit them to me, for transmission to Plunkett. On Saturday, February 13, I met him in company with the late Con Collins (afterwards T.D. for Limerick), also a member of the I.R.B. We lunched together in the Tyrone Restaurant, Cathedral Street. After lunch I brought Tomás and Con to 61, Middle Abbey Street, the office of the Irish Journalists' Association, of which I was secretary, and there

Tomás … submitted some plans and details. I remember that he had two or three maps of areas in Fingal, drawn by himself, with positions marked on them, and some explanatory papers. I listened attentively to his explanations and it is recorded that I submitted his plans and papers to Plunkett at the next meeting of the Volunteer Executive, four days later.[4]

In a discussion with the writer, Piaras Béaslaí confirmed these statements and paid tribute to the military skill and sense of Thomas Ashe as being equal to the best the Volunteers had. The maps and designs he produced included everything. *'Bhí gach aon rud ins na léarscálacha úd.'*

The Fingal Volunteers were trained for swift, sudden movement on the principle of the flying column which was used with such success at a later stage of the war against the British. There were active Volunteer companies in Lusk, Swords and Skerries, with smaller groups at Donabate and Santry.

Christopher (Kit) Moran of Swords, a fighter of Ashbourne, described to the writer the diligence with which the Fingal men pursued their training. Something on the lines of a military college was established at Turvey, between Swords and Corduff, in an abandoned farm. There, in a detached house which may be seen off the road on the way down Turvey Hill, a meeting was held every week. Lectures in military tactics were given 'by a man named O'Duffy', probably Eimar O'Duffy, who was a poet and novelist as well as a military instructor. Hearing it more than fifty years later from Kit Moran, and affirmed with all the pride of a soldier in his battalion, no one can doubt the verve and eagerness of the Fingal youths at their training:

The best men in North County Dublin met there. They were there from Skerries, Swords, St Margarets, Lusk, Turvey and elsewhere. O'Duffy seemed to have been university trained; some of his lecture material was theoretical and of no use; at the same time he gave us a great deal of useful knowledge. Ashe was looked on as the boss. Another man closely associated with Ashe was Dr Hayes of Lusk and, of course, Frank Lawless. We had the fastest hundred men the world ever produced in that sort of way, for speed, strength, vision and crack-shot ability. We were so well trained we could hide behind an apple tree.

At Easter 1915 the Fingal Volunteers took part in manoeuvres which might have been a rehearsal of the task they were assigned a year later. This was an exercise mounted over a front extending from Blanchardstown to Santry and included sending a detachment south into County Wicklow.

Published reports of the second annual convention of the Irish Volunteers held in Dublin on 31 October 1915 put Thomas down as representing Lispole. Delegates attended from all over Ireland. Kit Moran's account to the writer states that an election of officers took place and that Thomas Ashe was there elected commandant in charge of the Fingal area. It adds that the Volunteers grew stronger than ever after that convention. Dublin Castle sources give figures that amply confirm this.[5]

On St Patrick's Day 1916 there was a full muster of the Dublin Brigade of the Irish Volunteers in College Green. Brother Allen of O'Connell Schools, North Richmond Street, stopped to view the Fingal Volunteers marching into Dublin, headed by the Black Raven Band with Ashe leading. 'You couldn't take your eyes off him.' In the parade the Fingal Battalion occupied the space in front of the London and Lancashire Insurance Company. Kit Moran witnessed there what might be called the first act of the rebellion. A car containing British headquarters staff personnel drove down Dame Street from the Castle. Ashe's order rang out: 'Don't let that car through.' The British officers were obliged to turn back and go another way. 'That was the first clear act of rebellion.'

11

'THERE WILL BE GLORIOUS DAYS FOR IRELAND YET'

We have got the honour from God to live in the years that are at present, and to see men lay down their lives in the spirit our fore-fathers laid theirs down. It is an honour only few generations, and only choice generations of the people of Ireland, have got; and we should thank God that we have lived in the years of Irish Nationality, so militant and so self-sacrificing ...[1]

It has taxed all the ingenuity of chroniclers and historians to re-construct the events of the week leading up to Sunday 23 April 1916, the date set by the Military Council of the IRB for the rising in arms which was to proclaim the Irish Republic. Whatever the exact sequence of events, two things that happened within a short time of each other reduced immeasurably the power of the in-surgents' blow. One was the capture of the arms ship *Aud* off the Kerry coast on Friday 21 April. The other was the realisation late on Thursday 20 April by Eoin MacNeill that a rising was planned and his despatch throughout the period Friday to Sunday morn-ing of countermanding orders which caused disastrous confusion to the main insurrectionary plans.

It is a striking tribute to the resolution and resilience of the in-surgents that these shattering blows set back the date of the Rising only twenty-four hours. The loss of the 20,000 stand of arms in the

Aud meant that the insurgents would be seriously short of arms if they turned out in full strength. As it happened the small forces which turned out to fight were inadequately armed and not too plentifully provided with ammunition. Thomas Ashe's own Fifth Battalion is a case in point. Though all members of the battalion had guns, these were of miscellaneous standard and effectiveness. This lack they remedied throughout the week, however, by capturing other supplies. MacNeill's countermands were issued at too late a juncture to enable the Military Council to redraft its plans. His efforts succeeded in confining the Rising to Dublin. His actions drew a storm of controversy on his head and he was bitterly attacked. Thomas Ashe, one of the greatest fighters the Rising of 1916 produced, never spoke a word of blame against him.

Early on Good Friday 21 April, Ashe became aware that all was not going according to plan. About midday he was with Diarmuid Lynch in an office in O'Connell Street when a copy of one of MacNeill's orders revoking Pearse's authority was brought in. Ashe was astonished and disturbed. Lynch went away to report it to Clarke and Connolly. Shortly afterwards Thomas MacDonagh arrived. Ashe pointed out to him that it was tantamount to a reversal of the plans for Easter Sunday. MacDonagh reassured him that MacNeill had withdrawn his opposition and all was well.

Volunteer Tommy McArdle recalled events of Easter Sunday. As a member of the Black Raven Band he took part in the Foresters' parade after last Mass at Lusk. He was told the Volunteers were to mobilise at Rathbeale Cross at 3 p.m.:

> Thomas Ashe took charge at Rathbeale Cross [said Tommy]. That was the first time I saw him take charge. We manoeuvred around

until about 7 or 8 p.m. and we had our tea in Lawless's yard. Meantime a dispatch rider came out from the city to say the Rising was off. Tom Ashe was so sure it would be on that he couldn't accept that it was off. He went into the city himself to check and returned about 11 p.m. I remember well his last words to us that night: 'Guard your arms as you would guard your lives. You never know the moment you may be called on to use them.'

Ashe spent the night at Dr Hayes's house in Lusk. Like many others, he was puzzled in the confusion caused by MacNeill's countermands. His cousin Pádraig Ághas relates that on the Saturday or Sunday night before the Rising Ashe was in Liberty Hall, headquarters of the Irish Transport and General Workers' Union and of the Irish Citizen Army. The Citizen Army officers were gathered there. A mood of depression and disappointment prevailed in the reflection that all their preparations seemed to have come to naught. He saw that night many a strong man in tears with the cruel shock of shattered hopes. That weekend, his cousin relates, he received his instructions for action as battalion commandant from James Connolly. Connolly was commander for the Dublin area of the forces of the Irish Republic and Ashe, serving under him, could have asked for no commander closer to his own sympathies. He, like Connolly, relying on the inspiration of their predecessor Wolfe Tone, looked to the men of little or no property as their main support in carrying out the task they were now setting their hand to.

The Rising, which was put back twenty-four hours by the calamities that befell the leaders' plans, was re-timed to commence at midday on Easter Monday. Paddy Doyle, a member of the local circle of the IRB, was told at a céilí in Lusk that night that he was to turn out the following morning for mobilisation.

Early that morning Ashe received from Joe Lawless a written order from Patrick Pearse to strike at one o'clock.[2] Clear and positive, it was in welcome contrast with the confusion of the day before, and there was an end to wavering. It was the order Ashe was waiting for, and he received it with a comment that might have come from an ancient hero tale, that this day would be remembered in Ireland forever more. He sent out instructions that the battalion was to mobilise at Knocksedan Bridge, two miles west of Swords, at 10 a.m., and started himself on his motorcycle to spread the news amongst his men. 'We mobilised at the band room,' said Paddy Doyle. Father Togher gave Confession to all who wanted it. He knew the Rising was on and being a good Irishman did nothing to stop it. 'We marched down the laneway and met Tom Ashe on Daw's Bridge. He greeted us warmly: "Good old Lusk! I knew you wouldn't let me down." There were twenty or thirty of us.' Richard Kelly and a group of his comrades, all keen racing fans, were going to cycle to Fairyhouse. Following the previous day's call-off they did not think there would be any action this Monday. Near Corduff they got a whistle from Joe Kelly who told them the Rising was on. It was Tom Peppard who had apprised Joe one night in Holy Week that Easter was the time. Joe turned out on Easter Sunday, only to be disappointed. When Peppard called to him on Monday to tell him Lusk company was mobilised, Joe was puzzled what to do as the news of a rising was yet uncertain. He did not want to ask leave from his job at Lusk Workhouse until he had definite information. He went to Turvey to check with his cousins Charlie and Bartle Weston.

The Westons, like himself, were IRB men. He found they had taken their rifles and gone. 'Going back towards Lusk,' said Joe Kelly, 'I met the Lusk Company of Volunteers, fully equipped and cycling in order, and against the tree-lined background I thought it was one of the finest sights I ever saw. Leading it was Captain Eddie Rooney. I shouted "Is it on?" and they replied "Looks like it."' Joe Kelly went to the workhouse, got his rifle, called back to his home, where his younger brother Pat joined him, and set out for Knocksedan. On the way they met the local sergeant of police. 'He didn't even look at us. He didn't want to see us.'

The sergeant clearly did not want to see them although he must have had a fair idea of what they were up to. That Monday morning Dr Richard Hayes was told, 'in strict confidence', by the postmistress of Lusk that a coded message, which she was able to interpret, had come through on Holy Saturday, addressed to the sergeant of the RIC at Lusk. It was an instruction to arrange for the arrest of Ashe and himself.[3] Perhaps in his heart of hearts the sergeant was in sympathy. Joe and Pat Kelly cycled through Swords to Knocksedan Bridge. It was mobilisation point for the Fifth Battalion.

We take up the thread of our narrative here from Thomas Ashe's brief note, written into Éamon de Valera's prison autograph book, now in O'Connell Schools' library. It reads, in translation from Irish:

Thomas Ashe, Commandant (under James Connolly). The 5th Battalion mobilised at ten o'clock, Easter Monday, at Knocksedan.

All the acts and thoughts of Ashe's life since boyhood were an almost unconscious preparation towards this day. Only afterwards did his colleague in Corduff National School, petite, pretty Mary Monks, realise the full meaning of what he said and did on his last day at school. She recalls the occasion in a letter to the present writer:

> After discussing the possibility of a fight for freedom he remarked: 'Should the fight begin on Good Friday, we will surely win, for we will have Brian Boru with us!' He then cut all the flowers in bloom in the school garden, placed them in my arms with a request that they should be put on the altar in front of the Blessed Sacrament on the following day – Holy Thursday, 1916.

His housekeeper Mrs Thornton, who had seen him come and go many a time before at all hours of the day and night, and read nothing unusual into his apparently casual departure that weekend, bewailed when looking back over the events of the week: 'Poor Mr Ashe, he never told me he was going.'

It might be asked, what were they going out to fight for, and the simple answer would be 'for Irish independence'. The answer might go further and include the many complexities which are summed up in the words of Lionel Johnson: 'A dream, a dream, an ancient dream.' This was the battle rendezvous sung from time immemorial by the Irish poets, prayed for at firesides in the seanachaí's aspiration, stamped into the Gaelic mind through the centuries of desperate endurance. Now the compulsive urge of the dead generations renewed the ancient challenge; this was the march of the Rapparees, of the men of '98, of the Whiteboys and Ribbonmen, of the gallant Fenians and of all the legions who had fought against the ruthless suppression of the Irish nation. In the background lay the trials and travails of a decade of centuries, the traditions and reckonings that survived in the little thatched laneways of the west, in the lichened stones of Gallarus, in the cracked bricks of the old shaky slums of Dublin and Belfast. They went out to fight for the proud and intangible things of life. Tangible and material things that are the right of a free society counted too. Arthur Griffith and Sir Robert Kane had spoken well on their behalf. Fair play and equality to all the nation's children, to all, not to any faction or segment, for as Sir John Davies, no particular friend of Ireland's, had noted, there was no nation on earth which loved equal and impartial justice more than did the Irish people, and Thomas Ashe with his men marched to get it. As Connolly and Larkin had spoken for the city workers, so had Ashe thought in terms of the farm workers and country men and boys who wrought life out of the soil. That Easter Monday he led his men across the roads and fields of Fingal in an act of challenge to an empire.

In his small army were Fingal's best and bravest sons, the Mc-Allisters of Turvey, their cousins the Westons, and their cousins, the Kellys; four Lawlesses shouldered their guns and marched; there were the Taylors and the Wilsons and the Doyles, who in the person of Paddy Doyle maintained the link with 1798; the Black Raven bandsmen were there; there was nineteen-year-old Thomas Rafferty, who could not ordinarily join in the manoeuvres as his employment on the government farm at Lusk did not permit, but who promised to be there when the time came; there were Jack Crenigan and 'the Rover' John McCann, described by his comrade John McAllister as 'the bravest man a country ever had'; Captain Richard Coleman led the Swords company; there were men from Skerries and St Margarets. Thirty turned up at Knocksedan, but many more joined during the day, until by evening there were between sixty and seventy men under Ashe's command. Their weapons were oddly assorted. They had twelve or fifteen modern service rifles, a dozen Martini single-shot rifles, some Howth Mausers, twenty or thirty shotguns and some revolvers. Their ammunition supply was less than plentiful. They all had bicycles, useful for mobility in the flat countryside where they operated. Ashe had his motorcycle, Dr Hayes his car. A bread van was commandeered later at Swords.

Thomas Ashe's task was to disrupt and destroy enemy communications in North County Dublin. His first step was to make the important Great Northern Railway between Dublin and Belfast impassable by blowing it up at Rogerstown Bridge. That night he camped at Finglas. Dick Kelly remembers getting instructions from Ashe to go to a certain point where he would meet a man, whom he was to challenge and escort back to camp. It was Dick Mulcahy who, with Tom Maxwell and Paddy Grant, had been out near Howth Junction to cut telegraph connections with Britain and Belfast. The three joined Ashe's force. That night Ashe sent a party to Blanchardstown on a diversionary tactic. At ten o'clock next morning he got a message from Connolly asking could he send forty men into the city to reinforce the garrisons there. Reviewing his strength, Ashe decided he would send half the number for the present, and twenty men, with Captain Richard Coleman in charge, marched away into Dublin, where in the GPO and the Mendicity Institution they added to the glory of Fingal.

Moving rapidly from point to point across North County Dublin, Ashe struck now here, now there, setting a guerilla pattern which was followed with great success in the War of Independence. He now had a force of about forty-five men, divided into four sections, three to pursue warlike operations, the fourth to take charge of camp and provisions, the latter duty to rotate between sections. In swift decisive moves he disarmed Swords and, following resistance, Donabate barracks, and added their arms to his supplies. Garristown barracks was empty of rifles as they had been sent away. At all places he dismantled telephone and other communications. Food was commandeered as necessary. A lamb from Craigie's farm at Finglas supplied a meal which the men declared was the best they ever tasted. Messages came through from the GPO, Mollie Adrian of Oldtown acting as courier, a heroine ranking with the bravest. 'There will be glorious days for Ireland yet,' wrote Connolly to Ashe, and Ashe rejoiced in the inspiration of that message in hours of crisis, trial or victory. He recalled it at Ardfert when he commemorated Casement:

I had the pleasure during Easter Week – in fact I think it was on Wednesday of Easter Week – of receiving a dispatch from Jim Connolly, who commanded in Dublin. His dispatch said, amongst other things: 'The Republican Flag still flies triumphantly over Dublin City. There will be glorious days for Ireland yet'… think of the mind of the man who saw clearly from behind the barricades of Dublin streets that there would be glorious days for Ireland yet.[4]

Within Dublin city the Republican forces were standing up to heavy pressure from the enemy and the battle was moving to a climax.

12

ASHBOURNE

Thomas Ashe's military operations that week are acknowledged by his commanding officer in a celebrated document. It is an order of the day from 'Headquarters, Army of the Irish Republic, Dublin Command', dated 28 April, and in part reads:

> To Soldiers:
> This is the fifth day of the establishment of the Irish Republic … The men of North County Dublin are in the field, have occupied all the police barracks in the district, destroyed all the telegraph system on the Great Northern Railway up to Dundalk, and are operating against the trains of the Midland Great Western … Never had man or woman a grander cause, never was a cause more grandly served.
>
> James Connolly
> Commandant-General
> Dublin Division.

On the morning of the day that order was issued, Friday 28 April, Ashe and his men were encamped at Borranstown. For the day's campaign he proposed to capture Ashbourne Barracks, cut the Midland Great Western railway line at Batterstown so as to hold up troops expected from Athlone and, should circumstances permit, capture another barracks to complete the day. About 9.15 a.m. he detailed two sections of the battalion for 'a special job' [we follow mainly Jerry Golden's narrative] and led them, cycling in file, towards the Dublin–Slane road which passes through the village of Ashbourne. Near Rath Cross he halted them for instructions. Pointing out a large two-storey building which fronted the main road two hundred yards away towards Ashbourne, he told them this was Ashbourne RIC Barracks, which it was their task to capture and disarm. He sent half the force to take up positions to the rear of the barracks and there await the signal for attack which he would give presently. With the rest of the men Ashe worked his way towards the front of the barracks, surprising on the way a sergeant and two constables, one of whom escaped. He made prisoners of the other two but the sergeant, who offered to take a request to the garrison advising surrender and was given a white flag for the purpose, skipped nimbly through a gap in the hedge and got away. Ashe located his men in positions facing the barracks and then, standing on a fence in full view of the building, he called on the garrison to surrender. The indifference to personal danger, such as he displayed on this occasion, gave his men confidence in battle. 'That crowd would follow him anywhere,' as Paddy Doyle put it. A volley of fire greeted his call for surrender and he took cover. The garrison had been reinforced, the windows were protected with steel shutters loopholed for defensive firing and barriers had been put up in front of the building. The garrison was clearly confident that it could hold out. Ashe gave the signal for attack and the Fingal men raked the building with fire in an attack that lasted half an hour. Part of the Volunteers' equipment consisted of homemade hand grenades, and two of these, thrown at the barracks with perfect timing, exploded with a deafening noise and shook the building to the roof. A white flag tied to a rifle barrel was pushed through an upper window. The defenders were surrendering. Ashe was on his way into the yard when a sudden and unforeseen development changed the position completely. A short distance to the north-west of the barracks, and visible from it, on the road to Slane, was Rath Cross. As Ashe was entering the yard to take the surrender, 'we all heard the hoot of motor horns and looking back up the road in the Slane direction we saw several motor cars all loaded with RIC coming towards the Cross Roads'.[1]

There were in fact some twenty cars containing about eighty police, although estimates vary more or less.[2] Their arrival was completely unexpected and placed Ashe and his men in a difficult, not to say vulnerable, position. He reacted quickly. Golden continues:

> The Commandant then ordered one of our men to get round to the men at the rear (of the barracks) and get them up to attack the R.I.C. on their left flank and he ordered the remainder of us to rush to the cross roads and hold them against the police and prevent them from spreading out and surrounding us.

The Volunteers rushed up the road towards the cross; some got into the ditches at one side while others got up on the bank on the opposite side and all opened a brisk fire on the approaching cars. Now began the real battle. The result of Ashe's move was that the police convoy was halted before reaching Rath Cross and contained in that particular sector of road for the whole of the ensuing action while the Volunteers, though outnumbered, kept closing their grip on them. The police got out of the cars and took cover in the ditches along the road. Paddy Doyle told the writer:

The section that stopped the police from coming through played a decisive part in the battle. They were Section Leader Charlie Weston, Michael and John McAllister, Bennie McAllister, Richard Aungier and Mick Fleming (and Paddy Doyle himself) – they were the men who stopped the convoy coming in on top of us. The first car was only fifteen yards away. Mick McAllister was the best shot I ever saw. He played an important part in the battle.

Tommy McArdle confirms Mick McAllister's prowess. 'He could shoot a trout jumping out of a river.' The Volunteers holding the cross kept up a continuous fire on the police positions for half an hour until those who had been attacking the barracks from the rear came up on the police left flank and opened fire on them. Meanwhile Ashe sent a messenger to the camp ordering the rest of the men to come with all the spare ammunition and join the attack. His plan was that these men should enter the fields about two hundred yards from the main road and divide forces, one group to attack the police right flank and the other their rear and so press in and surround them.

Step by step the Volunteers closed their grip. During one of their positional changes forward Tommy Rafferty of Lusk was killed. He was wearing a bright-coloured bandolier which might have attracted the enemy fire. His body was taken to a cottage nearby. The behaviour of the Volunteers under fire was cool and ordered, their leader setting the example. 'He wouldn't draw back from anything,' said Jack Devine. 'Tom Ashe was a desperately fearless man. He didn't mind being under fire. Our hurling experience was a great help for giving us a sense of discipline.' By rapid, systematic fire and skilful use of terrain to conceal their true numbers, they created the impression amongst their opponents that a much superior force was attacking. In actual fact the police outnumbered them two to one, if not by more.

For some five hours, in the lush Meath countryside, the crisp sounds of battle echoed, with bullets whining through the air, sometimes to their fatal mark, sometimes to lodge in grass and hedgerow. Over the crack of the service rifles could be heard the heavy report of the Howth guns and 'Shinny' Kelly could be identified by his friends during the action by the loud crash of his Howth Mauser. Captured police carbines, with loads of ammunition to fit, were used by Jerry Golden, Mick Fleming and Dick Aungier. Jack Devine, located in a deep ditch full of briars, felt 'the grass being cut from under my fingers with the bullets'. In Frongoch camp afterwards, a wondering Clareman asked him how come the clothes at the back of his neck were scorched. The whizzing bullets at Ashbourne did it but he was too occupied to notice.

Ashe's plan of containing the enemy force in the segment of road on the Slane side of Rath Cross and closing in on them was successful, although the surrounding party, Tommy McArdle remembers, had to retreat twice. Ashe has recorded, briefly, his instructions to Lieutenant Mulcahy at a vital stage of the encounter: 'Bring down the camp reserve. Charge the police line from the Slane end. I'll support you from the Cross.'

That, says McArdle, corresponds exactly with what did happen. This order was carried out and the final stages of the battle are here described in Jerry Golden's words:

At about 4 p.m. we who were at the Cross Roads heard, during a lull in the firing, a shout, 'Charge,' and on looking up the road we saw about 300 yards away Lieutenant Mulcahy and about seven men charge down on the police with fixed bayonets. When the police saw them, those who were able to run threw their arms on the road and rushed into a labourer's cottage which was just about fifty yards from the Cross Roads on the right-hand side towards Slane. We immediately opened fire on the police as they were huddled together trying to get into the cottage and after about ten minutes we heard the shout 'We surrender' and they marched out on the road ... The Commandant then ordered firing to cease.

The stone cottage, standing yet, was occupied then, as now, by the Brunton family, and its present owner John Brunton, then a lad, can describe in lively detail how the police sought refuge in it. At the crossroads they encountered Ashe and his men, who met them with effective resistance. They surrendered. They were astonished to find their attackers so youthful and so few in number. One of them, showing signs of frenzy, shouted to the others: 'Are you going to surrender to a lot of schoolboys?' But his colleagues pacified him. At the same time the barracks garrison, some twenty in all, came down the road bearing a white flag and surrendered to Ashe. On his asking their officer, a district inspector, why he had not tried to attack them during the battle, the DI replied that he had already surrendered and would not break his word.

The police lost eleven men, including DI Harry Smith, killed in the closing stages, and County Inspector Alexander Gray, who died later of his wounds; between fifteen and twenty were wounded. In the years of the land revolution Gray had been district inspector in the Dingle area where he became notorious for his acts of repression on behalf of the local landlords. His death seemed to mark the end of an era, as the world to which he gave allegiance came crashing to ruin. Two Volunteers were killed: Tommy Rafferty as related and John Crenigan, not yet twenty, who was shot dead towards the end of the conflict; four or five were wounded. Over ninety rifles and a large supply of ammunition fell into Ashe's hands, besides an almost embarrassing number of motor cars. Official reports, loath to admit the facts, said the police surrendered only when they had practically used up all their ammunition but the ample stocks captured by the Volunteers contradict this.[3] In fact, the large supply that fell into their hands put an end to their ammunition problems for any future action.

The grim task of clearing up the field of battle took an hour, with Dr Hayes attending the wounded and Mollie Adrian helping capably with bandages. The Volunteers sent to Ashbourne for a priest to give spiritual attention to the dying. The battle over, Ashe treated his opponents with every kindness and consideration. He arranged with the senior surviving police officer for the removal to hospital of the wounded men and placed all the cars necessary at his disposal. Joe Kelly remembers them walking up and down discussing matters, Ashe offering the police officer a cigarette, the officer's promise to use the cars only for the removal of his wounded, not for the conveyance of another attacking party. When order was restored Ashe lined up the remaining police near the cross and, standing on a fence, addressed them in brief and effective words, telling them they might return to their homes but at the peril of their lives not to be found again in arms against the Irish Republic.

Thus was fought the battle of Ashbourne, where victory was won by the resource of Ashe and the valour of his Fingal Volunteers. Sophists might argue that as battles go it was a small affair.

The same might be said of Lexington and Concord, actions that loom large with meaning in modern history. The role of Ashe and the Fifth Battalion during Easter Week, culminating in Ashbourne, was significant in its context. It was an act of defiance against a powerful military system. It set an object lesson in guerilla tactics that was copied with success in the later phase of the War of Independence, not to mention campaigns in various other parts of the globe since then. The veteran of the Boer War John MacBride, looking out on the Dublin hills from Jacob's Factory and reflecting gravely on the lessons he learned on South African terrain, thought the Rising ought to have taken place in the countryside and not in the cooped, confined city streets. The result of Ashbourne might be cited in his support. It was, in conjunction with the major battle for Dublin, a preliminary step in the dismantling of the British Empire. Like Lexington and Concord, it re-echoed across the globe.

When everything was put in order, Ashe mobilised his men and marched back to Borranstown camp where they had something to eat. The wounded Captain Eddie Rooney was taken away to a friendly house to have his injuries attended to and get a night's rest. Sentinels were located at mile intervals. 'In case of attack,' said Jack Devine, 'our orders were to hold our enemy in check until we got the men and supplies away safely from camp, should we have to retreat. There was no attack and next day, Saturday, we rested.' That evening they moved to Newbarn, where they pitched camp in a deserted farmstead well protected by outer walls and buildings. There was cheer and confidence in the air.

All too soon the bright hopes faded. The following morning, sentries intercepted a police officer bearing a white flag, who brought from Dublin the unlooked-for news of the surrender of the republican insurgents and an order in Pearse's own hand to lay down arms. The Fingal Volunteers, whose morale was high, could not be brought to think of any such thing as surrender. There was bewilderment, disbelief and non-acceptance.

In order to check the exact position of things, Dick Mulcahy accompanied the police officer into Dublin. He was taken to Kilmainham prison, saw Pearse, who confirmed that the order was genuine, and brought back word to the Fingal Battalion that for the present the battle for the Republic was over. For Ashe and his men, who had tasted victory all that week, it was a bitter disappointment. 'I took my rifle,' said Joe Kelly, 'and I think I was going to smash it against the wall. One of our officers told me that would do no good. Then I think I broke down. Our spirits had been so high. We were now well-equipped, having the police rifles and ammunition.' Some of the men wanted to take to the hills like Michael Dwyer in 1798 and hold out; a few did not wait to surrender at all. Tommy McArdle said goodbye to Ashe and went away to shelter in Dempsey's at Grace Dieu. Michael McAllister, bonniest of fighters, sheltered for a while in the district and, after adventures, made his way to the States. A young Volunteer named Holohan got away to New York and gave an account of the battle to John Devoy, who saluted on behalf of Irish America the valour of Ashe and his men. Thomas Ashe the soldier accepted the decision of his commanding officers and advised his men that their duty as soldiers was to obey, much against their wishes though it might be. Paddy Doyle has a vivid impression of the scene in the yard at Newbarn, where he saw Ashe throw his Luger pistol into the clump of ivy at the back of an old shed, not wishing to yield it. 'I could swear it is there yet.'

The Volunteers proceeded to Swords, where they were put in open lorries and taken into Dublin. 'This will start a lot of writing,' said Ashe to Dick Mulcahy. Of those who did write none wrote less than Thomas Ashe, which is a pity, as his account of the battle would have special authority. There are some brief words in Irish which he wrote in de Valera's autograph book:

In Finglas on Monday and Tuesday, in Swords on Wednesday, in Donabate the same day, in Garristown that night, in Ashbourne on Friday, in New Barn on Saturday. I got Pearse's notice on Sunday morning – we were taken prisoner that evening.

Ashbourne barracks is no more, but on Ashbourne plain stands a memorial commemorating the two heroic soldiers who fell in defence of the Irish Republic, Rafferty and Crenigan. After the battle Tommy Rafferty's mother was sent for and her arrival on the scene has been described by Ashe in poignant words:

On our side there were two men killed; one patriot from Lusk, a fine manly fellow, who ran from his work to take up his rifle when we sent out the call. His body was taken to a house in Ashbourne, and the women of Meath, who had heard the rifles ringing the whole long day, were in the house with the body of young Rafferty. They stepped aside when his mother entered, trembling in fear and sorrow for the young fellow who lost his life, and for his mother, an old woman. She entered and looked at the dead body of her son, and moved the long locks, and, looking up towards Heaven, she said: 'Thank God it is for Ireland you died.'[4]

In a prison letter to his sister Nora, Ashe expressed in similar terms his admiration for the nobility of this mother in her hour of grief.

Ashe's brief span of life after his release in June 1917, the stress of the times, the numerous and urgent demands on him, his concentration on the duties of the hour, these things never left him with the leisure in which to write his own account of Ashbourne, though he foresaw what writing there would be. Once, at a social gathering in Mícheál Ó Foghludha's house, Gothic Lodge, Cabra Road, a great nationalist rendezvous, he drew for enquiries a hasty sketch of the battle on the back of an official OHMS envelope, while he explained to those present the fortunes of the day. Drawn offhand from memory, it shows how familiar he was with the terrain over which the battle was fought. When finished, he handed the sketch to a young lady who was following his account with rapt attention. She was Miss Claire Archer, who later married Diarmuid Ó hÉigeartaigh, secretary to the First Dáil. The sketch has survived the vicissitudes of time.

13

THE ECHOES OF KILMAINHAM

'After the surrender,' related Paddy Doyle, 'the lorry brought us all to Richmond Barracks. We were put into an old room; on the following day we were put into the gymnasium. Johnny Barton, the big G-man, walked round looking at everybody and picked out big Tom Ashe, John MacBride and others. Seán MacDermott was there too. Tom sang a song for us the last night we were there together, "My Colleen by the Lee". He was a grand singer. He was in the best of spirits and he had everyone else the same way. No one complained. Then we were separated. Tom Ashe, MacBride and the others were taken away and we were shifted off to Knutsford on the 3rd of May.'

Ashe was taken away to face court martial. Trials by court martial became the order of the day, a state of affairs foreshadowed explicitly by Prime Minister Herbert Asquith when he announced in the House of Commons, on 27 April, that martial law was to come into effect immediately all over Ireland.

The same afternoon General Sir John Grenfell Maxwell sailed for Ireland to take over command of the British troops, set the civil functions aside and assume the power and authority of a dictator in governing the country. What can be said about him has been made most of by his eulogist Cyril Falls. His previous military experience included a command in Egypt and Gallipoli. From this theatre of war he had been moved in circumstances that left him with a dislike of civil authority, and he may have approached his Irish assignment with the resolve to set at naught any doubts of his efficiency. His instincts were militarist and in the next few weeks he allowed them full scope. As a result, whether he pleased his superiors or not, he has become numbered with the great execrated of the world. We quote here his announcement of 11 May from British headquarters, Parkgate, Dublin, twelve days after the surrender of the Irish republican leaders:

> In view of the gravity of the rebellion and its connection with German intrigue and propaganda, and in view of the great loss of life and destruction of property resulting therefrom, the General Officer Commanding-in-Chief has found it imperative to inflict the most severe sentences on the known organisers of this detestable rising and on those Commanders who took an active part in the actual fighting which occurred. It is hoped that these examples will be sufficient to act as a deterrent to intriguers, and to bring home to them that the murder of His Majesty's liege subjects, or other acts calculated to imperil the safety of the Realm will not be tolerated.[1]

At the time this statement was published twelve leaders of the Irish Volunteers, who had fought in uniform and observed in war the highest standards of chivalry, had been sentenced to death by court martial and executed by firing squad. Their names were: Patrick Pearse, Thomas MacDonagh, Thomas J. Clarke (executed 3 May); Joseph Plunkett, Edward Daly, Michael O'Hanrahan, William Pearse (4 May); John MacBride (5 May); Cornelius Colbert, Éamonn Ceannt, Michael Mallin, Seán Heuston (8 May). Two more, James Connolly and Seán Mac Diarmada, were executed on 12 May.

Nearly all were friends of Ashe but some of them were linked with him in the closest bonds of comradeship and sympathy. Nora Ághas tells of the admiration in which he held Patrick Pearse and his educational work at St Enda's School and of how he would try to help along St Enda's by encouraging his friends to send their children there. With Seán Mac Diarmada Thomas had been on terms of intimate friendship and there was much that was similar in their characters. Between Connolly and Ashe there was not only friendship but complete rapport in social ideals. Tom Clarke he admired beyond all, for his long sufferings and his inflexibility, and with him John Daly of Limerick, the indomitable Fenian whose nephew Ned, no less indomitable, fell before Maxwell's firing party.

General Maxwell's hope of deterring intriguers has an odd ring when placed cheek by jowl with the behaviour, not many years old, of Edward Carson, Frederick E. Smith and Sir Henry Wilson. A proper logic might suggest that these men, on the score of intrigue, ought to figure at the receiving end of a firing party, instead of being, as they were, elevated to the places of honour and power they presently occupied. However, the Irish people were not at liberty to indulge aloud in such speculations. Martial law was in force and Sir John Maxwell was thorough. He was rewarded with the GCB [Order of the Bath] in November.

On 11 May, the same day as Maxwell issued the statement quoted, it was announced that Thomas Ashe had been sentenced to death by field general court martial and the sentence commuted to penal servitude for life. A similar announcement was made regarding Éamon de Valera. The actual trial seems to have been held on 9 May.[2] There is no record available of Thomas Ashe's court martial. Of the 1916 courts martial, generally speaking only fragmentary reports, derived from various sources, are available, with the single exception of Eoin MacNeill's. An intention by Asquith to have them published was reversed by his successor Bonar Law on the ground that 'in present circumstances it would be most detrimental to the public interest' to publish them.[3] It is to be hoped that they are not irretrievably lost, although some of them may well be. The writer sent an enquiry to the British Prime Minister, Mr Harold Wilson, and received a courteous reply from his secretary dated 5 September 1967 saying that no trace could be found of the court martial proceedings relating to Thomas Ashe, which might have been destroyed, since not all proceedings of courts martial are preserved. Such fragments as we possess were related to us by Gregory Ashe.

The first question asked of Ashe at his court martial was: 'What hope did you think you had of defeating the British Empire?' to which he replied: 'A soldier does not question the difficulties with which he is faced.' Later, on release, he said he was sorry he was not shot, as never again would he be so spiritually prepared.

Doubtless the death sentence was no less than he expected. In Kilmainham prison, in the solitude of his cell, he faced the prospective consummation with absolute serenity of mind and soul. He described the moment briefly in a prison letter, dated 12 April 1917, to his friend Séamus Ó Donnchadha, recollecting 'the happiness I felt while awaiting the sentence of death in Kilmainham prison. It was a beautiful experience.'

Gregory Ashe was in New York, in the employment of a grain company, when the Rising broke out. He was laid up with a bad attack of tonsillitis, and confined to bed, when Dr Jim Nunan came in to attend him. 'Any relative of yours in the Dublin Rising?' asked Dr Nunan. Gregory did not know, but felt fairly certain his brother was in it. Some time later Father Tom Casey came in with a newspaper. It carried the announcement that Ashe had been sentenced to death.

It has inevitably been asked why Thomas Ashe and Éamon de Valera, both of them senior officers who had fought with signal distinction in the Rising, were spared the death volley and given penal servitude instead. Mr de Valera, now president of Ireland, in an interview which he gave on his eightieth birthday, answered queries about the commutation of sentence. He said he had seen documents which appeared to him to show why he did not share the fate of others. On these documents there was a line drawn across a list of names and his was first below the line. The executions were taking place from day to day and resentment was growing in America.

> I think the British Government did not wish to exacerbate American opinion [said the President] and when the pressure was coming on, Mr Asquith, the British Premier, said: 'We shall have no more executions except those.' I was tried on the same day as Seán MacDermott and Tom Ashe, who was also a Commandant – the fact was that I got off the same as he did.[4]

De Valera thinks that what saved his life was that, on the surrender, he was taken to the Royal Dublin Society grounds in suburban Ballsbridge instead of to one of the city barracks, and kept there until Thursday, when he was removed to Richmond Barracks. He did not consider his American citizenship to be a factor in the commutation.

What is beyond doubt is that, in the aftermath of Easter Week, Ashe stood very close to death, almost certainly closer to it than de Valera. For the information which follows we are indebted to the president's biographer, Thomas P. O'Neill who, in the course of his researches in the Public Record Office in London, consulted a memorandum, dated 9 June 1916, which had been submitted to the British Cabinet by the attorney-general, J. H. Campbell, KC. Having detailed events in Ireland which caused him apprehension, including Dr O'Dwyer's celebrated reply to General Maxwell, the attorney-general went on to say:

> Then followed the reprieve of the man who was the leader of the party that murdered nine members of the Royal Irish Constabulary at Ashbourne, a reprieve to which I was strongly opposed, while I was entirely in favour of leniency towards the rank and file.[5]

The man specifically indicated here is Thomas Ashe. He is like-wise the only man individually so indicated in the entire document. The fact that the attorney-general was strongly in favour of his execution shows what a bare shadow intervened between Ashe and the firing squad.

The ways of fortune are strange. A few short years earlier, J. H. Campbell was one of Sir Edward Carson's lieutenants in the rabid, anti-constitutional campaign directed against Home Rule. He fomented disaffection, sedition and rebellion. No magistrate or constable invoked against him a Defence of the Realm regulation. Yet a few short years more and he would become elevated to the bench and in the fullness of time, as Lord Glenavy, occupy the chair of Seanad Éireann, an institution the existence of which might be speculative were it not for the sacrifices of men like Ashe and his comrades. And now here was James H. Campbell, attorney-general and subscriber to the Carlton Club, arrayed in the trappings of law, martial and otherwise, against the rebel republican commander Thomas Ashe, and doing his utmost to send him to death. The fact remains, however, that Ashe survived the hostility of the attorney-general.[6]

What did Thomas Ashe think saved him? In the quiet conviction of his mind he believed that more things were wrought by prayer than the world knew or dreamed. Time and again his thoughts must have gone back to those days before Easter Sunday when he placed offerings of freshly cut flowers on the altar at Lusk. Few comrades knew Ashe's thoughts and ways more intimately from early years than his cousin Pádraig Ashe, who shared in his confidences as boy and man. We have already related Mary Monks's recollection of how Ashe collected a mass of flowers from the school garden to lay on the altar. It may have been this same occasion which Pádraig Ashe writes about to the author:

> The last thing he did on the Saturday before that celebrated Easter Sunday was to collect all the flowers in his garden and arrange them neatly on the altar of the Virgin Mary in Lusk church and he believed strongly in his heart that it was her intercession saved him from the firing squad after Easter. This devotion and reverence for the Virgin Mary was in his heart from early youth.

So Ashe believed. And so it well may be. The victories of a man's faith lie beyond our knowledge.

There is in existence a photograph which was taken during his brief stay in Kilmainham. It shows him standing in shirt sleeves, between four British soldiers, in a narrow enclosure, wearing still the strong walking boots and gaiters in which he must have strode the Fingal terrain during Easter Week and holding in his hand what looks like a tin mug. Captive though he is, he dominates the scene, rising head and shoulders over his escort, his splendid appearance enhanced by the drabness of his surroundings.

He was removed from Kilmainham to Mountjoy jail. From there he wrote to his sister Nora on 13 May, the day following the execution of two men who were very dear to him, Connolly and Mac Diarmada. He asked Nora to put certain affairs of his in order:

Dear Nora,

I am sure you are very much troubled over me for the past few weeks. I expect you know before this of my presence here. The term looks long, but I am facing it in a most optimistic mood. Prison life, so far anyhow, is not so bad as one views it from the outside.

Be sure and write home as soon as you get this. They must be in a queer state. Let them go on with their business as if nothing happened to me. That is exactly how I look on it.

I am anxious too that you should write to Fr. Hoey, P.P., Lusk, telling him that owing to circumstances I must resign the Principalship of Corduff N.S. and thank him for his many acts of kindness to me.

I think you should call to Corduff if possible, and remove any of my belongings that you think useful. I leave all this in your hands. You might give Dalton's *History of Ireland*, all the volumes, to Fr. Togher, C.C. of Lusk, as he and I were friends.

Some of my salary and pension payments should be got from

the National Board. I give you permission to get them. If you succeed you might pay £5 to Mike Casey, and some small amount to
the Educational Co. of Ireland and also some to Browne and Nolan.
Otherwise let them wait.

I am leaving my motor-bike to Dan McAllister of Turvey, Donabate, Co. Dublin. Write and tell him so. Also tell his youngest sister,
Nellie, that I have been asking for her.

I wish you would also write to Judge Arthur O'Connor, Co.
Court judge of Somersetshire [*sic*], England. Father will tell you all
about him.

Write to Fr. O'Mahony, St. Mary's College, Rathmines.[7]

When I next get leave to see a friend I'll let you know.

Give my love to everyone and remember me in your prayers.

Your fond brother
Thomas Ashe.

Ten days later, he was transferred across the Channel to Dartmoor.
But not before he had received from Nora, who in the interval was
allowed to visit him, the joyful news that his father Gregory had
fully approved his part in the Easter Rising. Ashe, who revered his
father, faced prison with a light heart.

14

DARTMOOR

The Irish prisoners were dispersed throughout Great Britain, some six hundred being interned in Frongoch camp, North Wales, and hundreds more in Knutsford, Wandsworth, Stafford, Wakefield, Lewes, Dartmoor, Glasgow, Perth and other places. The story of Ashe for the next thirteen months is summarised on a postcard addressed to him by May McAllister of Turvey. It reached him in HM Prison, Dartmoor, an address to which is added, in his own handwriting, 'Lewes, Portland, Pentonville'. Such was his prison odyssey.

He was taken from Dublin under escort on 23 May 1916 and sent with some sixty-five other comrades to bleak Dartmoor prison, Devonshire, in the south-west of England. It was an abode known to former Irish patriots. Its grey walls had held the dashing Fenian Captain of Hussars John Boyle O'Reilly. There Michael Davitt received the treatment which undermined his health. Ashe is entered in the prison records as 'q 102 Life'.

After the excitement and action of the Rising, the unforgettable moments and memories of those early mornings in Kilmainham, and the emotion of lying for a period in the shadow of death, he composed his thoughts to the prospect of spending a long time in prison. This did not daunt him. There would be time for thought and prayer, and Thomas Ashe, man of action though he was, was very much a man of spiritual reflection.

The day after he arrived he wrote his first letter to Nora. The rules did not permit any reference to politics but, as he told her: 'It is easy to guess on what our thoughts mostly will dwell, and the object of our prayers too will be fairly evident,' and it is not hard to surmise that he dwelt on the events of the last few weeks and their possible effect on Ireland's future. He told Nora as much about his thoughts and situation as the rules would permit:

24 May 1916

Dear Nora,

We arrived here yesterday and had a very pleasant journey from Dublin. The sea was very calm, and therefore the trip was a pleasure but the railway journey was very long. England from Liverpool to Bristol is nothing but chimney stacks and a heavy fog seemed to hang over the land. But from Bristol southwards there are not so many large towns. The scene is pastoral, and looks like parts of Ireland very much. The country round about here is hilly and we saw some very nice scenes on our way.

We all felt in the very best of spirits, and I feel so too. Prison life might do us no harm, as thought and prayer are two things that I feel sure can be indulged in, and these surely will do us good. It is easy to guess on what our thoughts mostly will dwell, and the object of our prayers too will be fairly evident. You should be sure and join with us in the latter that our petitions may be heard the sooner. Continue in the same and get all your friends to do likewise.

How are they all getting on at home? I hope father is himself again. No need for fear and depression of spirit in anybody at liberty, when we are not suffering from such things. I hope Jack Begley is increasing his prayer guild daily. I am delighted he has done this. Praying will give us more assistance than grieving.

Be sure and tell all my friends that I remember them all daily. I generally run over the whole list and I try to think what they are all thinking of. I am glad they remember me and please tell them so. Give my love to Nellie [McAllister] … I hope she is keeping up a brave heart. Write to her often and cheer her as I feel that she will think things very lonely. But there are happy times in store for us all. Give my best regards also to her sisters and mother. I would have given a lot to see her before I left, but it was impossible … Make no mistake and thank Father Hoey for me for his kindness. I don't think there is any use in his keeping the school for me. He must appoint somebody … He is very good and so is Father Togher. If you'll remove my things be sure and search the school for books of mine. There are two copies of St. Enda's Annual there, and I want you to be certain and take them and keep them safe for me. I am also anxious that you should keep a file of the daily papers, commencing three weeks ago for me, and any weeklies that you may think worth keeping, too. How is Paddy in Dunbeg? I have just been thinking of him for some days past. Tell all his brothers and sisters that I have been asking for them. I am sure Miss Monks was a bit upset over my imprisonment. How did Mrs Thornton take it? I want you to write to Mrs Rafferty of Lusk and offer her my sympathy for her son. Or better still tell Father Togher do it for me. She must be a noble woman for what she said. I'd like to write you a list of people I'd like to be remembered to but it would cover more than these pages if I did. So be sure and tell all my friends as you meet them or as you write to them of this. (How is Kit Griffin?) I am afraid it will be impossible for you to come over here and see me. It will be some time before I will be allowed to see a visitor, and the journey over is too long. Tell this too to Nellie. I have permission to receive a letter from you in answer to this. Be sure and follow the instructions on the front. Also get words of cheer from all the friends you can for me that my spirits might be kept up and my heart be encouraged. This applies specially to Nellie.

Never tire of asking for prayers for me and I am sure I need only suggest this and you'll do it. Also I know that you'll do all the other things I have asked for too. Tell them at home to mind my dog and to be sure and care for her in every way ... Give my best regards to everybody. And especially to the children of my school, of your own, and of home.

With love to Nellie and to you and to them all at home.

I am your fond brother,
Thomas Ashe.

He received Nora's reply on 6 June:

Cappamore
Co. Limerick
Ireland
4.6.16.

Dear Tomás,

No need to tell you of the joy your letter gave me and of the relief it was to know at last where you were. We had no idea but that you were still in Dublin altho' rumour had it that you were sent to Portland. Now to come to business. I was glad to hear that you and all the others were in good spirits for that is how we want ye to be. When I got your letter I wrote and told many of your friends and I waited till to-day to get back messages. I can't write them all in full for as Minnie said it would take a ship to hold them all – suffice it to say that I have got messages of love, respect, regard from young and old, from great and little. I shall begin with Nellie – she wrote me a very nice letter by return post saying that when she heard you were in Portland she wrote to you there, she sent all kinds of loving affectionate remembrances and also from her mother and Annie. She said her brother Dan was home again from England and that he wished to be specially remembered to you and that he said you should finish his photo before the winter set in. Nellie told you not to work too hard. She gave me an invitation to go and spend some time with them when I go to Lusk again.

I had two letters from Miss Monks. In the first she told me that Mr Welply, Dr Starkie, Mrs and Miss Starkie were out with her at the school the day before. They stayed for ¾ of an hour and went way very well pleased. Fr. Hoey would not appoint a teacher – he's getting a substitute till July and then he says 'we'll have poor Mr Ashe back again.' In her second letter she sent messages from all. The first prayer at school each day is for you. She's minding all your flowers and geraniums. She would like to hear from you as you were always so kind to her. The children answered splendidly at Confirmation … Mrs Thornton sends kind remembrances and says she hopes she'll have you back again. When I was speaking to her she could do nothing but cry and say 'Oh Boys! Oh Boys! Poor Mr Ashe and the poor Doctor.' She's a kind old woman. I had no letter from my Father but you know what he would say. He's keeping up grand – better far than you would think. And as for Matt – you know what he would say too. They both pray hard for you anyway. Minnie and Hanna and John and all the children send messages of love. All Min's boys pray for you – even Teddy doesn't forget his prayers for Uncle Tom and all the Irish boys. Minnie says everyone is related to you now at home … She tells you pray, sing, and live constantly with God. Paddy in Doonbeg and Eileen and Peg also sent their share. Paddy is going to see you in August, or Christmas at the very latest. You can guess the message he would like to send. He said he was dreaming that you and he were on the hill a few nights ago, fighting as usual the old game … Miss Hayes was here to see me one day and I met her in town yesterday and took her up to Barrington St. We went in to see John [Daly] – he's very weak now, but oh! if you could only hear him you'd stay all your life in Eng[land] to earn one word from such as he. I am attending to all your little business but I have not been for any of your things yet. However I may go up for the Whit weekend. I was in Gothic Lodge when in Dublin and it would break one's heart. No trace of poor Mícheál and Brighid is still away. Nora is the same as ever. I had to bring her some memento of you when coming from Lusk. And now dear Tomás I have told you all. You are never absent from my thoughts and prayers. Remember me to D. Lynch & the Doctor.

God bless you all, with love,

Your sister,

Nora.

P.S. Tom, I have kept the papers for you. I think there are more prayers said here for you than there are at home. I gave your messages to the children. All your friends here send best love and wishes. Don't forget to give D. Lynch and Dr Hayes my love. I have kept all the letters for you too – so you'll have them to read when you come back. I met Seán Hurley who sends you a wireless, unsaid message and a solid, sound shake hands. Kit has also put in a claim to go to see you. Goodbye now and write next time to Father. Let Nellie wait, she's young.

Best love again to all our boys,

Your fond sister,

Nora Ashe.

Ashe's prison correspondence is full of the warm and affectionate wishes of his own family and relatives. They rallied to him in his hour of trial and supported him, fully and decisively, in his views and actions. His legion of friends gave him their full-hearted admiration and support, and their messages lifted up his spirits. The rules forbade prisoners to receive or send any references to political doings, but his correspondents got around this by using the allegories familiar to students of Irish literature with which to convey their message and indicate changes in political thoughts and trends in Ireland. References to Kathleen's improving health were let pass by blissfully unconscious censors, as were expressions in disapproval of her neglectful and nefarious stepmother, and if they wondered at the interest the prisoners might have in 'the state of the crops' or the qualities of 'the Grand National horses' it does not seem to have struck them that the words had any other significance beyond their face meaning. Yet the censors were alert and strict, and not easy to pass, and many letters received by Ashe are scarred with their deletions. Some of them may be seen in Kilmainham Museum.

He was naturally eager to hear news of the world outside and of the reactions to the Rising of his friends and relatives. Commissioner Starkie certainly did not approve, nor was Ashe worried much about what he thought. There were many people, like his relatives and friends in Kinard, Dunbeg, Ardfert, Dingle and elsewhere, whose good opinion he was far happier to have. His thoughts wandered a great deal to Fingal, especially Lusk and Corduff. It cheered him greatly that Father Hoey proposed to keep his job open for him until he should return, although Ashe doubted whether Father Hoey would succeed in this. He was particularly anxious that the school and its surroundings should be kept in as good order as always. He wrote to Nora on 28 June:

Dear Nora,

The letter of the National Board to you regarding my salary for April, etc., which I saw some days ago, prompted me to ask for permission to write you a special letter concerning my school. This permission has been kindly granted; hence this letter.

Now you left me in the dark very much regarding a lot of things in your last letter, although I was delighted with it otherwise. It was a most companionable letter and I have read it often since. But as I have said it left me in the dark. If Fr. Hoey, the Rev. Manager, states that I would be soon back again in the school, why did you not give me his grounds for so stating? It is quite evident that his reasons for thinking so must be strong ones, considering that he is only appointing a locum tenens in my place. Now I'd like to know for certain why Fr. Hoey thinks he'll have me back again so soon, and furthermore in the event of my return at no far distant date will the locum tenens immediately resign in my favour, and also has the latter been appointed and if so who is he, etc. Of course he'll live in the official residence. Then I think you should remove all my clothes, letters, books, particularly my books on painting, pictures, and my gun, dog and motor licences which latter I am sure you will easily find. Also any other things you think necessary. Furniture need not be removed I think.

To the lady teachers you might tell the following: Ask Miss Monks to look after my flowers, and to see that all the beds are kept in order and free from weeds. Also to be sure to take up all hyacinths, tulips, etc., for drying. I am sure she will do this. I would write to her but I am in prison, and prison rules must be kept. However I am quite certain that she'll do what I ask.

Ask Miss N. McAllister to look after the drawing and to be sure that my pictures are not injured in my absence. I received her letter and was terribly sorry I couldn't answer it. I certainly am delighted at the interest she is taking in things since my leaving and please tell her so. I sincerely thank her too for the message she sent in your letter. Ask her to tell her brother Dan to keep my motorbike for me, and to take all the care he can of it, and also that I have invented (it is only in my mind so far but all details are complete) a lamp suitable for motor-bikes and motor cars, of which I'll say no more until my return, except that it is going to beat all the acetylene and electric lights so far used in efficiency, beauty and cheapness.

Let Mr Patrick Hanafin take care of my dogs, and particularly care of my setter, which they must be careful will be taught no bad habits such as rabbit hunting, etc. I was delighted to hear how they all remembered me.

Could you find out the Inspector's and the Resident Commissioner's report of their visit to my school for me. Be sure to thank Fr. Hoey for his kindness and don't forget.

Tell Mrs Thornton to keep the school as clean as ever, and that I'll get back sometime D.V. I'd like if you sent me Fr. O'Leary's Irish Book 'Séadhna' [*sic*]. I may get permission to read it here, and anyhow it won't get lost. There is a copy in my house.

I think you should not ask the Commissioners to refund my pension premiums. That can wait. If you have asked for a refund I think you should withdraw your letter.

How is the attendance at my school keeping up? I am sure there are a lot of my books in the school. Be sure they do not get lost, particularly two copies of St. Enda's School Annual. Be sure and get them for me and keep them safe.

Any other school matters that you think interesting let me know of them.

Give my love to all,
Your fond brother,
Thomas Ashe.

Nora's answer, dated 7 July, from Cappamore, County Limerick, reached him on 10 July. She would have written earlier only she had been away to attend the funeral of her old friend John Daly of Limerick, a man whose inflexible Fenian character Ashe had found a great source of inspiration.

Mary Monks had written to Nora to explain how matters stood with regard to the school. Father Hoey was awaiting Ashe's return to resume teaching and had made up his mind to appoint nobody in his place until the summer holidays. Then he would make no permanent appointment as it was his firm belief Ashe would soon be back again. Father Hoey seemed to share in a general view that there would be an amnesty. He did not want any of Ashe's things removed because he preferred that Ashe on his return should find everything exactly as he left it. Mrs Thornton was taking scrupulous care that everything was kept trim and tidy. Mary Monks was attending to his flowers, the grass was neatly cut all round the school and the children had been only too willing to help. The school was redecorated and looked brand new, and Father Hoey was going to have Ashe's house redecorated as well. There never was such a wonderful bloom of roses all round the house. Everyone still called it Mr Ashe's house. Pat Finnegan, one of Ashe's pupils, was given charge of his potato crop. The children were attending catechism examination. Dr Starkie did not ask many questions, apart from enquiring was Ashe in the school up to the day he closed it for Easter and some other queries. He left no report. Both Father Hoey and Father Togher came over to the school very often and were taking a particular interest in it. Father Hoey said Corduff was now his favourite school. It is easy to see that both Father Hoey and Father Togher held Ashe in the highest regard. There was a special message from the children of Corduff School that must have cheered Ashe's heart. 'The children all send you their best love and wish to tell you that they are minding your apple trees and are keeping your flowers free from weeds. They also want to tell you that they are praying very hard for you.' Kathleen, Mary Monks's younger sister, was happy to take charge of his geraniums and to see that his favourite seat down at 'the Arches' by the seaside, where he used to while away the time singing and sketching, was kept in proper style and order against his homecoming. Father Hoey often spoke of the glorious mass of hyacinths which Ashe sent him for his altar. At home in West Kerry his cousin Patrick Hanafin was taking good care of his dogs, especially his favourite red setter. Nellie McAllister had taken charge of his drawings and her brother Dan kept his motorcycle in perfect condition, cleaned and oiled, and was more than interested in Ashe's idea for a new type of motor lamp. Nora had sent him *Séadna*, one of his favourite books, and asked when he would have permission to receive visitors, as she would like to go over and see him.

Fellow prisoners of Ashe in Dartmoor included Éamon de Valera, Eoin MacNeill, Desmond Fitzgerald, Harry Boland and Austin Stack. Stack's first meeting with him in Dartmoor took place under conditions of prison discipline which ruled out conversation:

> Here I recall my recognition of Tomás at exercise in the prison yard on the morning after my arrival at Dartmoor, my nod to him as he limped around the inner 'ring' and his smile of welcome in return. It was a happy 'meeting' though we had no chance of getting nearer than thirty feet or so to one another that day. Indeed it was weeks before we got much nearer, except one Sunday when we were able to touch one another's hands – in chapel after Mass.
>
> Tomás was in hospital with a wound or injury to his knee for some time after my arrival.[1]

The knee injury was described by the prison doctor as synovitis. When he recovered from it Ashe returned to the prison workshop, where his seat was close to Stack's. Stack gave him such news as he had of events from Dublin and learned a great deal of Irish from his companion. Ashe was more than keen on the language and was constantly trying, not only to improve his knowledge of it, but to make it predominate in his mind over English. He talked of his visit to the United States and expressed sadness at the thought of all the men Ireland could not afford to lose, especially her Irish speakers, who became lost to her forever through the lure of the dollar or the necessity of seeking a living in America. His fellow convict, Councillor Thomas Partridge, a popular figure of the Labour movement, has recorded that Ashe was 'one of the most inoffensive men, a man of noble character. He would spend his day (in jail) singing the grand old traditional songs of Ireland. He cheered the men at work, as he sang them under his breath.'[2]

Letters were always welcome. From Lusk Mary Monks wrote and gave him the local news. Father Togher had volunteered as a navy chaplain and would soon be leaving. He had been to Corduff School many times and felt very lonely after Ashe. Father Hoey had appointed a successor to Ashe in the principalship of the school after the summer holidays. He had been very reluctant to do so, and only pressure from the Commissioners of National Education had finally compelled him. They had threatened to withdraw grants from the school unless he did.

> The children are very good and are praying hard for you [wrote Mary]. The school looks very nice, but really it can never again look as nice in my eyes as it did before Easter. I think I'll never again be as happy as I was then.

She was caring for all his flowers. Mary Monks had worked very hard throughout the summer, upheld by the thought that she was keeping the school in order for him.

We will never forget you here and shall pray night and day for your speedy release. With very best love and kind remembrances from all your friends and a special remembrance from Mother and Kathleen.

I remain,
Your sincere friend,
Mary Monks.

Mary Monks's letter, dated 20 September 1916, bears the prison stamp of 3 October.

There were many empty places in the familiar circle of friends. Nora Foley, writing to Ashe, says that Gothic Lodge is very lonely now. Her brother Michael was interned in England. 'No, we never have a game of bridge now, who is there to play?' She had been out to Corduff with Nora Ashe and thought it was such an empty deserted place. 'I don't know how you ever lived there.' But to Thomas Ashe Corduff, Lusk and the sky over them were home and heaven.

He wrote to his father on 4 September:

Dear Father,

I am sure you have been anxious to hear from me since my committal to prison, but I found it impossible to write any but purely business letters up to the present. Besides I thought writing to Nora would suffice for you all. I am quite well and feeling a lot more content than perhaps a lot of you at home. There are 65 of us here altogether and all are, as far as I can see, feeling just like myself in health and spirits. I missed my summer holidays a good deal, but I hope I'll live to enjoy many a summer holiday yet in freedom. I hope all at home are well. Remember me to everybody and let no one be troubled about my being in prison or about my long term. When I am not in the least put about over it myself nobody else should. At the same time ask all the neighbours and friends to pray for a speedy delivery from prison for us all. Give my love to all the children at home and in Dingle, also to Minnie and Han. Tell Matt that when I'll meet him next I'll keep him in news for a month.

Your fond son,
Thomas.

The same day he wrote to Nora:

Dear Nora,

My letter this time is rather strange looking. I have got permission to write a number of letters on this sheet and I want you to cut each out and forward it to the person to whom it is addressed. You can receive answers to them all and transcribe these answers on foolscap paper and send all on to me. You can fill four pages of foolscap unruled. So that by taking care of your writing and of the space you can send me as much as would fill a volume. I am in the best of health although I had some trouble with one of my knees. Regarding my state of mind: I have always been an optimist and am one still. All the boys seem to be in the best of spirits. I have received *Séadhna* [*sic*] for which I thank you. Did you get all my clothes? Take care of them. Fr. Hoey's idea has not worked out anyhow. Did you ever hear from A. O'Connor? Were you at the G. League annual dance this year? I suppose my usual place was filled up. I could now have visitors but instead I'll ask permission to write in November. This place is too far away to come to and the visit is too short. So I prefer to write in this manner and receive replies. You can send me all the news except political, and four pages of foolscap will contain a good deal. Send my compliments to P. Ryan, Peadar, Jerry Lynch, John Dowd, George McDonnell, Maggie, Seán Ó (?), Róisín Breathnach, etc., etc. Do you hear from Gregory? Send him my love, and ask him to write to me through you. Friends can put off their visit to me until later. Tell them this.

Your fond brother,
Thomas.

The correspondence arrangements suggested by Ashe in this letter were carried out in full detail by Nora Ághas. She would re-address his letters to his friends, receive their replies, copy these into the allocated number of foolscap pages and send them on to Thomas, who was in this way enabled to receive a welcome and varied amount of correspondence.

On 3 October he received a letter from his father, Gregory Ashe of Kinard. Reading through it we do not wonder how it was that Gregory Ashe had such a far-reaching influence on his family, and on his son Thomas. Only a man of finest mind could have written it.

Prison date stamp Oct 3–1916
Cappamore
Co. Limerick
20th Sept. 1916

Dear Tom,

I received your letter and words cannot express how happy I felt. All are well at home. I had a letter from Gregory a fortnight ago and he is well. He met Fr. Joe Moriarty and Fr. G. Ashe, Minard, in Springfield. Be quite sure you have my prayers and the prayers of all your relations and neighbours east and west, north and south. They all make enquiries for you of me and of everyone belonging to you whom they meet and they all pray fervently for you. Yesterday at Mass they all asked me if I had heard any news from you and I was proud and glad to be able to tell them that I had a letter from you the previous day. My dear and loving child, do not be discouraged. Be cheerful and perhaps we may soon meet again. I say again you may rest assured you have the prayers of the whole parish and of the little children at home and at school. I gave your message to Matt and he was delighted … Goodbye now dear child and may God bless you and keep you safe. All at Kinard, Dingle and all your friends wish to be remembered to you.

Your loving Father.

A cheerful letter to his sister Minnie, Mrs Michael Devane of Dingle, dated 13 November 1916, shows a spirit immune to prison conditions:

Dear Minnie,

I feel I owe you a letter so here goes. I have just spent six months in prison, the shortest six I've ever spent in my life. Time flies here surely. If the world outside took a lead from a prison the wheels of time would run far smoother I think. Still in looking forward my term looks stupendous. So far anyhow I'm in the best of form and full of hope. The letters I get from Ireland often make me sad. The whole country seems to be crying. I hope it is crying for itself rather than for us. Otherwise there is absolutely no need for tears. Give my love to all the friends in Dingle and outside of it. I'll write again for Christmas or the New Year, but of course I'll write to others then. I hope you all are well, and that all the children are adept at Irish conversation. I'll look out for that whenever I'll get back. I am very sorry I must cut this note short but Nora will give you any news there is in the rest of it. Nora will tell you how to answer this.

Your fond brother,
Thomas.[3]

Shortly afterwards Ashe and his colleagues were transferred to Lewes prison. It was a welcome change. His reaction to it may be noted from his next letter to his father, dated from Lewes, 13 December 1916:

My dear Father,

I am glad that I have got this opportunity of writing to you for Christmas. As you can see I have been removed from Dartmoor Prison to Lewes Prison since I wrote last, and I assure you I am delighted with the change. I was glad to see by your letter that I am not forgotten at home. I often turn my thoughts towards Kinard and you all, and would very much wish to be among you, but let this not make you believe that I am homesick. I have been so often away that I suffer only very little from this. My health always remains good, and I expect the active open air life I spent in the past is standing by me. I hope all at home are well. And all my friends about and in Dingle too. Remember me to them all or they will surely forget all about me, and I wouldn't wish that. Whenever I get my liberty I'll be most anxious to see that all my nephews and nieces can speak Irish. That work rests with you and I hope you won't forget them. I am sorry that I won't be home for the Christmas holidays this year. I'll miss the shooting very much, and I am sure snipe and woodcock will be very plentiful. However I have acquired fairly good control of all my desires, and to miss a luxury or two doesn't make me in the least unhappy. I am sorry I didn't learn more Irish songs from you as humming airs quietly to myself is the greatest pleasure I have. I even have composed some airs to while away the time and once I have succeeded in this I intend to compose some more. So that I'll be independent of all Kerry airs after a while. Give my love to all for Christmas and my good wishes for the New Year, and be sure and pray for me. You need not answer this letter until you hear from me again.

Your fond son,
Thomas.

His father replied shortly afterwards:

Dear Tom,

I received your letter some days ago and was glad to learn you were well and in good health and spirits. All at home and your friends and cousins in Dingle are well. I hear from Gregory about every two months. I pray for you morning, noon and night and you have the prayers of all the people of the parish, both young and old. All the neighbours and strangers alike make inquiries about you, want to know how you are and surely one could hardly answer them all. Be courageous and cheerful and never despair. Keep a stout heart and you will pull through all right. The people are longing to see you back again, the little boys are always speaking of you and asking me when are you coming again. Matt is well and we often discuss the situation. Dear Tom pray for me and for your brothers and sisters. We do not forget you.

Your fond and affectionate
Father.

15

LEWES JAIL

Maxwell was recalled from Ireland on 5 November 1916. Agitation in favour of amnesty for the prisoners increased. The Irish Party did commendable work in putting pressure on the British government in the House of Commons. To this, and to American opinion, the British government, led since 6 December by David Lloyd George, was obliged to respond by liberating the Frongoch internees and the Reading prisoners, most of whom reached Ireland in time for Christmas.

Only the convict-prisoners, sixty-five in Dartmoor and fifty-seven in Portland, all sentenced for life, and a small group of short-term prisoners, remained in British custody. Early in December they were all removed to Lewes prison near Brighton. Although the climate of Lewes was cold and moist, the restrictions were not as severe as in Dartmoor and presently, through the prisoners' own initiative, they were eased a great deal more. Reports reaching them from time to time about the reawakening spirit of Ireland encouraged them to rebel. The prison rules did not permit them to speak to each other except at exercise time and only then as a privilege. They ignored the rules and talked at all times. The authorities threatened them with penalties. The prisoners persisted and Vincent Poole, one of a celebrated Dublin family with a long Fenian tradition, was sent to a punishment cell. The prisoners called a strike immediately and Poole

Corduff National School. *Author's collection*

Portrait of Thomas Ashe
by Seán O'Sullivan.
*Courtesy of the National
Museum of Ireland*

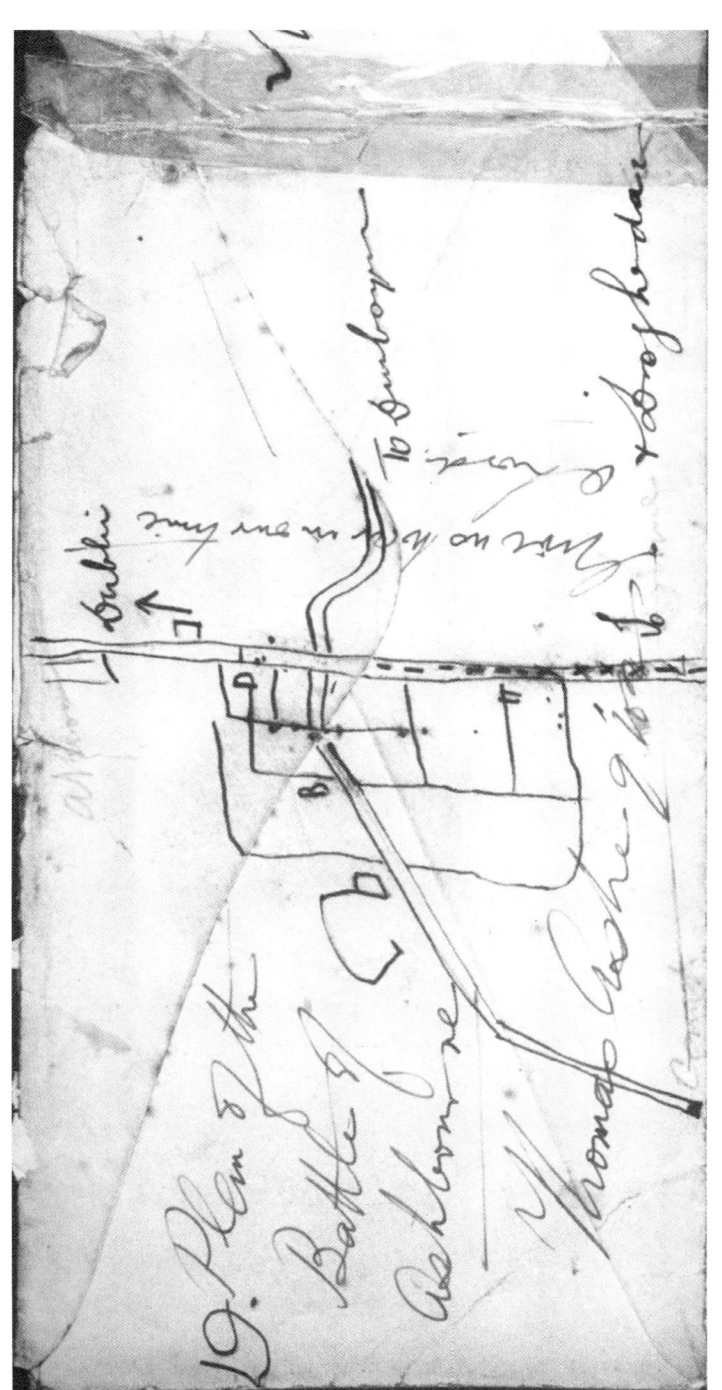

Ashe's impromptu sketch of the Battle of Ashbourne.

Thomas Ashe between guards at Kilmainham, 1916. *Courtesy of the National Library of Ireland*

Thomas Ashe after release from Lewes Prison, 1917. *Courtesy of Mercier Press*

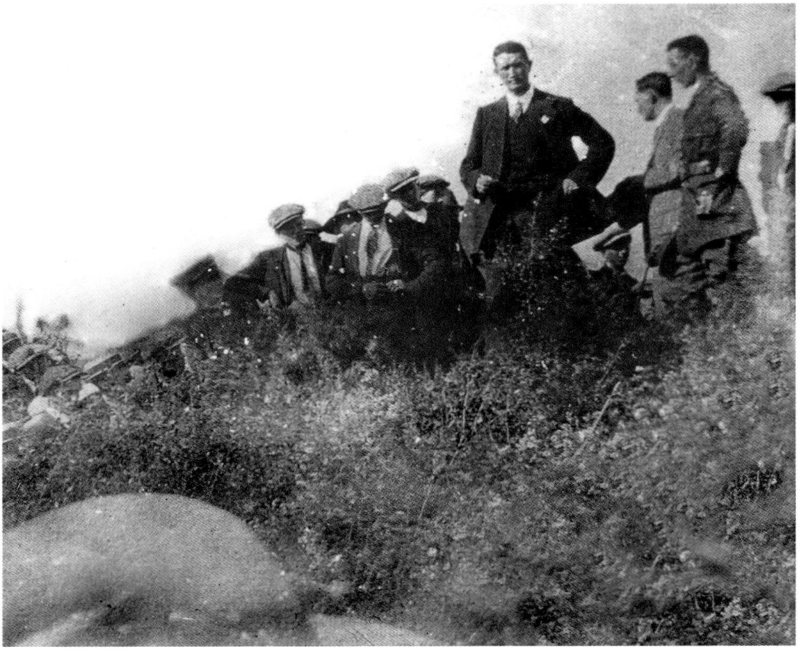

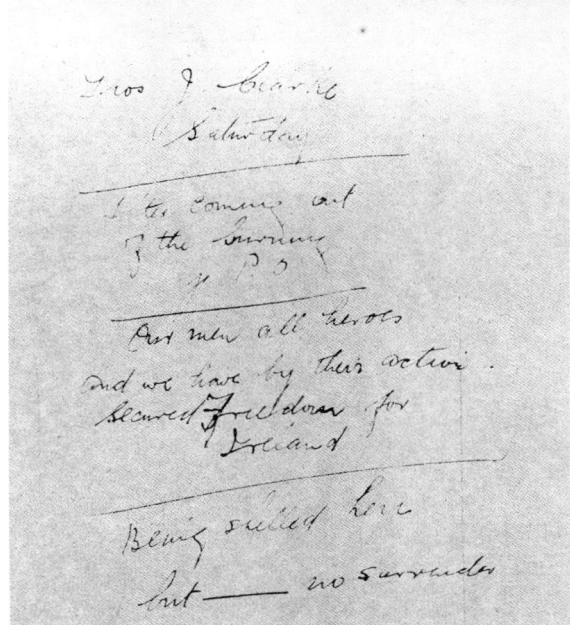

Thomas Ashe at Casement's Fort, August 1917. *Courtesy of Mercier Press*

Thos J. Clarke
Saturday

the coming out
of the surrender
of P.O.

Our men all heroes
and we have by their action
secured Freedom for
Ireland

Being shelled here
but —— no surrender

Notes for speeches made by Ashe.

No. 179

ORDERS

By Colonel H. G. H. KENNARD,

Commanding Dublin District.

Lower Castle Yard, Dublin, Friday, 31st August, 1917.

DISTRICT ORDERS.

1.—Courts-Martial.

The detail of Officers as mentioned below will assemble at the Garrison Office, Lower Castle Yard, Dublin, at 1.30 p.m. on the 3rd September, 1917, for the purpose of trying by District Court-Martial :—

Thomas Ashe (civilian) of Corduff, Lusk, County Dublin.

And such other accused as may be brought before them.

PRESIDENT.

Major L. Swinton Browne, Indian Army.

MEMBERS.

A Captain, H. J. B. Whitehead (H.S.) Garrison Bn. Royal Irish Regiment.
A Captain, L. S. N. Palmer, Royal Dublin Fusiliers.

The O.C. Det. (H.S.) Garrison Bn. Royal Irish Regiment, will provide the necessary stationery, and detail an Orderly to the Court.

The proceedings will be forwarded to the G.O.C.-in-Chief Headquarters, Irish Command, Dublin.

2.—Attached.

The undermentioned men will be attached to the Army Service Corps for rations with effect from 1st September, 1917 :—

No. 12486, Private J. McGinley, Royal Irish Fusiliers.
No. 14832, Private T. Hennessey, Royal Irish Fusiliers.

G. STRATFORD BURTON, *Major.*
Garrison Adjutant.

JOHN FALCONER, Printer to His Majesty's Stationery Office, 53 Upper Sackville Street, Dublin.
[466] Wt. 9083/69. S. 230. 8/'17. G. 5.

Court-martial order, dated 31 August 1917.

CHARGE SHEET.

The accused THOMAS ASHE of Corduff, Lusk, County
Dublin, civilian, is charged with doing an act prohibited
by Regulation 42 of the Defence of the Realm Regulations,
namely, attempting to cause disaffection among the
civilian population.

1st Charge.
REGULATION No.42

Defence of the
Realm Regulations.

in that he

at Ballinalee in the County of Longford, on the 25th day
of July, 1917, with the intention and for the purpose of
causing such disaffection as aforesaid, did speak and
publish certain words and speeches tending to cause such
disaffection as aforesaid, including among others, words
and statements to the following effect:-

"Form military Societies. Train, arm and equip
"yourselves. A man who is trained is far better than
"a man who is not. If it had not been for the Rebel-
"lion of Easter Week, there would not be such a fine
"crowd of young men present as are here tonight, for
"there would have been conscription in Ireland, and
"they would be out fighting for England A great many
"people in Ireland think we are out for another rebel-
"lion, not just exactly another rebellion, but if I
"saw my chance, and England were overpowered or defeat-
"ed on the Western Front, I would have no hesitation
"in calling out my men again as I did in Easter Week,
"1916."

No I — Tried already for Reb

The Br Party say they — No II
have stopped conscription.

If E. were overpowered there
would be nothing else to do. — No III

Signature *Frederick H. Shee*..... Com....
Commdg. 2nd (H.S.) Bn. Bn. Royal Irish Regt.

‡ The Unit with which
the accused is in
custody.

‡ Commanding ....

Place .....Dublin.....

Date .....31st August 1914....

TO BE TRIED BY COURT MARTIAL.

Place .....Dublin.....

Date .....21.9.17.....

Ashe's funeral going along the north quays of Dublin.
Courtesy of the Bureau of Military History, Military Archives, IE-MA-BMH-CD-227/35 (Fintan Murphy collection)

The graveside scene. *Courtesy of the National Library of Ireland*

Group, including members of the Ashe family, at the commemoration of Thomas Ashe in De La Salle College, 22 April 1966.

A handshake in memory of Thomas Ashe at the Ashe commemoration in Dingle, 4 June 1967. *Courtesy of The Kerryman*

was released. A pattern was set by the men, which they followed with perseverance.

Prisoners, on entering a new prison, had permission to write a special letter, known as a reception letter. Ashe wrote the special letter permitted him to his sister Nora just before Christmas:

My dear Nora,

I haven't received an answer to my last letter from you yet, hence I am sure you will be surprised to hear from me so soon again. But as you can see I have changed my residence since I wrote last and I assure you I am heartily delighted with the change. So this letter is what is called a reception letter, as it is allowed when one enters a new prison. So I don't want you to answer this until you hear from me again. I thought I'd feel my absence from Ireland very much during Christmas, but I think it will not give me very much trouble. All such feelings and disappointments are mostly a matter of sentiment and I have fairly rid myself of all sentiment; at least I have brought it into order and under discipline. Hence I am going to feel quite happy during Christmas. But fearing that all my friends will think this rather cold of me, as I am quite certain you'll tell them, I want you to send Christmas cards for me to the following: M. Griffin, P. Ashe and Mrs, Mrs Fitzgerald (K. G.), Hanna Flynn, T. Nunan, Miss Mahon, Birr, P. Ryan, The Foleys, Maighréad, Róisín Breathnach, N. McAllister, M. Monks, and any other of my friends that you wish. You should have found a rubber stamp of mine in my house and it will do very well for my signature. Also send cards for me to the two Fr. Hayes, Fr. M. Ryan, Fr. Wall, Fr. Toal and Fr. Fullerton. If they wish to write to me at some future date they could do so through you, but as I have stated above any letters you receive for me you may keep until you hear from me again. I have received O'Kane's *Grammar* from H. Flynn since I wrote to you last. I am certainly very thankful to her for sending it. My Irish books are great friends to me and they help me to spend the time beautifully. I think I'll have *Séadhna* [*sic*] off by heart soon. I had a lovely journey here from Dartmoor. The south of England looks beautiful even in December and such great cities as there are everywhere. No wonder they build vessel upon vessel to protect them. I wonder will we ever see any tall chimney stacks in Ireland except those of the distilleries and breweries. Who knows. Give my love to all my friends and remember me to all at home when you return for Christmas. I am quite sure they all believe I am dying with anxiety, lonesomeness, homesickness, etc., etc. I am not and tell them so. I look upon my imprisonment as St. Columbcille did on his banishment, which of course you may keep to yourself for fear of scandalising anybody. I have the advantage of the Saint though inasmuch as I'll get back to Ireland some day, but his banishment was for all time. And as I know from his writings that he felt his exile very much, I ask his prayers daily for my speedy return. I don't know whether he is the accepted patron saint of Irish exiles but I have adopted him as mine anyhow. In which I think I am wise. I expect to be allowed to write soon again and I think I'll get far better facilities for writing than I enjoyed up to the present. So you may expect to hear often from me, and I hope that will please you. Give my love to all my friends and send the first leaf on to Father.

Your fond brother,
Thomas.

P.S. Since writing this letter I am told that I may receive a reply so you may answer back as usual. I will look out for an early reply. With best wishes for Christmas and the New Year.

Tomás.

As far as prisons went, it was a change for the better. He could have writing materials and as many books as he liked. In Lewes he wrote his unfinished novel, also his poem 'Let Me Carry Your Cross for Ireland, Lord'. He taught his fellow prisoners Irish. William Cosgrave has described the zeal with which Ashe taught his colleagues:

> Those who knew him, and those who were his students, learning the language of their country from him in a foreign jail, realised the depth of his love for Ireland, and the greatness of his wish for the preservation of the language, because every moment of his recreation was devoted to its teaching, and when he had retired to his cell it was to write out exercises for the morrow to give to those students who could not attend the lessons he gave.[1]

'He was a great reader of the Bible,' recalled Nora Ághas. 'He read it constantly in jail. In his letters he would refer to passages in it, chapter and verse, which might apply to the politics and events of the day.' He spent hours reading his favourite Irish poets. As time went by, the rules with regard to writing and receiving letters were relaxed. Extra correspondence was permitted at Christmas and Ashe was delighted with the shoals of cards and letters he received. Towards Christmas 1916, he wrote to Nora:

> I'll write to Nellie McA[llister] for Christmas. I am still in good health and am delighted with my Irish books. Reading shortens the day very much for me. I am glad that Síle Ó Gara is so much better. Give her my best regards and tell her of my delight at her improvement ... I was surprised to hear of my school, but of course I expected that long ago. I supposed my teaching days are over. I am not one bit sorry. If you are writing songs at home so am I here. I'll write

again for the New Year. So I hope you'll have a good lot of news collected for me by then. Give my best regards to Fr. Mat [*sic*] Ryan if
you ever meet him, and also to all my old friends.

One of Ashe's favourite correspondents was Mary Monks. 'Of
all the letters I receive M. Monks writes the best. I love to read
hers always.' So he wrote to Nora before Easter 1917. He asked
her to tell his friends to send him the poems of Tomás Rua Ó
Súilleabháin, Eoghan Rua, Seán Clárach and one of Father Patrick
Walsh's Irish anthologies with words and music. 'Get M. Monks
to write to me often.' He also delighted in the newsy, cheerful
letters of his cousin Michael Hanafin and their political allusions
which were Greek to the censor. Among his correspondents
was Siobhán Ní Fhloinn, now Bean Uí Thalbóid of Clounalour,
Tralee, whose father, William Flynn, as head centre of the IRB,
had helped in the decades after 1860 to establish and consolidate
republican tradition in Tralee and district. A strong promoter of
the Gaelic tradition, she writes to urge himself and de Valera to
compose short stories in Irish in the manner of *Íosagán* and *An
Mháthair*. His faithful soldier friends of Fingal did not forget him,
the McAllisters of Turvey, Charlie and Bartle Weston, Joe Kelly
of Lusk. Always welcome were letters from Catherine Mahon
of Birr, who wrote pungently and prophetically about the ills of
the Irish Party which she did not much like. His college friend,
Michael Sheehan, wrote regularly. And of course his cousin
Pádraig wrote as often as permission was available. Amongst
his correspondents was Madge Daly, sister of the executed 1916
leader and member of a family whose distinction in the history
of the Fenian and republican movements has no peer. The closest

ties of friendship and sympathy had bound Ashe with the family of John Daly and Tom Clarke. A little of what the family suffered may be understood from the following letter written early in 1917 by Madge Daly to Ashe, in answer to a note she received from him at Christmas:

Dear Tom,

I am so glad to get your note and to learn that you are well and full of trust and hope that God is working out all things for the best. I believe that now with my very soul and expect to meet you soon with that belief verified by fact. Mrs C[larke] and her boys are with us now. She was very ill for a long time so that we expected to lose her too, but she is now on the mend. Daly is at St. Enda's, Tom and Em. are going to school here and are growing strong. My mother is also in poor health and does not seem to improve but perhaps with the Spring and fine weather she may. Laura, Nora and all the others are only fairly well, but if good friends, kindness and sympathy and honour for the dead could help, we'd have all we want. All the Reading and Frongoch men are home now, but one. E. Blythe was arrested since and interned in his home place. We hear that you are allowed to speak to one another now, if so give my love to Seán McGarry, Frank Fahy, D. Lynch, P. Beasley, S. O'Sullivan, T. Hunter and all our other friends. According to popular reports, you are all growing wings since Easter, but I hope you'll shed them before you get back. I do not want to meet my friends changed in any way, and I don't think saints would do in Ireland now. As to all the various reports of doings here – fret not – the past was glorious but please God the future will outshine it.

With love from all here,
Your friend,
Madge Daly.

The seagulls, hovering free over Lewes, reminded him of Doon-shean and the Trá Bheag. Writing to his cousin Pádraig on 12 February 1917 he says:

Dear Paddy,
… How are all your people at home? I wonder what they think of me? I'd give a good deal to have a chat with you just now. But it is impossible. I often see seagulls here and they remind me of Kerry. Like St. Columbcille I send a message with them to the West from a very heavy heart. Be sure and offer up your prayers for our speedy release.

Yours affectionately,
Thomas Ashe.[2]

Another friend who kept in touch with him was Cathal Brugha. They probably first met each other in the Gaelic League, for the objects of which they both worked with an absolute devotion. Cathal Brugha fought in the South Dublin Union in the Rising. He was a man to whom surrender or defeat were unknown terms. He fought. He fought until his body was sieved with shrapnel and bullets, and still faced his enemy, defiance in his eyes and a song on his lips. No hero of legend outranks him in spirit. So terrible were his wounds it was thought he would not survive. But he did, and years after, in the most tragic encounter of the Civil War, his slight body was shattered a second time, his opponents then being his former comrades, and he died, as he lived, knowing nothing of compromise, retreat or surrender. Between Ashe and himself there existed a complete accord, as this letter shows. Brugha wrote from Ennis, County Clare. At that time he was recovering from his wounds and going from place to place on his bicycle, reorganising the Volunteers.

Queen's Hotel,
Ennis,
26.3.17.

My dear Tomás,

I was delighted to get your letter and especially to hear that you are in such good form notwithstanding your present surroundings. It must of course be a great relief to be able to speak to one another even for an hour or so in the day. Though your absence is a loss to the language at home, still by all accounts it is compensated to an extent by your being over there. I understand you are turning out some great students. Our friend Austin will soon I believe under your able tuition be as good as a native speaker. I hope he takes things as lightly as you apparently do, but I'm sure he does for his heart will never fail. Tell him I'm looking forward to having some interesting discussions in Irish with him on his return. Tell Willie Cosgrave that I well remember the night he refers to – or rather I can never forget the extreme kindness I received from himself and one or two others. Everything else that happened the same night and for two or three days afterwards appeared more like a dream to me than anything else. I have come on a lot since then, thank God, tho' I cannot yet walk much – about 100 yards at a stretch is my limit. I have nothing to complain of however for I can cycle fairly well with my left leg and I feel the right one getting stronger each day. The doctor says that when the warm days come again I'll be all right. So you see my football days are not over yet. Bean a tighe desires to be remembered to yourself, Con Collins, Finn Lynch, and Pierce Beazley and Nollaig sends a special greeting to you. We have your photo in the dining room and she remembers you distinctly. When you call up, which please God will be soon, she will easily recognise you and welcome you in the language you love best. Remember me kindly to all my friends over there. Good luck to you now my dear Tomás.

Cathal Brugha.

Nora came over to see him at Easter. Father McLoughlin, the prison chaplain, received her with courtesy and kindness. He saw to it that she had a hot meal, which was very welcome, for the early April weather was bitter and the journey across had been tedious and cold. She had the happiness of speaking to Thomas for some forty-five minutes and for shorter periods to Austin Stack, Frank Fahy and Con Collins. In the course of their talk Ashe let fall a compactly folded piece of paper, the size of a half-crown, at her feet. She picked it up unobserved and kept it in safety. It was a message to Michael Collins, which she delivered to him later. Her brother looked well, though thinner. She was intensely relieved at having seen him for herself and could now reassure their father and all the family that they need not worry. She wrote from Cappamore on her return (letter dated 18.4.1917) to say how she enjoyed her visit and was glad she went:

> You see there is nothing like seeing things for one's own self and now that I have seen you, Father and all at home will feel more content. I thought you looked well but rather thin ... Your clothes make no difference to me – in fact I rather liked you in them. I can see 'For Ireland's sake' all over them and I would as willingly wear them myself ...
>
> On the whole I enjoyed the trip well and I must say all the English people with whom I had to deal treated us most courteously.
>
> M[ichael] Collins called at G[othic] Lodge the evening I came back and I gave him your messages. He understood about the N. Aid and said he would do as you ordered. I shall send my letter to him next time so that he can put in his piece. I'll find it handier to do that. All the girls asked for you and the others – in fact we were besieged with kind enquiries ...

The letter which follows, though incomplete, is one of the most revealing in Ashe's correspondence. For it I am indebted to Rev. Bro. Bernardine, FSC, formerly president of De La Salle College, Waterford, and now of St Fachtna's College, Skibbereen, County Cork. Ashe was writing to his friend Bro. Séamus Ó Donnchadha, who was teaching in St Mary's College, Mullingar. The first part of the letter is missing.

… From what I hear of Ireland off and on I am glad we are suffering. Future historians will say that we and our little sacrifices were a good deal the cause of the murmuring of the New Ireland that I hear away in the distance. We have had many a young Ireland. I sincerely hope the present one is not a pretender. I am sure you would like to hear from me about Easter Week but I am sorry to say that that is a closed book to me while here but I may be allowed to say that few can tell as much of its beauties as I. Its religious effect on us all is the one most in evidence here. You know how careless we were when outside. The Parish Priest of Lusk used call me a modernist and an anticleric but I don't know if he could understand the happiness I felt while awaiting the sentence of death in Kilmainham Prison. It was a beautiful experience. I hope that your health is the very best. It is a grand thing to be healthy and to live in Ireland particularly in the midst of lovely Tipperary. Strange that Tipperary is my favourite county in Ireland. To Kickham I owe this. If we only had his Tipperary to-day! If we have you must tell me about it. If you ever meet Fr. Matt [*sic*] Ryan remember me to him. I hear a good lot from Kerry, even from Dingle, poor Dingle of the public houses. Even some of my friends write and say it is the fashion to claim kinship with me in Duibhneacht, but there was always a lot of blarney there.

Do Chara,
Tomás Ághas.

Séamus Ó Donnchadha's reply is dated 24 April 1917. He writes:

> Nora has written me a full account of her recent visit, and has told
> me something of her thoughts. For her you need have no uneasiness,
> no undue concern for her feelings on your behalf. From the first she
> has borne up nobly ... with thoughts and feelings ever with you.

Canon Sheehan's classic *The Graves of Kilmorna* was on the literature course. Brother Ó Donnchadha did not fail to point out to
his class the comparison between its hero, Myles Cogan, and Ashe.

> I have read them your letter and they have asked me to send you and
> your comrades the assurance of their constant remembrance and of
> their best prayers for you all that God would fill your hearts with
> courage and consolation, alleviate your hard lot and soon restore you
> all to freedom.

In earlier years Brother Ó Donnchadha had taught in the Dingle
Monastery where he was associated with Ashe in Gaelic League
work, and Ashe's letter had revived memories for him. He goes
on:

> I remember the Feiseanna at the Monastery and the plays and the
> foundation then laid down. And the football matches near the Sta-
> tion and I recall particularly one match up behind McDonnell's of
> Kilnaglera and I see you and Pádraig as vividly this moment as I
> viewed you then, now more than ten years ago ... You have described
> the effect of your present lot upon your spiritual outlook and your
> thoughts while lying under sentence of death. Everything is exac-

tly as I expected. Fire tests gold and sufferings the true man ... J. McGuinness is certain to have pleasing news from the neighbourhood very soon ... Go neartaí Dia do chroí ...

Séamus Ó Donnchadha.

It will be seen that the reference in the above letter to Joe McGuinness, the Sinn Féin candidate for South Longford, is in a hopeful vein. It becomes necessary to survey briefly the course of events since the Easter Rising and the changes in public opinion which could hold out a prospect of success for a republican against the long-established Irish Party in a by-election contest.

16

AFTER THE RISING

Although the Rising was a military failure it proclaimed a victory of the spirit that made for far-reaching and permanent results. As a protest against the centuries-old domination of Ireland by her neighbour, its occurrence in the middle of a great war waged, said the headlines, for the freedom of small nations, projected the Irish cause dramatically into the centre of the world's attention. It immediately posed the problem to the United States, whose help was being sought by the Allies, of how relevant was Ireland's claim to the objective the Allies were advertised to be fighting for.

As the rafters of the GPO crashed in flames and its garrison withdrew to Moore Street, the slight-framed, frail-looking man who was the soul and centre of the revolutionary movement, Thomas J. Clarke, refused to contemplate surrender. Amongst Thomas Ashe's papers, in his own handwriting, is a note expressing briefly Clarke's sentiments as enemy forces closed in. It documents one of the most fateful moments of Ireland's experience. The note, as written, reads:

Thos. J. Clarke
Saturday

After coming out of
the burning G.P.O.

Our men all heroes

and we have by their actions
secured Freedom for Ireland

Being shelled here
but – no surrender

The first signatory of the Proclamation had stated a position from which there was no retreat.

First public reactions had been totally adverse. Comments by people in the early part of the week were noted in his journal by the Irish writer Peadar Ó hAnnracháin, who was detained in Cork city by the turn of events and heard such expressions as 'Drawing down trouble on the country', 'Destroying the good accomplished by the Irish Party', 'The idea of fighting the British Empire!', 'Bringing disgrace on the country'.[1] What Peadar Ó hAnnracháin heard was typical of the country as a whole.

Yet within a few weeks as deep and fundamental a change as ever moved a country's conscience affected Ireland. Slowly the public recovered from the impact of the Rising and its poignant aftermath. The executions carried out by order of Sir John Maxwell had wrought the strange and dramatic alchemy on the nation's personality not foreseen by his impercipient military mind but sensed with uncanny accuracy by Pearse.

How immediate in fact the effect of Maxwell's action was may be judged from a letter written on 10 May 1916 (even before the executions had ended) by George Gavan Duffy to a correspondent, in which Duffy relates:

I have just returned from Dublin, where the feeling even among Redmond's people is intensely bitter. They were, of course, against the Rebellion while it lasted, but hundreds have moved completely around since the military atrocities began; in fact nothing could have been better calculated to revive the spirit of the 'Jail Journal' than General Maxwell's performance.[2]

For months to come Ireland's true thoughts were repressed under martial law or checked by the vigilance of the censor. Strongly though feelings ran underneath, it was felt unsafe to utter any opinion that ran counter to the imperial. Yet the weekly review *Irish Opinion* was bold enough in its first issue (17 June 1916) to mark in these words the changing mood of the country:

> The reaction against materialism and self-seeking has been complete. The Ireland which has emerged from the conflict of Easter Week is a holier and purer and better Ireland than the Ireland which we knew before Easter ... The collapse of the insurrection has not left the country nerveless and prostrate. Far from it. The events of the past few weeks have had an integrating effect on the Irish people.

Early in November 1916, two former presidents of Arthur Griffith's Sinn Féin organisation, John Sweetman and Edward Martyn, wrote letters urging that no policy was better designed to meet the present occasion than Sinn Féin's.[3] The name of Sinn Féin had been associated with the Irish Volunteers and the Rising and as a result it had acquired high favour amongst the public. From the currency and honour it received it was but a step to enquiry about its meaning and philosophy. The Rising had created a situation in which the public mind became receptive to the teachings of self-reliance and abstention from the British parliament that Griffith spent years advocating. To the original stratum of Sinn Féin nationalist teaching was added a rising and confident militancy.

At Christmas 1916 the majority of the Irish prisoners were released. These included the six hundred held in Frongoch, North Wales, amongst them Michael Collins, and the Reading prisoners, with whom was Griffith. Their return to Ireland gave a powerful stimulus to political thought and initiative. The period was one of transition and profound change, which, for the present-day historian, remains unsatisfactorily documented. Amongst those who challenged British rule and along with it the Irish Party, there were different nationalist groups which at times jostled one another. In the course of discussions and negotiations between them, sharp clashings of opinion occurred.

The contest resolved itself into one between two main groups: republicans and old-style Sinn Féiners. Two cardinal principles of the old Sinn Féin programme were acceptable to the republicans: abstention from the British parliament and the complete recasting of Ireland's economy, commerce, education and institutions on the basis of self-reliance and self-endeavour. Their differences centred on the political form which autonomy should have. Up to 1916 and perhaps for some time after, Arthur Griffith favoured the idea of a dual monarchy on the Austro-Hungarian model. The republicans rejected this absolutely and would have freedom under no other shape or definition than that of an independent republic. A writer who studied Griffith's policy and interviewed him personally, Shaw Desmond, has written that after 1916 Griffith wanted a separate and distinct Irish monarchy, but the Rising dealt a mortal blow to the monarchical concept in any form and Griffith presently discarded the idea for reasons of unity. The differences between himself and the republicans were reconciled in the revised Sinn Féin constitution of October 1917, when a united and cohesive movement of great determination defined its political objective as an independent republic. This, however, is anticipating events.

A new topic of discussion was introduced in the form of a proposition that Ireland should put her case to the Peace Conference expected to take place at the end of the European war. The notion of such a conference came from America. The American tradition of idealism and liberty was being given eloquent voice by President Woodrow Wilson. He enunciated principles with respect to international fair play and the autonomy of nations, which were readily and gratefully accepted in Ireland. America was coming to be recognised as the greatest power in the world. What her president had to say commanded attention. Speaking to the United States Senate on 22 January 1917 he stated:

> I am proposing, as it were, that the nations should with one accord adopt the doctrine of President Monroe as the doctrine of the world: that no nation should seek to extend its policy over any other nation or people, but that every people should be left free to determine its own polity, its own way of development, unhindered, unthreatened, unafraid, the little along with the great and powerful ... I am proposing government by the consent of the governed.

And much more to the same effect. Nothing like it had ever been heard from the head of a European state. The clarion of liberty from Washington was welcomed by oppressed European peoples with hope and optimism. In Ireland a distinguished figure in the

Labour movement, Louie Bennett, echoing the hopes it aroused, called President Wilson's speech:

> ... a charter of human liberty ... It will find quick response and able advocacy from the lovers of liberty in every nation who have cherished and worked for a similar ideal in spite of scorn and derision and failure ... I wish that this magnificent manifesto of the American President would capture the mind and imagination of the Irish people.[4]

When the United States entered the war shortly afterwards on the side of the Allies it made the defeat of the Central Powers a certainty. It was taken for granted that President Wilson would uphold for Ireland the principles to which he had committed his country and himself on entering the war. In the event he proved himself unequal to the ideals he had proclaimed. Old atavistic prejudices were staked deep in his heart. When he was confronted, in Versailles, with the freedom of Ireland versus the *status quo* of the British Empire, he murmured, out of his fund of philosophical formulae, that Ireland was the great metaphysical problem of the age, and proceeded unhesitatingly to let her down. Ireland did not care a fig for metaphysics. She wanted freedom.

A parliamentary vacancy caused by the death of the old Fenian James J. O'Kelly occurred in North Roscommon on 22 December 1916, practically coinciding with the release of the Irish prisoners. Activist groups composed of Sinn Féin, the IRB and the Irish Volunteers combined to select Count Plunkett, scholar and savant, and father of the executed 1916 leader, to contest the seat. They placed no formal policy before the electors of Roscommon but the selection of Count Plunkett was understood to represent the principles of the executed men. It was the first time any section of the public had the opportunity of showing in effect whether they gave moral support to the act of insurrection accomplished in the previous year, and in electing Count Plunkett by a substantial majority on 3 February they recorded their approval of it decisively.

A month after his election Count Plunkett, at the Emmet Commemoration Concert in the Mansion House, Dublin, announced his adherence to the primary Sinn Féin principle of abstention as advocated for many years by Griffith. Because of the importance of his statement on that occasion it is well to quote it extensively:

> I stand for Ireland a nation ... Men [in North Roscommon] came to me with tears in their eyes, feeble old men, who had crawled across the snow to vote for me, and they whispered in my ears that they were out in '67. People might say, what is the moral of the Roscommon election? Well, there are 82 constituencies pledged to some form of Home Rule, and the moral of Roscommon is that we are going to take these 82 seats. It is a hard road. The struggle may be a difficult and uphill one, but I am prepared during the few remaining years that God may give me to carry the fight into every constituency in the land ... I have pledged myself, and North Roscommon has ratified my pledge, that I will not go out of Ireland. I would not even mention the name of the place where I would not go to, because I deny the right of any country to own Ireland, to a single inch of the soil of Ireland, and I deny the power of any nation but the Irish nation to control Ireland. I assert that I will accept nothing but complete and perfect independence for Ireland. People may say, that is a difficult thing to do, but where is the difficulty? We are on our own soil; we are among our own people; we hold Ireland. The Irish Party went to Westminster, and there they tried to bring a case against

the devil in his own court. They need not have been surprised by the result. They were outnumbered and outcheated ...

After an appeal to rebuild Irish industry and trade Count Plunkett went on:

> Ireland will put her case before the Peace Conference, because that will be a gathering not under the control of English Ministers, and it will have to consider the claim of the small nationalities that are asserting their rights to liberty. The Conference will give the same consideration to the case of Ireland as to that of the other nations. Ireland will not even wait for the sitting of the Peace Conference to begin the business of self-government. Ireland must dispense with the men who pervert her voice, and make it known to England and to the outside world that she will not rest until she is free from end to end. There will be no use in bringing before the Peace Conference the false belief that Ireland puts her hope in Parliamentary representation. Ireland will never again allow England to speak for her. Ireland will not relax her efforts, or lower her flag, till she has won ...[5]

Count Plunkett now sent out a circular letter to all public boards and bodies throughout the country inviting them to send representatives to a convention he planned to hold in the Mansion House, Dublin, on 19 April. With its representative authority, he said, the convention would claim sovereign status for Ireland and ask the powers at the forthcoming Peace Conference to give it their recognition. A considerable number of public boards welcomed the invitation and sent delegates who, along with representatives from Sinn Féin, the Irish Volunteers and other organisations, formed a large assembly at the Mansion House on 19 April.

There was much discussion and divergence of opinion. At a critical moment Father William Ferris intervened to soothe ruffled feelings. Count Plunkett wanted to dissolve Sinn Féin and all other organisations and start a completely new one. Griffith urged that a federation be formed to which any national organisation might affiliate, provided it accepted abstention and supported Ireland's appeal to the Peace Conference.

Following this suggestion a committee was formed to coordinate existing national organisations. After the meeting a group of men went to Sinn Féin headquarters at 6 Harcourt Street to make preparations to contest a vacancy that had occurred in South Longford.

17

ASHE AND COLLINS

On 3 April 1917 a parliamentary seat became vacant in South Longford. The proposal was made that Joseph McGuinness, a native of the county, who was locked up in Lewes jail, should contest the by-election. There would be no question of his entering the House of Commons if elected. The proposal was taken up with spirit by the separatist groups, although they did not fail to appreciate the risk they took in putting forward a candidate in an area where the strength of the Irish Party appeared unchallengeable. McGuinness's own consent had to be sought and Michael Collins, whose energy and influence were becoming felt in republican ranks, sent a messenger to Lewes to ask his approval.

McGuinness opposed the idea totally. Before making his refusal definite he decided to consult his colleagues, and the question was accordingly considered by Piaras Béaslaí, Richard J. Duggan, Thomas Ashe, Éamon de Valera, Tom Hunter, Diarmuid Lynch, Seán McGarry, Con Collins and others. With one exception they all decided that McGuinness should decline. They held the view that they represented the republican and separatist ideal in its most uncompromising and absolute sense and that for one of their number to acknowledge, however indirectly, a British parliamentary institution in Ireland by standing for it was contrary to their principles. McGuinness himself was in full agreement with this view. The one exception was Ashe. He disagreed and urged that their colleagues in Ireland should have full discretion in this matter. He pointed out that they were in touch with the people and saw the tide of Young Ireland rising in their favour. They were not giving recognition to the British parliament but giving the people an opportunity to support Irish freedom. It would add strength to the republican movement if they availed of the advantage offered them in this contest and went all out to fight and win it. So reasoned Ashe with his colleagues but without success. Harry Boland alone supported him. The rest did not. Joe McGuinness sent off a message to Dublin rejecting out of hand the suggestion that he should contest a parliamentary seat. Michael Collins, intent on securing hegemony for the republican influence within the newly formed movement, decided to ignore the message from Lewes, grasp the opportunity that presented itself and proceed with his plans to get McGuinness elected. His Lewes colleagues disapproved of what he did and some of them, like Seán McGarry and Con Collins, seem to have let him know the fact in hot and forceful terms. Collins at that moment must have blessed the support of Thomas Ashe. 'You can tell Con Collins, Seán McGarry and any other highbrows,' he wrote to Ashe, 'that I've been getting all their scathing messages, and am not a little annoyed, or at least was, but one gets so used to being called bad names and being misunderstood ... your general idea of things is quite correct and it was the first bit of encouragement I got.' That extract is taken from the letter, fully printed below, from Collins to Ashe, which must be read in the context of the events related in this and the previous chapter. It is a document of the first importance in illustrating the stresses within the Sinn Féin movement in its transitional and reformative stage. On the personal plane, it shows the close and confidential relationship that existed between Ashe and Collins, and the reliance which Collins placed in the judgement of his older colleague.

A Thomáis a chara

I see Nora has dated this Apl 24th but I didn't receive it until yesterday so don't blame me for *all* the delay – today is the 2nd May. Well, I couldn't do anything yesterday as I was taken up nearly all day with young Cullen. Poor fellow! You can tell Con Collins, Seán McGarry and any other highbrows that I've been getting all their scathing messages, and am not a little annoyed, or at least was, but one gets so used to being called bad names and being misunderstood. If they only knew of the long fights I've had with A[rthur] G[riffith] and some of his pals before I could gain the present point! The difference we had with him in the old school has been continued and grows more intense according as the new school passes into working order. Talking of that new school, you'll be interested to hear that the new master is going strongly and vigorously for the highest salary – as claimed for instance by poor Tom – and you know what that represents. Curiously enough the pupils are supporting him most enthusiastically and are gaining fresh supporters every day. Our assistant approves too in a general sort of way. You know how difficult it is to get an expression of opinion from him – *distant,* strange, stand offish as he always was. As of old the inspector is the obstacle and continues to place every obstruction against the thought of the matter being laid before the school committee, helped by the 'melancholy boy,' Joseph and friends. On the other hand the position from the point of view of the master and the pupils has been strengthened considerably lately by a very strong pronouncement of the Rev. Manager in favour of the highest salary. It was made in no uncertain voice and among the most influential gentlemen of his acquaintance, causing quite a flutter of annoyance in some quarters. The only thing the pupils have in common with Master Arthur G[riffith] is this question of the school committee. On other points he is pretty rotten, and for that reason some of us have been having fierce rows with him. In view of this it is rather disgusting to be 'chalked up' as a follower of his, and the refusal, though expected by me, was certainly a bit disconcerting. The only way to save the situation was to go on and this has been done. It is possible that the point may be gained and the effects will be far reaching. For instance it will be an immense gain to those of us who are anxious to have the matter brought before the school committee, not mind you but it is possible that that committee will let us down. Even so, a big point of principle will have been conceded, *an dtuigeann tú*? To ensure against everything being lost through such a decision the pupils continue with unabated fervour in their old ways – first and foremost. This latter I want to impress on them above all things and I am sure you and the other ex-schoolmasters will be happy to hear this. You will be weary of all this shop but just one more point before I go off it. Did you hear of the circular which the new master sent out? I am sure you did. Lots of people did not approve but principally they preserved silence until it had been rejected in many places. But it was accepted in many places also. And whether accepted or rejected, various managerial boards up and down the country were found even for five minutes to discuss the much talked of and now old question of the highest salary. The case for this was put very clearly in many unexpected places and though kicked out etc. the idea was implanted and is spreading. There is and need be no fear that the pupils will abandon their first position and even if the Rev. Manager should fail that will not deter them either.

I have received strict injunctions to give you kind messages from Dick Mulcahy, Diarmaid Hegarty surnamed The Parson, from Gearóid O'Sullivan now known as George, from another man whose name I didn't catch, but I tried to look intelligent about the matter. Was at Mass this morning at Mount Argus. There was a very good crowd and Fr. Eugene preached a very spirited sermon, thus things go on. Please give my love etc. to Seán McGarry – I'll write to him without fail tomorrow or Saturday – Con Collins – tell him I have my bike back again, but his will be useful to the Parson. Donnacha Callaghan – I was trying to tap his late boss for a sub. the other day and I hope to get it yet – Finn Lynch, the Plunketts, J. J. Walsh, Jim Sullivan, Conn Donovan, Diarmuid Lynch, etc. Well now goodbye. Forgive me for talking so much about the school, but one has so little interest in anything else in this place. I was forgetting that you had been away so long and you may not even understand my references. But for God's sake don't think that Master A[rthur] G[riffith] is going to turn us all into eighty two'ites. Another thing, you ask about Eoin [MacNeill] – well we did not approach him and by the Lord neither shall we. Otherwise your general idea of things is quite correct and it was the first bit of encouragement I got. How I wish Seán were *here*. You've no idea how he is missed.

With every good wish and kindest regards,
Yours Mick C[ollins].

There is a key to certain references in this letter in one of the manuscript volumes used by Ashe for his literary studies in Lewes jail. Two volumes in which he wrote contain the draft of his unfinished novel about Moynalty. In the first volume there are pencilled notes within brackets, interspersed here and there at the end of paragraphs, which appear unintelligible in themselves. But when read in conjunction with the above letter they clarify it immensely. Here are the notes, with the page numbers in the MS, in which they occur:

Vol. I	P. 5	(highest salary	C. Ind.)
	P. 6	(Inspector	Sasana)
	P. 7	(Rev. M.	Almain)
	P. 8	(Ireland	Parish)
	P. 9	(Ass	Dev)
	P. 10	(Sch. Com.	P.tionól)
	"	(Organisation	Pupils)

Most of the references are obvious enough. *Highest Salary* means complete independence, understood by Ashe and Collins to mean a republic; *Inspector* means England; *Rev. Manager* means Germany and the *Assistant* appears to mean De Valera; *School Committee*, on which Ashe has written the gloss *P.tionól*, probably means the Peace Conference announced to take place after the war; *Pupils* probably means the Volunteers but might also mean the republican or IRB organisation. At a guess, 'the melancholy boy, Joseph and friends,' could mean John Dillon, Joe Devlin and the Irish Party.

This letter from Collins, along with other references in Ashe's correspondence, goes to show that he held a primacy in the IRB corresponding to that indicated by General Richard Mulcahy, who writes in *An tÓglach*:

> At the time of his death he was President of the Supreme Council of the Irish Republican Brotherhood; notionally, he was successor to Pearse as President of the declared Republic of Easter 1916.[1]

General Mulcahy in a conversation with the writer confirmed his statement that Thomas Ashe was president of the Supreme

Council and stated that documentary evidence of the fact was in his possession.

The letter also shows, amongst other things, that there were sharp differences between Collins and Griffith and their respective followings, that Eoin MacNeill was not in favour with the republicans, and that the republican organisation would 'continue with unabated fervour in their old ways' no matter what the outcome, an assurance which Collins felt would be welcome to Ashe, as indeed it was, and the meaning of which is plain enough. The reference by Collins to 'the refusal' which, though expected by him, 'was certainly a bit disconcerting' is no doubt an allusion to the refusal of the Lewes men to sanction the candidature of McGuinness.

In the event, the judgement of Thomas Ashe and Michael Collins was clearly vindicated by the victory of Joe McGuinness in the South Longford election. The result was declared on 10 May: McGuinness 1,498; McKenna, 1,461.

Between Thomas Ashe and Michael Collins there was a firm bond of comradeship. Collins, who was his junior by five years, admired Ashe for his idealism, his fighting qualities, his determination and, where principle was concerned, his unswerving rocklike immutability. Both were members of the IRB, in which Ashe occupied the premier position, and they were very much in agreement about policy. From the beginning of 1917 they were in frequent communication. Nora Ághas remembers bearing a written message from Thomas to Collins on the occasion of her visit to Lewes prison to see Thomas. In the course of this visit she also talked to Stack and other prisoners. She related to the writer:

Austin Stack gave me a written message from Tomás to bring to Michael Collins, and I gave it to Michael when I returned. Tomás and Michael kept in constant touch with each other. They were great friends, each holding the other in high regard, and very much in agreement about policy. They admired each other's qualities. Austin Stack used say that had Tomás lived his influence on Collins would have prevented Collins from falling into the error he did when he signed the Treaty. Austin thought Tomás would have a stabilising influence on Michael which would keep him on the right road.

In one of their conversations, after Ashe's release from prison in June 1917, Collins expressed his grave disappointment at the total failure of Cork to rise at Easter 1916. To Collins's local pride in all that pertained to Cork it was a galling blow. 'But Tomás,' said Collins with his chin stuck out, 'when fighting begins again, Cork will take a greater part in it and I'll see to it that it does,' a resolve on his friend's part which Ashe encouraged. Between these two men there was complete understanding. They both formed a deeply felt part of the historical experience of Ireland. Both died young, in vastly different circumstances, each creating in death a profound tragedy and leaving their country to mourn the irreplaceable.

18

STRIKE AND RELEASE

The Lewes prisoners chose a committee to guide them as to policy and tactics. The first body was too unwieldy, leading to disagreement and confusion. A suggestion of Piaras Béaslaí's was adopted. It was that the surviving officers of the Dublin Brigade should assume control in order of their seniority. According to Béaslaí's proposition de Valera would be camp commandant, Thomas Ashe vice-commandant and Thomas Hunter adjutant. After consultation this was agreed. So runs Béaslaí's version. Peadar Clancy of Clare, a Portland and Lewes man, has related an account which differs in certain important details from that of Piaras Béaslaí. The writer received it from Gregory Ashe, who took the keenest interest in his brother's career, made close and detailed enquiries about every phase of it, and is aided by an excellent and retentive memory. We give here some details of events in Lewes related by Peadar Clancy who was himself a close friend of Ashe.

The three surviving commandants in Lewes – Ashe, de Valera, and Hunter – formed a committee in which none of them held precedence over the other. They each had equal authority, all projects had to be discussed between them and all decisions had to have their united approval. A general strike of the Lewes prisoners in demand of prisoner-of-war status had been agreed between the three men, to take place on a certain day. It involved the breaking up of the prison as an act of protest against their continued non-recognition as prisoners of war.

Some time before it was due to take place, Ashe received a written message from de Valera, countersigned by Hunter, saying it was called off. Ashe did not agree with this decision and went to see Hunter, whose reply was inconclusive. Ashe went to see de Valera, showed him the order, and asked what was the meaning of it. De Valera explained that the time for a strike was inopportune. Ashe flatly rejected the idea that the time was inopportune and insisted firmly on the original decision that the strike must take place on the day appointed. It did accordingly take place. Ashe possessed a mind that was very much his own.

Volunteer Thomas Peppard, now (1968) living in Rush, County Dublin, gave me an account of the strike, which arose out of a breach of the no-talking rule by Richard Kelly:

> I was involved in it also, but Kelly got penalised. The Governor, who was not at all a bad man but was following the instructions given himself, told us we would have to obey the rules and not talk during exercise. There was a pause. Then Tom Ashe spoke up, put the prisoners' case and put it very effectively.

Heartened by the assurances of support from Ireland, the committee had sent forward their request for recognition. The position is briefly stated by Ashe and Austin Stack as follows:

> Our leaders presented an ultimatum to the Home Office stating our determination to no longer agree to our treatment as convicts and to take on ourselves the status of prisoners of war. This was refused and

an attempt was made by the prison officials to enforce the convict code with the utmost stringency.[1]

Ashe and Stack state their reasons for requesting to be treated as prisoners of war:

Firstly, owing to the fight of Easter Week, which of itself gave us that right; and secondly, we having found that Irish opinion in general, through the voice of their Public Bodies, demanded that right for us; therefore we thought we would be wanting in our duty to our country if we did not agree to the desires of the Irish nation.[2]

They were assured of Irish support in their actions. There are many passages in Ashe's correspondence which reflect the change coming over Ireland but perhaps none more striking than this account from a letter of Nora's:

q 102.   Cappamore
T. Ashe   Co. Limerick
7.5.17.   5th May 1917

My dear Tomás

There was a requiem High Mass on the 4th of May at dawn (4 o'c. Irish time) in the Cathedral at Limerick. I went into Daly's the night before and Dr Hayes's sister and brother were in too. C. Colbert's brother and E. Dore were up at Daly's as well. It was a glorious morning with a rosy dawn and as we approached the Cathedral we saw crowds of people already there. They were standing all round, young and old, lame and blind and feeble and the swanks you would not expect to see at all. The crowd numbered over 5,000 people. In the church nobody except a very few knelt, they all stood to make more room. Mass was celebrated by Father James Hayes and all the young priests of the diocese were there. It was a sight I shall never forget ...

Prisoner-of-war rights having been denied them, they struck. They declined to work. They broke the prison windows and cell furniture. The authorities decided to remove the leaders of revolt from the prison. De Valera and Harry Boland were sent to Maidstone. Ashe and Piaras Béaslaí, chained together (a proud recollection of Piaras's), were removed with others to Portland, on the coast of Dorset. The writer was told by General Richard Mulcahy that Ashe, at the time of his leaving Lewes, had been elected president of the IRB Supreme Council.

'We went back to Portland,' recalls John McGallogly of Dublin. 'Peadar Clancy was with us. We refused to use the same bath as ordinary criminals. They gave in to us and installed a separate bath. By that time the strike was on two weeks.' In Portland they continued to ignore the rules and were placed in punishment cells. They cheered themselves, and the criminal convicts, by chorusing rebel ballads, to the intense delight of Father Kiely, the chaplain, who in his day had seen and cheered for Michael Davitt, rebel of an earlier generation. 'Actually for four weeks we acted as prisoners of war, ignoring all rules of the convict code,' said Ashe and Austin Stack in their joint statement already cited. Ashe, like the others, had his hair close cropped and his moustache shaved off.

The march of outside events helped to bring their imprisonment to an end. The Sinn Féin-republican victories in the Roscommon and Longford by-elections were evidence of a separatist trend which disturbed Lloyd George. There was, besides, a vast segment of United States opinion which he wished to cajole. On 16 May he wrote to Redmond suggesting, among other things, 'a convention of Irishmen of all parties for the purpose of producing a scheme of Irish self-government.' While the good intentions of Lloyd George in this matter are in serious doubt, Redmond accepted them in sincere faith, and preparations towards a convention were set in progress. One of the conditions Sinn Féin made before it would agree to participate in the convention was that prisoner-of-war treatment be accorded to the Irish prisoners at Lewes and Aylesbury.[3] Bonar Law announced in the House of Commons on 15 June that the Irish political prisoners were being released so that the convention might meet in an atmosphere of harmony and good will.

Ashe was already on the way with his comrades from Portland to Pentonville prison, London. There they were joined by their colleagues from Lewes, Parkhurst and Maidstone. The governor of Pentonville told them that they were being released as an act of grace which might assist in the promotion of the Irish convention. They rejected this view. 'Our real belief is that the course of the Government's action in liberating us was because they wanted to terminate, to them, the very awkward position of our action in assuming the attitude and status of prisoners-of-war.'[4]

At Pentonville they were each given a suit of cheap civilian clothing to usher them back into the world, placed on a special train to Euston, and sent to Ireland by way of Holyhead and Dún Laoghaire. Mementoes of his sojourn as a convict, which Ashe took out with him, were his convict's cap and the stiff cloth pad with his prison number q 102. The latter was presented to Kilmainham

Museum by Nora Ashe at Easter 1966. Another item he retained was his travel ticket, a slip of paper from London (Euston) to Dingle via C. of D. Kingstown. Governor Marriott returned to his father at Lispole some property he had left behind in Lewes. This included his watch and chain, locket keys, Agnus Dei and a book.

19

RETURN TO KINARD

Pádraig Ashe got a lift from Limerick in a Dublin-bound car in time to be at Dún Laoghaire pier for the arrival of the released men. He saw the tall figure with close-cropped hair coming down the gangway off the boat but did not recognise him at first. It was his cousin Thomas, who came towards him. They greeted each other with the eagerness of long-parted comrades. In Dublin they retired for a quiet drink and a chat to a public house in Hill Street owned by a man named Corbett, of Nenagh. Ashe had a problem on his mind which he proceeded to explain to his cousin.

He had been selected by a large majority of the Lewes prisoners, who were in effect the officer body of the republican movement, to stand as candidate for East Clare where a parliamentary vacancy had occurred. Thomas said he was reluctant to go forward. Pádraig asked why. 'Because,' explained Thomas, 'a small but solid group is supporting de Valera with great persistence. If I accept I believe it may cause disunity in our ranks.' Pádraig strongly advised him to go forward and from his own knowledge of Clare, where he was teaching a long time, he assured him of certain victory. Thomas remained unwilling on account of the division which he feared his acceptance might cause. The man for whom he expressed his personal preference as candidate was Peadar Clancy. Clancy was a tall, personable young man, a splendid speaker in Irish or English, a native of the county where his people were well-known and widely connected. Two of his uncles were priests of the diocese and their support would count well. Later, on their way to a hotel in Gardiner Place, Ashe and his cousin met Austin Stack. 'Well, Tomás, what about it?' said Austin. 'Are you going to accept and go forward to Clare?' 'No,' said Ashe, 'it might cause disunity.' To William Cosgrave's enquiry he made the same reply. Cosgrave's comment was that if there were any elements of disunity in the movement the time to weed them out was now and not later.

That evening in Fleming's Hotel, Gardiner Place, a meeting of the released men was held at which Ashe was proposed by his cousin Pádraig as the choice of the Lewes men for the vacancy in Clare. Ashe stated that he did not wish to go forward. De Valera was then proposed and accepted. Gregory Ashe commented regretfully on his brother's decision. 'He ought to have accepted the candidacy for Clare. He would have been elected flying and with his status as MP no prison authority would have dared to treat him as they did. He would have lived. He would not have died as he did at their hands.'

It can be argued that Ashe's unwillingness might have sprung from a natural inner reserve and reluctance to be in the limelight. It is in that way his cousin Sheila Gunning remembers him. 'He was a man who would not put himself forward. He was not a show-off type.'

Ashe, with Stack and Timothy Brennan, set out for home on 20 June. Arriving in Tralee after midnight they were given a tumultuous welcome by great crowds who packed the streets and roared their approval of the felons. Bonfires blazed in the streets and away on the hills, windows were illuminated and ranks of men in military formation saluted them, a significant proof of the mood of Ireland's young men. Tired out, they rested at O'Donnells of Ballyard and next day, after a visit to Casement's Fort and relatives in the area, Ashe and Stack left by motor for West Kerry. Months earlier Ashe had wondered what did they think of him at home now. After that evening he could have no doubts.

There are not many places in the world where nature is displayed with such agreeable effect as in the highlands of West Kerry. With hill rising behind hill, in number and variety and shape, all encompassed by a silver surround of sea, it might be a canvas created by an enchanted hand. On that glorious June evening bonfires blazed on every hill of these to rejoice in the homecoming of Thomas Ashe. Through the night long they burned, on the hillsides, in the villages, by the roadside. Crowds set out in procession from Dingle to greet him at Lispole and were joined by contingents from all the villages on the way. There was nothing organised about it. It was the spontaneous and deeply felt gesture of a whole countryside. A close friend of Ashe and witness of the historic occasion, Mrs Talbot of Tralee (Siobhán Ní Fhloinn) has related to the writer:

> … Thomas Ashe was our honoured visitor. He, with his friend, Austin Stack, came to Tralee and westward to the Dingle Peninsula. He spoke at many meetings en route. Unlike present-day meetings, they were spontaneous gatherings of the people who assembled at the crossroads to bid welcome to Tomás and Austin. I can vividly recall the groups of black-shawled women at Abha na Scáil and Lios Póil who stood with lighted candles awaiting their arrival. Tomás spoke to each group in the lovely Gaelic tongue.

At Lispole Ashe addressed the crowds and went on, escorted by a large concourse of neighbours, up the hill to his home at Kinard. Here he received the warmest and to him the most welcome greeting of all, from his father. The neighbours, gathering after, filled the house to the door, stretching hands out to clasp his, with words of welcome and encouragement. His father wanted to hear about Ashbourne. On a large sheet of paper which he mounted on an improvised blackboard Thomas drew a sketch of the engagement, explaining move and counter-move in detail, while everyone listened with rapt attention. It was one of the few occasions he was given time to describe the battle.

They were expected in Dingle. It was past midnight when they arrived but no one in the town thought of going to bed. Night was turned into day with torchlights and tar barrels in honour of the visitors, and the crowds clamoured for a speech. Ashe addressed them in The Mall, after which they dispersed quietly to the remote villages of the coast and countryside. Ashe went back to Kinard for the night. He spent the next night in Dingle at the home of his sister Mrs Devane. While visiting at his step-uncle's house he had dramatic evidence of the change taking place in people's minds. There was a knock at the door. Two RIC men stood there to tell him he had their support.

That evening in Dingle he received a telegram summoning him to Clare for the by-election campaign on behalf of de Valera. He left next morning, never to see his home again. Mrs Talbot remembers the scene at Listowel station when he was on his way to Ennis:

The town of Listowel was literally closed down whilst the entire population congregated on the platform to wish him God-speed. He addressed the crowd from the railway carriage and then withdrawing for a few moments re-appeared at the door wearing his felon's cap, a souvenir of Dartmoor. At the moment there burst from the assembled throng, led by Tomás, 'The Felons of Our Land.' It was something to remember ...

Ireland's attention shifted to East Clare. The vacancy had been caused by the death in battle at Messines of Major Willie Redmond, the popular younger brother of the parliamentary leader. Patrick Lynch, KC, a native of the county, ran for the Irish Party against de Valera. The issue was placed before the public by de Valera and Sinn Féin with a clarity that left no room for doubt. Up to this stage in by-election contests Sinn Féin had not been specific as to its objective. Sinn Féin declared in Clare that it proposed to achieve the republic for which the 1916 leaders had died. Other points to which emphasis was given were the peace conference, abstention and self-reliance. Fionán Lynch writes:

> Tom Ashe, Gearóid O'Sullivan and myself were stationed in Killaloe for the week before the election. Tom was about the only experienced public speaker amongst the prisoners in penal servitude and he was equally fluent in Irish and English. He had spoken in public frequently at Gaelic League gatherings in Ireland and he had accompanied Father Michael O'Flanagan [error for Diarmuid Lynch] on a fund-collecting mission for the Gaelic League to the USA where he had to address large meetings at dozens of centres. He was, therefore, a great asset at Sinn Féin meetings and was much sought after.[1]

There are amongst Ashe's papers some faintly pencilled jottings for a speech written by him on the notepaper of the Old Ground Hotel, Ennis. The first three points read:

1. Easter Week. Our rights and guiding star.
2. Our object the Republic and the Peace Conference.
3. Pearse's last words.

There is also a reference to Dr O'Dwyer, a man much admired by Ashe, as he was by all, for his crushing reply to Maxwell. The last few lines on the sheet read:

The young men to stand by Ireland ready to support her claims and the old men by their votes to show the world Ireland's determination.

On the back are further points for speeches numbered as follows:

1. Pleasure & Meeting.   Jem Connolly
2. Pearse's last words
3. Republic, etc.
4. Easter Week & compromise
5. Prison & ourselves
6. Sinn Féin Clubs
   Political and Military
   The Unknown.

Cathal O'Shannon records that a local man told him of Ashe's speech at Feakle, which made a great impression.[2] Along with O'Shannon, Ashe, by way of relaxation, viewed the sights of Loch

Gréine celebrated in Merriman's famous 'Midnight Court'. 'It is grand to work here in Clare,' he wrote to Tommy Peppard. 'The whole country is with us and we expect a clear win.'

Polling took place on 10 July.

The result was: de Valera, 5,010; Lynch, 2,035. A wave of exultation spread through the ranks of Sinn Féin. Here was a large and important area of Ireland expressing, by its election of de Valera, its support for the Rising in which he was a major participant and for the republic which was announced in the Proclamation. The lord lieutenant of Ireland, Wimborne, wrote to the British Cabinet on 14 July to say that:

> … in a remarkably well-conducted political contest sustained by excellent candidates on both sides, the electors on a singularly frank issue of self-government within the Empire versus an Independent Irish Republic, have overwhelmingly pronounced the latter.[3]

The Freeman's Journal, which supported the Irish Party, stated the message and meaning of the election in its leading article on 12 July 1917:

> East Clare has declared for revolution by an overwhelming majority … In Clare the people were invited without qualification to vote for an Irish Republic and total separation from England, and five out of every seven of the electors … responded to the call.

So they did. Ashe was the first man to carry the news into Limerick city where he announced it to an enormous victory meeting. After the strenuous weeks of electioneering some recreation was called for. He relaxed for a short spell to join Seán McGarry and J. J. Quilty, of Kilrush, for some pleasant hours rowing on the Shannon, while he sang to the soft rhythm of the oars on the waters. In Mr Quilty's autograph book he wrote a few brief and salient facts about Easter 1916 and the Battle of Ashbourne. A photostat of the page on which he wrote may be seen in the excellent collection of Ashe items in St Canice's School, Finglas, organised by Eoghan MacCárthaigh.

20

AT CASEMENT'S FORT

The revolutionary forces, which collectively came to be called Sinn Féin, were becoming aware of their strength. Organisation proceeded briskly on the basis, indicated in Ashe's pithy notes, of clubs 'political and military'. Good speakers were in great demand and Ashe was one of the best. His sister Nora remembers him speaking in Westmoreland Street, Dublin, to a great meeting, and his full voice carried easily to the verge of the crowd. He addressed meetings in Kilmallock and Bruree, then went north and along with de Valera, Griffith and Count Plunkett spoke in Longford town on Sunday 22 July. Remaining for a few days in County Longford, he addressed a meeting at Ballinalee on Wednesday 25 July. Collins and Seán Mac Eoin were with him. It was a frank and forthright nationalist speech in his characteristic style, giving a clear intimation that for any fighting there was to be done, the duty of Ireland's young fighting men lay within her own shores. It was for this speech a warrant was later issued for his arrest. In fact Ashe delivered dozens of speeches in the same vein for which no charge was laid against him. John Devine of Lusk, who fought by his side at Ashbourne, remembers one he made about this time at Donabate, a rousing fighting speech it was – 'Tom Ashe couldn't deliver anything else' – and so much so that John Devine considered it was for it he was arrested. The truth seems to be, however, that the East Clare victory had given such a blow to the prospects of the Irish Convention, that the Cabinet had second thoughts on the policy of conciliation and was taking the gentle hint contained in the words of Lord Wimborne, who stated to it in the memorandum already part-quoted, that:

> Following as it does on a course of extreme leniency and concilia-
> tion which culminated in the general amnesty of political prisoners
> and tacit tolerance of seditious and secessionist propaganda [the East
> Clare victory], marks the definite failure of the policy to rehabilitate
> constitutional nationalism or disarm Sinn Féin defiance to English
> Rule.[1]

Defiance to English rule, in a nutshell, was what Thomas Ashe and his colleagues were sowing, broadcast by word and example. To meet present policy and necessities it was decided to reorganise the IRB, enforce its discipline thoroughly, engage whole-time organisers and amend its constitution. The draft of the revised constitution was drawn up by Thomas Ashe, Con Collins and Diarmuid Lynch. It was further revised by Michael Collins and Diarmuid Lynch and ratified by the Supreme Council.[2]

In August Ashe attended a meeting at the Keating Branch of the Gaelic League to further plans for the reorganisation of the Irish Volunteers.[3] It may have been shortly after the Ballinalee meeting that he returned for a short visit to Fingal, probably the part of Ireland, after his own home, that was nearest to his heart. Writing from the Grenville Arms Hotel, Granard, to Jimmy Kelly, he says:

> I have been in Fingal once or twice since my return, on a flying

visit, but I am going there next Sat. and will speak at an aeraíocht at Donabate on Sunday. I intend spending the week there among the boys ...

I am very busy since my return, but of all the welcomes we get wherever we go, and of all the honours showered on us I would prefer to be among the good men and true of the fighting 5th.[4]

John Devine recollects:

The day Tom Ashe and Dr Hayes came home after their release we met them outside the village and had a crowd there to welcome them. We had bought a lot of cartridges at bargain price from a decent man named George Carton. I showed them to Dr Hayes and Tom Ashe. Tom Ashe said with approval: 'So you're tearing to be at it again.' He made a great speech in a field at our aeraíocht in Donabate.

That was the speech for which he was arrested, said John Devine. No doubt it was one of many such. Mary Monks, writing to him later from Five Mile Point, Newcastle, on 1 August, said:

Dear Mr Ashe,
... I won't attempt to tell you how delighted I am that you are free again. You must have put in hard times – for you certainly looked like it. I would scarcely have known you. Did I ever think the last day we were in school together that you were about to make a new chapter for your book. Still, I must say I felt something strange was about to take place. I don't like to recall it ... Have you seen Fr. Hoey? He stuck to you very well through all.

The political changes that were taking place throughout Ireland were sweeping Fingal as well. The AOH, which was the powerful political masonry that had supported the United Irish League, was falling to pieces. Even in such ultra-conservative settlements as Rush and Malahide Sinn Féiners were appearing, to the astonishment of many. The popularity of Ashe was firmly established throughout Fingal. In person he was beginning to look himself again. There is extant a photograph of him in the possession of General Mulcahy taken shortly after his release from jail, which shows him with moustache grown, his wavy mop not yet regrown, rather thinner, with pipe in hand. He was being mentioned as a prospective MP. From all sides there were demands on his time. Mary Monks said to him, in the same letter quoted from above, 'I hope you are not killing yourself working. You never gave yourself a chance.' Into the short phase of eight weeks' liberty between his release and his re-arrest he crowded a phenomenal amount of activity. An impressive speech of his in the Mansion House is remembered for its demand to the British government to give up the bodies of the men executed after the Rising.

The old Norman city of Kilkenny offered a new arena of contest to Sinn Féin and the Irish Party in the form of a by-election. William T. Cosgrave of Dublin, a Sinn Féin pioneer who had fought under Ceannt in the South Dublin Union, was selected to oppose the Irish Party man. Cosgrave's precise approach to business lacked flamboyance. Knowing Ashe's abilities as a speaker and his capacity to communicate with a public gathering he asked that he be sent. His request is made in a note which in its brevity speaks volumes. It reads:

Victoria Hotel,
Kilkenny.
31.7.17.

A Chara,

I want Ashe.

Mise

W. T. Cosgrave.

Kilkenny, by electing Cosgrave on 10 August, shattered the claims of the Irish Convention, in session since 25 July, to represent the popular will, and confirmed that public support for the men of the revolution was rising to flood tide.

Early in August the annual Gaelic League Oireachtas was held in Waterford. It was a rendezvous for Irish-language supporters from all over Ireland. Ashe attended for a short while. Fionán Lynch remembers:

> I next met Tom Ashe ... at the Oireachtas in Waterford and after it was over we travelled together from Waterford to Mallow. He proceeded to Dublin while I went home to Kerry ... I think our last meeting before I saw him in Mountjoy was at 'Casement's Fort' on the first anniversary of Casement's execution where he gave the memorial oration.[5]

The first anniversary of Casement's execution, 5 August, was marked by a great public gathering at Casement's Fort, near Ardfert, where he was arrested on Good Friday 1916. It lies inconspicuously in a flat plain, a stone's throw off a byroad between Ardfert and the shorelands of Barrow, an old circular fortification the outlines of which are overgrown with bramble and whitethorn, but its association with the heroic personality of Casement has made it a hallowed place. The roar of the surf on Carrahane Sands, where he came ashore, is almost within earshot. On that glorious August afternoon 10–12,000 people gathered from all parts of Kerry to do his memory reverence. Their transport was such as they could provide themselves for there were no trains. There had been no press publicity; censors would have seen to that. News had gone round by word of mouth and the quickening pulses of nationality had drawn them from distant places. Three thousand men marched, some in Volunteer uniform, while three hundred horsemen, five hundred cyclists and many pipers' bands stirred the gathering with a martial pageantry. Willie Mullins, who marched with the Tralee Volunteers, remembers it as a day of such scorching heat that a drink of cool spring water was prized. Fervour was great. 'At that time the people had begun to realise what 1916 really meant and they showed their enthusiasm fully. Ardfert was a lively village that day. Ashe was a fluent speaker and appeared the ideal of what a man should be physically and mentally.' Willie Mullins had a fine photograph of Ashe, taken that day at Casement's Fort, which was used by Leo Whelan, RHA, when drawing the portrait in oils now in Nora's possession.

Con Casey of Tralee saw Thomas Ashe amongst a group which included Frank Fahy in his convict's cap, now become a head-gear of honour, Austin Stack and Fionán Lynch. Ashe's physical appearance made him the central figure, while his ability as an orator was obviously appreciated. Ashe had been chosen to give the memorial oration in honour of Casement and uttered one of the finest tributes ever paid to that gallant man. In the course of it he said:

Since my very childhood on the side of the hill or the shores of Dingle Bay, I heard old native speakers of Corkaguiney tell us of the prophecy of St. Columbcille. That prophecy stated an O'Donnell would land on the strand at Corkaguiney; that he would land on the sands of his native land, and that he would bring liberty to the shores of Ireland, which we are sighing after for centuries. Old people in Corkaguiney looked forward to this mystical O'Donnell to land on the Strand of Corkaguiney with a powerful army and powerful armaments. Back in the years of history many an eye similar to the eye of the old Irish speakers in numerous other countries outside of Ireland looked on many occasions for the mystical liberator of their country to come with sword and bayonet for their deliverance and it's no wonder that the people of Kerry thought that the deliverer would come with an army and armaments, and he did come. The mystical man of Columbcille's prophecy came; he came unknown, but I tell you he is not unknown today, nor will he be unknown tomorrow. He did not bring with him that great army; he brought no great powers in his train to back up his work for Irish liberty; but he brought with him a loving heart and an undaunted spirit that will live in Ireland as long as any man will live who believes in the Irish ideals of an Irish republic …

He spoke of Easter Week, the character of its idealism and of its effects on the youth of Ireland:

Our opponents tell us we were criminal idealists. You can see that the men of Easter Week were the most practical nationalists that ever lived in Ireland for the last 100 years. There was no dreaming about them or idealism but the dreams and ideals of absolute Irish liberty, and they worked for it and placed it on a foundation that it will never again be taken down from. I had the pleasure during Easter Week

– in fact I think it was on Wednesday of Easter Week – of receiving a despatch from Jim Connolly, who commanded in Dublin. His despatch said, amongst other things: 'The Republican Flag flies triumphantly over Dublin City. There will be glorious days for Ireland yet.'

Will you mark these words, my friends? Will you mark the words of Connolly; take them to your heart and think of the mind of the man who saw clearly from behind the barricades of Dublin streets that there would be glorious days for Ireland yet. Pearse and McDermott told me that the republican flag flies triumphantly over Dublin, and that they never withdrew those words. The Republican flag still today flies over Dublin city, and still flies over every county in Ireland, and any forces of Great Britain, and any army of England, will not drive the tricolour flag from the hills and fields of Ireland. It is there, and not only can we see it with our eyes, but we can feel it in our minds, because I have seen since I was liberated that there is a tricolour in the mind of every young man and every young woman from north to south, and from east to west, and though they may tear them down from the house-tops, they can never obliterate the tricolour nor the blood of Easter Week from the minds of the young men of Ireland. The last words, practically, the last words to his comrades, were told to half-a-dozen of our boys in Kilmainham by P. H. Pearse on the night before his execution. He told them in Kilmainham gaol that 'the Insurrection was a success. We have gained what we were out for. The Irish question is no longer a British imperial question. It is now an international one.'

No man could have been more appropriately chosen to speak in honour of Casement. Time and again he was interrupted by the applause of the crowds. Those who listened to him that day did not realise they were present at what was probably his last great speech.

21

A PRISONER AGAIN

A warrant was issued for Thomas Ashe's arrest under the Defence of the Realm Act (DORA) because of seditious things he was alleged to have said at the meeting in Ballinalee, County Longford, on 25 July. There is some mystery about this warrant. Enquiries made by the writer to trace the whereabouts of the original (if it has survived at all) led to no result. The *Police Gazette*, otherwise known as the *Hue and Cry*, for July and August 1917, contains no announcement of the warrant for Thomas Ashe nor any notice that he was a wanted man, although it carries announcements, with descriptions, seeking Robert Monteith and William (Liam) Mellows. It is therefore difficult to say on what date it was issued, but the manner in which the thing was done suggests that the authorities were less concerned with what Thomas Ashe said than with their design to place him under lock and key on no matter what pretext. It formed part of a general policy of coercing the republican leaders. The unusual manner in which the warrant originated was queried by Ashe himself. For example the statement of one of the police witnesses, Constable Martin Quigney, opens as follows:

> I was present at the meeting addressed by the accused, Thomas Ashe, at Ballinalee on the night on July 25th 1917. By *order* of my *District Inspector* I took mental note of the address he made to the people there.

Thomas Ashe underlined the words italicised above and placed on the margin the query: 'When did his order arrive?'

Nor is it easy to say when exactly Ashe became aware that the police were looking for him.

In *The Kerryman* of 18 August there is an announcement that the Dingle Feis would be held on the following Sunday, the 19th, and that Ashe would speak after the opening of the Feis by Count Plunkett. It is not known whether he proposed to go to Dingle for the occasion but since his name was advertised it is possible he may have planned to do so. Earlier that month he had sent a telegram to the County Kerry Feis, which was held in Castle-island on 15 August, regretting his inability to attend. In the event Piaras Béaslaí and An Seabhac deputised for him at Dingle Feis, while Paddy O'Brien, Michael Granville and many others helped to make the day a success. But there was extreme disappointment that Thomas Ashe was not present. Since the night before he was actually a prisoner in government custody.

Thomas Ashe was fully aware for many weeks that a warrant for his capture was out because he took the precaution of using, for most of the time, the safe retreat of Batt O'Connor's house, No. 1 Brendan Road, Donnybrook. O'Connor, a native of Castle-island, was a master mason and the builder of his own and other houses in the neighbourhood. With admirable foresight he used his craftsman's skill to build a concealed room into the structure of the house, which became a place of refuge and hospitality for guests who were evading government agents. Guests there included Michael Collins, whose fame was yet to come, and Thomas Ashe, one of the leaders of the republican movement most sought after by his friends and most wanted by the government. The

O'Connor family were only too happy to lavish every attention on their guest. Batt O'Connor's children remember him as a tall, fair, curly-haired man. His daughter Eibhlín related her memories of him to the writer:

> We as children remember him as a very gentle man during his stay with us and his delightful way with children, talking to us about his interests in country life, the Cause of Ireland and books … He had sung for my mother and father his poem 'Let me carry your Cross for Ireland Lord' and they were deeply impressed and one night they gathered us children around him and asked him to sing it to us. My father asked us to pay great attention. We were very impressed too and I remember it so well that summer evening with Tom sitting with his back to the dining-room window with the sun pouring in on him as he sang his poem. He had set it to his own music.

To be conscious of being wanted and watched for by his enemies was irksome to a man like Ashe who was naturally drawn to the unrestricted freedom of outdoor life. Besides, he was busy making plans for his future career. He had decided to abandon teaching and to study engineering at University College. He made arrangements to share a flat with his friend Michael Knightly, of Tralee, at that time a journalist on the *Irish Independent* and in later years the editor of Parliamentary Debates in Dáil Éireann. Ashe had a bent for mechanics and in Corduff used to delight in taking his motorcycle to pieces and putting it together again. Austin Stack records that Ashe talked about engineering with great knowledge and outlined many ideas for mechanical inventions which he hoped to perfect if he ever got the chance.[1]

Thomas Ashe was in the full glow of health and manhood,

and the prospects ahead, fraught though they were with the risks implicit in his line of politics, held out the challenge of life, adventure and national purpose which this young man of two and thirty faced with confidence. Suddenly and unexpectedly the blow fell.

On the evening of Saturday 18 August he went into the centre of Dublin. It was his first venture out for quite a while and he enjoyed the throb of city life and the pleasure of meeting friends. He bought a wedding present for a sister of Mícheál Ó Foghludha, and brought it to Gothic Lodge. Later Mícheál went with him into O'Connell Street. Bríd Ní Fhoghludha (Mrs Bríd Martin) writes:

> He came to us most week-ends and it was, unfortunately, on leaving our house, 5, Cabra Road, having brought a wedding present to one of my sisters, that he was arrested.

Near Nelson Pillar he waited for the Donnybrook tram to take him home again to Batt O'Connor's, chatting the while with Mícheál Ó Foghludha. Feeling a tap on his shoulder he turned around to be confronted by two plain-clothes detectives who had recognised him. His eight weeks of liberty were at an end. They placed him under arrest and took him to Chancery Place bridewell. There he was given in charge of the military, who took him next evening to the Curragh camp in County Kildare. He would have to face court martial once more.

Life at the Curragh was bearable enough. The rules were not severe and the soldiers in charge were friendly. He had permission to buy his own food and tobacco, and to receive visitors and letters. He had little hope of receiving a light sentence but planned to use what leisure prison might afford to continue his writing, finish his novel about Moynalty, compose poems and think about music. To his sister Minnie (Mrs Michael Devane) of Grey Street, Dingle, in whose home he had spent many carefree hours, he wrote:

> 221st. Inf. Guard Room,
> Curragh Camp,
> Co. Kildare.
> 22nd. Aug. 1917.

Dear Minnie,

I am sure you are aware by this of my arrest. It took place on Saturday in Dublin, and I was removed here on Sunday evening.

No definite charge has been preferred against me so far, but I have been arrested because of objection taken to a speech of mine at Ballinalee in Co. Longford.

I am detained in this Camp and I have nothing to complain of as regards treatment. I am buying my food, which is all right, so nobody need be troubled about me. The soldiers are not by any means severe.

I'll be allowed to write to my friends in future, and I expect to see any visitors who may call too. I would write to Nora, but I suppose she is in Dublin, or on her way there at present. My friends in the City are not forgetting me, and I hope nobody at home will be troubled about me in any way.

I remember writing in an album sometime ago, the names of the prisons in which I was detained last year, and I finished the number by writing 'To be continued.' Little I thought the next chapter would commence so soon.

I hope all are well, and cheerful. Remember me to everybody. For weeks I was hoping for a rest. So I am taking one now in rare style.

> Your fond Brother,
> Tomás.

The above letter is in the Dingle Library. Also there is the following note from Michael Collins which was probably sent to Mrs Devane along with it. Although undated it was written on 22 August.

> I saw Tom today at the Curragh. He is in very good form and all his wants are being attended to. There is no charge so far.
>
> He asked me to tell you that he is not allowed to write letters for the present. The present one was written before that order reached him.
>
> Michael Collins,
10, Exchequer Street,
Dublin.
>
> I am writing to Nora at Cappamore.

The same day Collins wrote a brief and hurried note to Nora:

> No. 10.
22/8/17.
>
> Nora a laogh,
>
> I've been down to the Curragh today to see Tom. He's in great form and all his immediate wants are being attended to. He is rather anxious to see you if you come up to town. I can give you all necessary instructions if you see me. His address is Keane Barracks Curragh Camp and he will be allowed to receive practically anything you send. For the present he is alright for linen, socks, tobacco and reading matter. In awful haste.
>
> Yours go deo,
Michael.

Collins was then secretary of the National Aid Association. He kept in close touch with Ashe, by what secret means we can only guess, kept his family and friends informed of developments and spared no efforts to help. Nora, who was at home in Kinard, decided to travel to Dublin from where she could conveniently visit him at the Curragh and be close at hand to look after his requirements. Kit Griffin arranged to travel with her. Mícheál Ó Foghludha made arrangements for their accommodation in Gothic Lodge. Already in custody in Cork barracks, awaiting court martial, were Ashe's colleagues Stack and Lynch. The following two letters of his, which the rules would have forbidden him to write, were probably conveyed out of the Curragh through secret channels which may have been organised by Collins. They indicate his cheerful good spirits as well as the fact that he had no illusions about the government's mind towards him.

23 Aug 1917

Dear Nora,

I got your note as I am only allowed *to receive* letters. I am glad that my two friends visited Dingle in my place. I hope the Feis was a success. I don't see how people should be disappointed over me, as I feel they should be fairly tired over me by this in Dingle.

Prayers indeed will do me no harm. By the way I was talking to Kathleen Monks last week and she told me that you promised to send her a photo of mine that you received from her last year. So far she says she hasn't got it. Send her one as soon as you can. I hope I'll be able to get those letters and P.cs. I'll get any letters sent here, but there is no need to mention the receipt of any from me.

Send my kindest regards to Finn and Austin. I'll bet them I'll be out before them. Give my love to all and keep the fires burning.

Mise
Tomás.

C/O Sergeant Taylor
221st Inf. Batt. Guard Room,
25 Aug. 1917.

Dear Nora,

I received yours and father's letters all right. I am glad to see how cheerful you all are. I feel likewise myself. No charge yet, and no word either of a courtmartial. I suppose I'll hear something though of it next week.

You needn't bother coming to see me, as if I am found guilty I'll be in Mountjoy and I suppose you can see me when you come to Dublin. I like the idea of a little rest in prison again, and I have little hopes of being left off lightly. I hope to be able to continue my writing, and if at large I could do but very little.

I am sorry the weather is so very bad. I hope it did not do a lot of harm in Kerry.

Remember me to everybody
Your fond brother
Tomás.

The evidence by which the government hoped to convict him was put forward by two police constables and taken down in writing in his presence in the Curragh on 27 August by Captain Guy Maclaw of the 3rd Hussars. The document is entitled 'Summary of Evidence in the case of Thomas Ashe, Civilian of Kinard, Lispole, County Kerry and Corduff, Lusk, County Dublin. Charged with an offence under the Defence of the Realm Regulations'. It is too long to insert here but will be quoted from presently. Ashe declined to cross-examine the witnesses and reserved his defence.

Two days later, on 29 August, he was brought back to Mountjoy. He travelled in a small, closed lorry under an escort of RIC and a military NCO. A young RIC man who was of the party remembers the prisoner handed over to them as a 'well-dressed and strikingly handsome young man of fine appearance and bearing', who chatted pleasantly with them on the way to Dublin and only showed annoyance when, on instructions, handcuffs were placed on him.

> On arrival in Dublin, we drove straight to Mountjoy, handed over our friend to the prison authorities, and left immediately, after an almost cordial farewell. I have just a sort of idea that his arrest had to do with a speech against recruiting for the British Army ... In ordinary circumstances this episode could have been completely forgotten as just a routine turn of duty; but little did either of us know that evening that in a few weeks time, the name of our prisoner would ring loudly throughout the civilised world. I am almost certain that we were the last people from the real outside world to have normal conversation with him. His name was Thomas Ashe![2]

Hostile reactions began to show throughout the country at the menacing pattern of the government's behaviour. The atmosphere of conciliation which it appeared was in the air at the time of the prisoners' release eight weeks previously had dissipated under the present policy of repression. Sinn Féin had given neither support nor recognition to the Irish Convention which was holding its sessions. They believed, with good reason, that it was a project conceived in no good faith and designed for the special attention of the United States, whose military support in war might be the more easily secured through the fiction that a genuine Irish settlement was by way of being arranged. The indifference towards it of Sinn Féin and the marked independence shown by its leaders and adherents were resented by the British, whose reply was to arrest. In the House of Commons one Major Newman put his sentiments to the chief secretary for Ireland, Mr Duke, in the form of a question whether he was aware that Volunteers in uniform attended the recent demonstration in Kerry in memory of Sir Roger Casement and what did he propose to do about hostile Volunteers. The chief secretary's reply on the occasion was not very conclusive but the numerous arrests of republicans were evidence enough that a positive campaign of harassment against them was going to be carried out.

Amongst those arrested was Ashe's friend and fellow-soldier of Swords, Captain Richard Coleman, member of a notable Fingal nationalist family. He was destined to die a tragic death in Usk prison. Austin Stack was arrested in College Green, Dublin, on the night of 12 August, and Fionán Lynch early the following morning at Kilmackerrin, County Kerry. They were both removed to Cork barracks to face court-martial charges under the much invoked DORA, Stack for inciting disaffection amongst the civilian population and wearing Volunteer uniform at Casement's Fort, Lynch for creating disaffection.

Public bodies throughout Kerry showed a spirited reaction at the arrests. A special meeting of the county council called on the serving Kerry MPs to resign from the House of Commons and passed a resolution in support of the 1916 Rising as 'not only perfectly justified but absolutely necessary for the preservation of the national interests of our country'. Dingle Guardians and other public bodies in Kerry passed similar resolutions.

The fortunes of Stack and Lynch are further related in the following letter from Austin to Nora Ághas, who was back teaching at Cappamore at the time:

(Austin Stack Remand)   H. M. Male Prison Cork
                                         28.8.1917.

My dear Nora,

... I am to be tried today ... And so Tomás is locked up also. Have
you heard from him as to when he is to be courtmartialled? Finian
Lynch is here with me and is to answer the charges against him today
... We had eight weeks of liberty but it was no holiday – nor did we
give ourselves much rest ... I hope you have had a nice holiday and
that you are not worried about Tomás. It will do no good and he
would be troubled if he thought you were anyway anxious. I understand he has a few fellow prisoners with him at the Curragh, and I
daresay they have visitors ...

                         Slán leat. Mise, do chara go buan
                                         Aoibhistín.

                                         29.8.17.

My dear N.,

Courtmartial took place yesterday. We were not acquitted and have
been sent back here awaiting sentence, which will probably be promulgated Friday or Saturday ... Am still feeling in good physical
form. Sorry I am not near Tomás though. We may be together yet.

                              Beannacht leat anois
                                    ó Aoibhistín.

Stack was given two years' hard labour and Lynch eighteen
months. They were both removed to Mountjoy prison in Dublin
where, for the present, they remained in a different wing from
Ashe, who was awaiting his court martial.

22

COURT MARTIAL

Mountjoy prison is a grey grim structure situated on the slopes of Phibsboro between the Royal Canal, North Circular Road and Phibsboro Road. In the stress of Fenian times it housed for a while O'Donovan Rossa, John O'Leary and many of the great leaders of 1865. These men have left literary memorials in none of which is there a word in praise of its hospitality. Here Thomas Ashe was confined, for the second time in his career, and awaited a court martial. After the comparative freedom of the Curragh the cold and airless character of the place was a decided change for the worse. Yet he preferred it to Dartmoor, and the rumble of the Dublin trams which he could hear in the distance was reassuring, if noisy. The morning after his arrival he wrote to Mícheál Ó Foghludha and asked him to call to Mountjoy to see him. Joe Dixon arrived to offer his legal services for his defence but Thomas had decided not to employ a lawyer. Mícheál Ó Foghludha wrote to Nora to let her know how things stood:

THE FOLEY TYPEWRITER TRADING COMPANY.
(TEMPORARY ADDRESS)
25, BACHELOR'S WALK
DUBLIN
30/8/1917.

A Nora,

Got yours. You will be surprised to hear that Tomás is back in Dublin, at Mountjoy. He was brought back last night by motor, and it was only this morning when I got a note from him that I knew about it. He asked me to go in to see him and I arranged with Mick Collins to go in, but unfortunately Joe Dixon went in to see him, as a Solicitor – which would not count as a visit in the ordinary way – but Tomás would not have him as that (none of them are defending themselves), the result was we could not go today, but I will go tomorrow. Joe Dixon says he is very well. I sent in some things to him today, and also his meals, so he won't be badly off. I'm getting the papers sent in each day too. What do you think now of coming up to see him that he is back in Dublin, or will you wait until later? After I have seen him I will write you again. Meantime you may be sure he won't be forgotten.

No news much. Let me know if you are coming up – we were expecting you last night. Tell Kit that she need not be afraid – I didn't agree with W[illiam] O'B[rien]'s policy soon after the war started so I gave it up for the Sinn Féin one, which I think is better.

I expect I shall write to you tomorrow night after I see Tomás. Let me know if you are leaving Dingle.

For the present
Mo bheannacht
M. Ó F.

Ashe wrote to his recent host Batt O'Connor:

Mountjoy Prison
31st August, 1917.

Dear Batt,

Of course you have heard of all my wanderings since I met you last. Isn't it a great world! I remember writing for a young lady, in her album, some time ago, the names of the prisons I had been in last year, and in fun wrote 'To be continued' at the end. How little I thought at the time that I'd be commencing the second round so soon.

No charge has been preferred against me so far. I have heard the evidence of the police though, and I suppose now that they are trying to find out what Section of the D. of the Realm Act my words come under. I suppose I'll finish up with Austin; but what does it matter. We and what we stand for will survive it all.

I hope Mrs O'Connor and the children are all well. Remember me to them all. I may be out with you again very soon.

I had a good time in the Curragh. The soldiers are decent fellows, and they allowed me do what I liked.

I expect to be courtmartialled next week. They don't seem to be in any great hurry.

There is quite a gathering of us here at present. I expect it will increase. The old game, like the two course rotation of the farmers, 1st year beans, 2nd year wheat, then beans, then wheat, and so on. Ireland's rotation is Coercion, Conciliation, Coercion, Conciliation and so on forever. 'Twill all fall to the ground some day though.

Any news of Con?

Remember me to all the friends.

do chara
Tomás Ashe.

P.S. I'll be tried on Monday in the Lower Castle Yard at 1.30.

T.A.

'We and what we stand for will survive it all.' Such was the faith in his cause of Thomas Ashe. While it is true, on present reflection, that a great deal of what Thomas Ashe stood for is far from being achieved, these words of his stand transmitted to history as part of the personal message he would wish to leave behind him.

In Mountjoy he was examined by Dr Raymond G. Dowdall, medical officer of the prison. The doctor checked his heart and lungs and found him fit. He asked Ashe was he in good health. Ashe said he was. Ill-health in any shape was indeed very distant from his thoughts. Writing on the same day, 31 August, to Madge Daly of Limerick, daughter of the Fenian Chief John Daly and sister-in-law of Tom Clarke, he made reference in light vein to the charges preferred against him:

> They seem to have picked out all the useless and harmless things I said, and I have been just thinking how hard it will be for me to claim any dignity at all in the matter. I suppose I'll follow the lead given by the Cork men.
>
> I have been longing since my release in June for a rest. So I've got it at last. If I only could get plenty air I wouldn't mind. I feel in good form. I had a grand time at the Curragh.
>
> I hope all at Barrington St. are well. I suppose it will be some time before I'll call again.
>
> Yours sincerely
> Tomás Ashe.
>
> P. S. I will be tried on Monday at 1.30 o'clock. Usual charge – disaffection among civil population.
>
> T.A.

Ashe's reference to the lack of air in his new abode is significant. In the crisis of a few weeks' time it will be noted that the only item of prison property he touched, and this out of sheer necessity, consisted of a few small panes of glass in his cell which he broke in order to get air.

Monday was 3 September. He did not receive notification of the date or time of his trial until three o'clock on Saturday afternoon. The official order from Colonel H. G. H. Kennard appointing the court is dated Friday 31 August and the court was composed of the president, Major L. Swinton Browne of the Indian Army, and two members, Captain H. J. B. Whitehead (HS), Garrison Battalion, Royal Irish Regiment and Captain L. S. N. Palmer, Royal Dublin Fusiliers.

The court martial took place in the Garrison Office, Lower Castle Yard. Ashe was charged 'with doing an act prohibited by Regulation 42 of the Defence of the Realm regulations namely, attempting to cause disaffection among the civilian population' at Ballinalee, County Longford, on 25 July 1917, by speaking and publishing certain words and speeches intended to cause disaffection including, says the charge sheet, the following statements:

> Form military societies. Train, arm and equip yourselves. A man who is trained is far better than a man who is not. If it had not been for the rebellion of Easter Week, there would not be such a fine crowd of young men present as are here tonight, for there would have been conscription in Ireland, and they would now be out fighting for England. A great many people in Ireland think we are out for another rebellion, not just exactly another rebellion, but if I saw my chance, and England were overpowered or defeated on the Western Front, I would have no hesitation in calling out my men again as I did in Easter Week, 1916.

Ashe prepared his own defence, although the time at his disposal was short. He examined the police submissions, and on the copies of the charge sheet and police statements given to him he jotted down annotations and queries refuting the evidence against him. His annotations on the charge sheet may be summed up in three points: first, that he had been tried already for the rebellion; second, that the Irish Party claimed it was they who prevented conscription; and, third, that if England were overpowered on the Western Front there would be no other course left but to call out his men again. The evidence against him was supplied by two police witnesses. It was based, not on their written notes taken down at the actual meeting, but on their recollection after the event, a recollection prompted by the instructions received by their superior officer. Their names are given in the contemporary press reports as Constables Bowers and Quigley, but in the present narrative we print their names as found in the official documents: Constable Thomas R. Byers and Constable Martin Quigney. Their summary of evidence is certainly not the most convincing and logical of documents. Newspaper reports of the trial are lopsided and inadequate and the same can be said generally of other trials by court martial in the period. A strict press censorship precluded any balanced version being published. Freedom to report as they liked might have made no difference, however, in the case of the Irish daily newspapers, which were one and all intensely hostile to the republican movement and supported the Irish Party, or England, or both.

Constable Byers was the first witness for the crown. Cross-examined by Ashe he stated he made a mental note of the speech at Ballinalee and later on wrote it out. Ashe asked to be shown the document. The president said it would be handed to the court and that the prisoner could ask questions regarding it. Questioned further by Ashe, Byers said it would not be correct to say that there were many military societies in Ireland at present. He admitted having heard of the Ulster Volunteers, the National Volunteers, Colonel Moore's Volunteers, the Redmond Volunteers, the Citizen Army and the Irish Volunteers. Ashe stated that he wanted to show that a remark such as he had made had often been made before and was not regarded as seditious. He wanted to prove that whoever drew up the charge drew up one that was not against the Defence of the Realm Act. In reply to another question Constable Byers stated that he had heard the Irish Party claim credit for keeping conscription from Ireland, but agreed that he never sent notes of their speeches to the district inspector. To a question from Ashe whether he signed a petition after Easter Week calling on the authorities to execute him, Byers answered, 'No.'

Constable Quigney corroborated Byers. He said he was sure Thomas Ashe was the man who made the speech at the meeting in Ballinalee. It was inclined to be dark at the time. He heard the accused man say at the meeting that he was not out exactly for another rebellion, and he afterwards said that he preferred to organise the country in Sinn Féin clubs in order that the people might be united and get a say at the Peace Conference. The accused also said that if he had seen England overpowered on the Western Front he would have no hesitation in calling out his men as he did in Easter Week. In connection with that statement, Constable Quigney did not remember the accused as saying that if England was invaded, following defeat on the Western Front, he would call out his men to protect the country.

We take the above account with little alteration from *The Freeman's Journal* of 4 September 1917. There follows this passage:

The President: Why don't you protect it now?

Accused: The question does not arise.

President: You waited too long.

Accused: I meant to protect Ireland not England.

If the exchange has been correctly reported, the inference to be drawn is that the president of the court, who by virtue of his capacity might be expected to be impartial, was in fact not so, but on the contrary, hostile. Courts martial are not noted for impartiality. From such a source Thomas Ashe could expect little mercy. He called no evidence in his defence. The prosecutor said in his address that the prosecution did not maintain that every word of the accused's speech was seditious. The charge was chiefly based on the statement that under certain circumstances the accused would call out the Volunteers as he did in 1916. To the president's query whether the accused had anything to say, Ashe replied that he had a lot. The president said he would write down only what he thought material to the charge, 'but I hope you won't give us a long dissertation on the rights and wrongs of Ireland. We all hold our own views.'

Ashe made a long statement, of which only a much truncated version appeared in the newspapers.[1] He protested against the short notice of his trial. He did not believe the statement of the police in regard to the statement about the Western Front. His idea was that if England were overpowered he would call out the Sinn Féiners to protect Ireland against anybody who would invade their country, be it England, France or Germany. The constables were confused as they had to make a mental note. The most choice item of their evidence was the statement in regard to T. P.

O'Connor. If he had not referred to T. P. O'Connor at Ballinalee he would not be there standing on his trial. He had made many statements in public, but had not been arrested until he criticised T. P. O'Connor. He would not mind going to prison for decent charges such as high treason or rebellion, as it was an honour to suffer for Ireland, but it was unfair to be sent to prison in order that Mr T. P. O'Connor might collect 40,000 dollars in America.

Thus far the excellent *Freeman's Journal*.

To balance it we include here a letter to Nora Ághas from Michael Collins, who had watched this event with the closest attention, in comradeship for the prisoner and in the fervent hope that his sentence might be light:

> Irish National Aid and
> Volunteer Dependents Fund
> Offices: 10, Exchequer St. Dublin.
> 3rd September 1917.

Miss Norah Ashe,
Cappamore,
Co. Limerick.

Many thanks for your card. Tom is being tried today. In fact his trial is proceeding as I am writing this. I was there for about two hours, but had to leave before it was concluded. The whole business was extremely entertaining, almost as good as 'Gilbert and Sullivan's skit trial by jury.' The President of the Court was obviously biased against Tom, and, although the charge is very trivial, and the witnesses contradicted each other, it is quite likely that Tom will be sentenced. However let us hope it will be light.

I presume that the same visiting arrangements will hold good until he is sentenced, and this will hardly be before the end of the week, in the usual way of courtmartial. But if you could possibly arrange it, it would be well to come up at once so as to make sure of seeing him.

Do Chara
Mícheál

The court stated that its decision would be promulgated later.

In a letter to Michael Sheehan, which Ashe wrote the day following his trial, he asked his friend to keep for a while longer the setter dog he had been promised. He would have taken the dog long since only things were so unsettled. Michael Sheehan was a good friend since the days in De La Salle College. He was now married with a family, and Ashe, referring to Sheehan's responsibilities, says, 'I wonder if some of us were ever made for responsibilities,' a reflection which could mean that settling down in marriage was something that did not seriously occupy his own thoughts. For although Ashe was immensely attractive to girls and although there were girls with whom he was very friendly, it is improbable that he contemplated marriage in the uncertain circumstances of his present life.

In Mountjoy he had a note from Richard Hayes, whose reappointment as dispensary doctor at Lusk was being contested by anti-national forces represented by Sir Henry Robinson. In the course of his reply to the doctor, dated 7 September 1917, Ashe wrote:

I have heard nothing of my courtmartial yet. Still I am expecting the verdict every day. I suppose you saw the account of the trial in the press. It was a rather tame affair. If I had a lawyer I'd have very easily got off ... It is rather disgusting waiting for a verdict as I am. I hope my anxiety will be relieved today.

With best wishes,

Mise
T. ASHE.

The verdict was officially announced on 11 September; two years' hard labour, with one remitted, to date from the day of trial, 3 September. It was altogether out of proportion to the triviality of the charge.

Ashe was told of it the day before and wrote to his father, who he knew would be awaiting the result with anxious heart. To relieve his father's concern he made light of the sentence:

Mountjoy Prison
10 Sept 1917.

Dear Father,

I have just heard of my sentence – one year hard labour. I was sentenced to two years but one has been taken off. Hard labour means nothing more than an ordinary sentence.

Pray for me that my health and courage may not fail me; with God's help they won't.

Remember me to all the friends and neighbours.

Your fond son,
TOMÁS[2]

23

MOUNTJOY JAIL:
PRELUDE TO TRAGEDY

The order of court martial was effective from 3 September. Under the regulations Thomas Ashe became, according to the formula which obtained in His Majesty's prison, a third-division offender. This meant in effect that Thomas Ashe, who had worn the uniform of an officer of the Irish Republic was, for a political speech, placed on a level with thieves, burglars, thugs and pickpockets, and given precisely identical treatment. In the 1860s the Fenian prisoners were similarly denied political status. Every effort was made to degrade and humiliate them, a policy which caused the fierce personal revolt of O'Donovan Rossa against the system. The design had not altered since then.

Over and above that, it becomes clear, in reading the inquest into Thomas Ashe's death, that a special animus against him appeared to have taken hold of the rulers of Mountjoy prison. While its meaning and raison d'être might be summed up in the word 'Ashbourne', there may have been a deeper and more subtle reason for the behaviour towards him which culminated in his death. This was his presidency of the IRB.

Could it be that the prison authorities, aware of Thomas Ashe's standing in the IRB, hoped to undermine the morale of the organisation by essaying to break the spirit of its chief protagonist? The suggestion is credible.

Part of the work the authorities expected him to do was sewing mailbags, the traditional task of criminal offenders. From the moment his sentence began he rejected the code which denied his political status and acted on this resolution. He was not told about his sentence until 10 September and on that date, as part of the conventional punishment which went with the sentence, he was deprived of his mattress. In the terms of his sentence the deprivation of mattress was to last fourteen days, but as the sentence dated from 3 September the deprivation, according to rule and custom, ought to end on 17 September. However, it did not.

On 11 September he asked to be brought before the governor of the jail, C. A. Munro. The governor being absent, Ashe was seen by the deputy governor, John Boland, who had formerly been in charge of Tullamore prison. Ashe explained that he would not obey any regulation or carry out any task which imposed on him a criminal mark. Boland was stiff and antipathetic. He warned Ashe against disobeying the regulations.

Ashe declined to sew mailbags. He declined to observe the silence during exercise which was expected of criminal offenders. Out in the wood yard he spoke to all he met. The prison rulers were outraged. Boland reported to his Prisons Board that prisoner Ashe, third division, objected to carrying out the task assigned to him by the regulations. The chairman of that body, Max Green, son-in-law of John Redmond, and dedicated to the interests of His Majesty's government, issued a warning about the consequences of disobeying the rules. The deputy governor called Ashe before him again on 13 September and uttered the menacing cliché of the consequences of continuing to disobey the prison regulations and refusing to work. I shall continue, replied Ashe, to disobey the regulations which make me out to be a criminal, for a criminal I am not. So battle was joined between one man of courage and a ruthless system which declined to acknowledge the most earnest convictions of man.

Ashe would sew no mailbags and would keep no silence. On Monday 17 September Boland called him up again. There was a charge against him of refusing to work in his cell and of talking to others. Boland ordered for punishment that he be deprived of secular reading matter for seven days and forfeit marks for days he refused to work. The governor's punishment book has the following record of the interview:

Sept. 17th. Thomas Ashe. Idling.
Mr Boyd says: 'Prisoner refuses to do any work. Prisoner says he has nothing to say.' Punishment awarded. Forfeit instructive books for seven days, also marks for every day he refuses to work.

This particular date, 17 September, deserves special notice in the history of Ashe's prison treatment. On 17 September that was the only charge standing against Ashe and that was the only punishment awarded against him. On that date he became a punished prisoner, serving his punishment for the offence with which he was charged, namely, refusing to work. No other charge was ever made against him apart from that one. No opportunity was ever given him of answering any other charge. There was no entry in the books of punishment before 17 September. That was the first and last entry of punishment. Yet on this important date of Monday 17 September there appears the first indication of a series of acts committed within the prison walls against the persons of Thomas Ashe and others, which ended in death for him and, no thanks to their jailers, might well have so ended for some of his fellow prisoners. The evidence of it exists in the form of a separate docket, *not* entered in the prison punishment book, which reads as follows:

> I hereby certify that I have examined prisoner 873 (Thomas Ashe), and I find him fit for close confinement, fit for scale punishment No. 1 and 2, also deprivation of mattress, fit for restraint in handcuffs, waist belt, muffs, restraint jacket or jacket in splints.

This document is signed by the medical officer of Mountjoy prison, R. G. Dowdall.

Rule 32 of the prison rules states that a man may 'not be deprived of his mattress for the rest of his sentence after the first fourteen days, except as a punishment. The punishment can only be inflicted as a result of trial and sentence.'

Thomas Ashe's sentence is recorded in Mountjoy prison documents as legally beginning on 3 September. Therefore he was legally entitled to be given back on 17 September the mattress of which he had already been deprived. He did not in fact get it back. The deprivation was continued. He was thus illegally denied the benefit of Rule 32 of the prison rules. In the case of Thomas Ashe there was neither trial nor sentence on any other charge. Yet he was so sentenced and deprived on Monday 17 September. And the extraordinary thing is that Dr Dowdall, whose name is signed to the special docket, stated that he was unaware of it. Why was he not? The question was put to him:

On the 17th September you had no knowledge that Thomas Ashe was sentenced to be deprived of his bed and bedding?

His reply was 'No.'

This is one of the mysteries surrounding the prison treatment of Thomas Ashe, and the officials of Mountjoy contributed nothing to solving it in the course of many opportunities given to them. The truth is that we will probably never know the full details of the bullying that brought Thomas Ashe prematurely to his grave.

24

THE ASSAULT
ON THE PRISONERS

Austin Stack, casting his mind back over the years, remembers
that a small group of court-martialled prisoners were already in
Mountjoy before Ashe was brought in to join them. They included
himself, Fionán Lynch and Phil MacMahon. Joe MacDonagh was
there, too, but was not a hard-labour prisoner, unlike the others,
having been tried and sentenced by a civil court in Dublin. He
was a brother of Thomas MacDonagh, the executed 1916 leader.
Thomas Ashe was court-martialled, and in due course found
himself in the 'wood shed', submitting for the moment to hard
labour for the purpose of seeing and consulting his comrades. They
were forbidden to speak or to receive letters or visits. 'As a result
of our little consultations,' said Stack, 'a decision is come to, and
a list of "demands" is written out and copied by every prisoner.
In our turns we interview the Governor and make our claim to
prisoner-of-war treatment in detail.' Stack was writing in 1928.[1]
Many years later, in April 1963, Lynch recalled the occasion. He
writes:

> After sentence Tomás was brought into our compound while we
> were at exercise and supposed to be walking in single file and not
> talking. When I saw Tom brought in I stepped off the path as if to tie
> my lace, stepped in beside Tom and shook hands with him and told

him what we had decided to do in order to insist on being treated as political prisoners – that, first we would try what was called the 'Lewes tactics,' that is, smashing up our cells as far as we could, and then, if all else failed, we should go on hunger-strike (in fact, circumstances forced us to go on hunger-strike immediately we had broken up what we could).

Tom said that, of course, he would fall in with what we had already arranged, but strangely enough he had a premonition that he would not survive a hunger-strike. I laughed it off at the time, saying he was about the heftiest man of the whole bunch of us, but I have often since thought that he must have been 'fey' or psychic. He was, of course, well-known to be a deeply religious man.

There seems to have been some confusion as to whether the prisoners' demand was for political or prisoner-of-war treatment. In essence, however, their claim was not for special treatment in itself but rather for the recognition of their political status and the principle that they were not to be classed as criminals. In the words of Tim Healy: 'Mr Ashe and the other prisoners claimed no luxuries, they claimed no conveniences, but they were claiming a status – the status of non-criminals...' The precise details of their request were:

1. Improvement of diet in quality and quantity.
2. Unrestricted conversation.
3. Work optional; but if Republican prisoners decide to work they shall do so together, and be allowed to converse, payment to be made for such work as per usage governs international prisoners of war.
4. Republican prisoners not to be required at any time or at any place to associate with ordinary criminals.

5. One letter and one visit per day.

6. Unrestricted smoking.

7. Receive newspapers, books and writing materials.

8. Parcels from friends.

9. Facilities for associated study and for class-work.

10. Cells not to be locked until 9.45 p.m.; light in cell until 9.45 p.m.

11. Association at work or otherwise throughout the day.

The foregoing details are taken from *The Irishman*, 13 October 1917, where it is stated they were received from Austin Stack. Amongst the Ashe inquest papers in O'Connell Schools' library there is a copy of a request submitted on behalf of the Mountjoy prisoners by Commandant J. J. Liddy which, apart from verbal differences, agrees materially with the one we give here.

MacDonagh placed these claims before the deputy governor on Monday 17 September. 'Nonsense,' said Boland, with impatience. 'I am not aware there is a war on. These demands are outrageous and will not be considered.' 'These demands,' said MacDonagh, 'are quite serious.' But Boland was adamant. Austin Stack recollects that nearly all the prisoners were lined up before the deputy governor on the occasion but he could not remember if Ashe was there. To Boland's rejection they replied that they would not work until they received prisoner-of-war treatment. They did not expect the deputy governor himself to give them any concession but they had some idea he would get in touch with the General Prisons Board and part of their plan was to give the Prisons Board a fortnight to negotiate with them, that is to say until 1 October. Should their request not be granted by then they proposed to go on hunger strike on that date. No doubt Boland's sentiments towards the prisoners and their request corresponded to the plea made on his behalf by his advocate Mr Hanna: 'It was a prison those men were in, and not a place of joy … What did they expect? There were between thirty and forty of them and they wanted things made as easy as they could. Did they think that it was a summer holiday?'

On Wednesday, they got their exercise together as usual about 6.30 or 7 a.m., before breakfast, and again between 11 and 12, before dinner. That afternoon they got no exercise. They waited a while until the ordinary prisoners had gone to work and when there was no appearance of their being allowed out, they began to ring their bells. A warder came to Stack's cell door and asked what he wanted. He said he wanted to be let out to exercise. The warder said he would see about it, went away and did not return. The bells were then tied up and muffled. Not all the prisoners rang their bells. Philip MacMahon, who on being transferred from Belfast jail had been put in the prison hospital and been discharged from there on Wednesday 19th, was deprived of his exercise although he rang no bell. The bells, however, were muffled and became useless for calling anyone. About an hour afterwards the political prisoners were transferred to another wing of the prison.

Joseph MacDonagh, who had no exercise on Wednesday, was the only one to be offered exercise on Thursday morning. He was brought out alone, which was the way prisoners under sentence of death were exercised, and asked to be brought back. The others tried to get the warder's attention by ringing the bells. Stack demanded exercise from a warder who told him wait a minute. Stack waited ten minutes and then rang his bell again. The bells were muffled once more. After they failed to ring and the warders did not come Stack began to kick the door with the heel of his boot. He heard a lot of knocking and hammering at the doors at the same time by the other prisoners. 'A considerable amount of noise and hammering' took place, as Stack recalled at the inquest, or as the deputy governor put it, 'there was pandemonium'. Suddenly Stack saw his cell door open; Chief Warder Ryan and a group of warders entered, took away his bed-board, table, stove, locked up the cell, came back, removed bedclothes, mattress, sanitary utensils, slippers, Bible and prayer book, everything except his personal clothing. Ten or fifteen minutes later a deputy chief warder and two other warders came and after much resistance removed his boots, having first pinned his arms. He was then left with his stockings on his feet until near locking-up time, about 4.30 p.m. He asked Warder Skelly was he going to be left without boots or slippers and the warder got him slippers. At that time he had done nothing in his cell. He had broken no glass in his cell window, nor had he threatened to do so. Neither had he threatened to damage bed or bedding. He saw no furniture broken, but he saw the furniture from all the other cells in his ward. Other prisoners had a similar experience. Phil MacMahon was reading his Bible when he was set upon. On that Thursday morning Thomas Ashe damaged nothing in his cell, neither his door, nor his wall bracket, nor his plank bed. At ten o'clock four warders entered his cell and removed his bed and bedding. They then tried to remove his boots. They were his own and he resisted. After a fierce struggle they took them off his feet. The explanation the prison authorities later gave for taking his boots was that he could use them for the destruction of public property. But he had destroyed nothing. Deputy Governor Boland stated that Ashe 'was taking part in combined action with others to defy the prison rules and upset the good order and discipline of the prison'. It was this illegality, committed against Thomas Ashe and some forty others at ten o'clock on Thursday morning, that caused the hunger strike to take place at once. The original date had been fixed for 1 October. The men refused dinner that Thursday, some hours after their cells had been emptied, and thus began the hunger strike, which took place in the first instance in protest against the aggression of the Prisons Board.

That some perturbation existed amongst the prison authorities is reflected by the fact that a meeting of the Visiting Justices was held in the prison at a quarter to twelve. Sir John Irwin, chairman, presided. Before the meeting, Sir John saw Ashe and MacDonagh. He went to Ashe's cell and asked what the trouble in the prison was about. 'We claim,' replied Ashe, 'to be treated as prisoners-of-war, not criminals.' 'Personally,' said Sir John, 'I do not consider you a criminal, but, as far as I know, from the rules governing prisons, there is no class in which you can be placed, in view of the fact that the court martial by whom you were sentenced did not order you to be treated as a first-class misdemeanant.'

'I am a political prisoner,' replied Ashe, 'and I claim to be treated as such. I do not ask to be released but I ask to be treated differently to the pickpocket and other criminals.'

Sir John Irwin pressed him to change his mind. 'I reasoned with him,' he stated, 'and pointed out that the forcible feeding, which he told me was intended to be carried out, might have a serious effect upon his health.'

This statement of Sir John Irwin is interesting. Evidently at the very beginning of their hunger strike it was known to Ashe, and accepted by Sir John Irwin, that forcible feeding was to be imposed on the prisoners. It is also of the utmost importance to point out that Sir John Irwin, chairman of the Visiting Justices, as shown by this observation, had no illusions about the ill-effects of forcible feeding. That being so, that was the time to act.

Firmly and justifiably, Ashe insisted on the principle of political treatment. His reply to Sir John was final: 'I am a political prisoner and am prepared to take the consequences.' Sir John Irwin then told him that a meeting of the Visiting Justices would be held in half-an-hour, and that he had already promised MacDonagh an opportunity to be heard before the committee.

Before seeing Ashe, Sir John, who was accompanied by the deputy governor, had spoken to Joe MacDonagh and expressed his concern at the present terrible state of affairs. MacDonagh told his visitor that on the previous Monday he placed his request for prisoner-of-war treatment before the deputy governor and had it rejected out of hand. Sir John then asked him would he speak on behalf of the prisoners before the Visiting Justices. MacDonagh explained that he had no authority to do so and would like to consult with Austin Stack first. Boland cut in to say he would not allow it.

At the meeting MacDonagh had only begun his statement on behalf of the prisoners when he noticed a document on the table before Sir John Irwin which he recognised at once. It was a request on behalf of the prisoners made to the deputy governor and signed by J. J. Liddy, Clare Brigade, Irish Republican Army. MacDonagh stated that it was unnecessary for him to say more as his request corresponded with what was in that document.

Hunger strike came up for discussion. Sir John said it was an intolerable state of affairs to have forty men going on hunger strike. MacDonagh pointed out that if the prisoners' request was not conceded they would go on hunger strike immediately and particularly on account of what happened that morning. By this he meant the denial of exercise and the stripping of their cells.

Sir John emphasised what a serious, what a terrible thing it would be to have forty men go on hunger strike. 'I suggested to him,' said MacDonagh, 'that it would be more awkward if one man were dead by that day week than to have forty men on hunger strike that day.' The tragic implications of this reply were seen afterwards. MacDonagh pointed out that the matter was very serious. Sir John asked him to influence the men against hunger-striking. MacDonagh stated that they were going on hunger strike because their requests had not been considered and because of the treatment they had that morning received.

One of the few documents which the officials were willing to reveal was a minute concerned with this meeting. It is an extract from the Visiting Committee Book of HM Prison, Mountjoy, dated 20 September 1917. It reads in part:

> The Deputy Governor (Boland) submitted a letter dated 11th from the General Prisons Board with reference to civilians awaiting trial by Courtmartial. The Committee found considerable trouble exists in the prison today. The prisoners undergoing sentences passed on them by Courtsmartial refuse to work unless they be treated as prisoners of war and are given privileges as set out in a memo prepared by prisoner J. J. Liddy, and forwarded to Prisons Board by the Governor.
>
> Prisoner Joseph MacDonagh appeared before the Committee, and stated that he and the other prisoners of his class demanded to have the terms of prisoner Liddy's memorandum given effect to. He further stated he declines to recognise any authority to treat him as

an ordinary prisoner, and if their demands are not conceded he and the others will go on hunger-strike.

The Committee found considerable damage has already been done in the cells by these courtmartial prisoners.

This note, signed by John Irwin, chairman, suppresses certain facts and sequences.

At the inquest the prison authorities' case was put mainly by Deputy Governor Boland. It was that the prisoners on Thursday took their ordinary diet until dinner, that after dinner pandemonium started in that part of the building where Ashe and the other Sinn Féin prisoners were confined, that they broke the furniture, windows and doors, made use of the wooden parts of their beds to break open the cells into each other, broke the gas brackets and did every damage they could to government property. That these men were all lusty, strong, healthy men, and that it became necessary to remove anything in their cell which might be used to damage property or create disturbance.

Boland stated that he removed the bed, bedding and boots early in the day without authority, on his own initiative and before he had communicated with the Prisons Board. He said there was a great deal of glass broken and this was the cause of the removal of the beds and bedding. Boland stated he did this to save public property from destruction. He admitted, however, that he could not point to a single item which had been broken or destroyed by Thomas Ashe. The only thing he could say was in general terms to the effect that Ashe was one of those creating a disturbance. Asked for evidence or witnesses to prove it he could produce neither. It is of interest to give his own statement:

It was said to me that all the prisoners undergoing sentence under the Defence of the Realm Act were creating a disturbance in the prison, and I went to the prison from my office to see what was going on. From my previous knowledge of Thomas Ashe I knew what he was prepared to do, and what he had already done. He had already told me he would defy all rules and regulations. When it was reported to me that the prisoners under the Defence of the Realm Act were breaking the prison rules and creating a disturbance I made no exception of Thomas Ashe or any other prisoner. I knew they were all out for fight to defy the application to them of the prison rules and regulations.

Enthusiastic as Boland was for rules, he could point to none that invested him with the power to inflict the punishment on Thomas Ashe he had inflicted. He could point to nobody amongst his large staff of about fifty who had any apprehension that Ashe would destroy his bed and bedding, from anything that he had done before. He denied that Ashe's treatment was connected with Ashbourne. He stated that he knew 'he was engaged in the destruction of prison property, and if he did not do as much himself as others, he was recognised as a leader of the others'. Boland took full responsibility for what he did in what he described as an emergency involving the destruction of prison property. He placed the value of the property from Thomas Ashe's cell, consisting of two blankets, two sheets, rugs, pillows, and plank bed, at £4, £5 or £6. He stated that none of the prisoners destroyed their bed and bedding, 'because they had not the opportunity' since they were taken out as a precautionary measure. He reported that Thursday morning to the Prisons Board what he had done and the Prisons Board approved his action. When it was pointed out to Boland that Ashe could not sit down, or lie down, except on the cold floor, and that when he lay down there was nothing he could cover himself with, his reply was that in the ordinary everyday working of the prison these regulations were strictly enforced. Questioned about the legality of keeping Ashe deprived of his mattress on the 17th, when it was due back, Boland tried to give his own interpretation of the rule and when it was pointed out to him that it did not stand up to examination he asserted that Thomas Ashe deprived himself of that 'privilege'. Sir John Irwin was present when the 'pandemonium' on 20 September was taking place, but Boland made no special report to him on the 'conduct' of Ashe. The deputy governor was unable to point to any specific act of Thomas Ashe on 20 September for which he was not already undergoing punishment, 'except that he was taking part in the shouting and the yelling to the other prisoners'. This he alleged to be 'a very serious offence coming from a man who was recognised by those prisoners as a leader.' He admitted that no offence was brought before the Visiting Justices on oath in respect of Thomas Ashe, and that the Visiting Justices had not the power to inflict on Thomas Ashe the punishment inflicted.

His case was the belief that, even if the prisoners had not been deprived of their mattresses, bedding and boots they would have struck anyway. He could give no special act on the part of Ashe to justify this belief. He said a report was made by the chief warder that others of the prisoners were 'worse' than Ashe.

Thus far the deputy governor of Mountjoy. The jurors who listened to his case were not prepared to support his sense of values in placing a few pounds worth of property against an assault on the prisoners and a gamble on their lives.

Stated briefly, what happened in Mountjoy prison was:

1. On Monday 17 September, a request was made by the Defence of the Realm prisoners for political (or prisoner-of-war) treatment.
2. On Wednesday afternoon they were deprived of their exercise. In protest they rang their bells and demanded exercise. The bells were muffled. They were transferred to another part of the prison. (Account of Austin Stack.)
3. On Thursday morning they were deprived of their exercise. In protest they rang bells, hammered doors, shouted and raised commotion. (There were some who did not.)
4. Their bedclothes, bedding, boots and cell effects were taken from them, a process in which force was used and assault committed on them.
5. Thereafter the alleged 'mutiny', i.e. hunger strike, occurred.

This sequence of events was proved at the inquest to be the correct one.

25

FIFTY HOURS

Battle was now joined in grim earnest between Dublin Castle and the Irish republican prisoners.

Austin Stack was the accepted leader of the men in Mountjoy. He it was who took the foremost part in giving instructions for the conduct of the strike. The Thursday night it began he appointed a committee consisting of Patrick Brennan, Thomas Ashe, Joe MacDonagh, Michael Travers and himself. He let the committee know of its selection by shouting out their names from his cell. He had an easier way of getting in touch with Fionán Lynch, who occupied the cell next to him, for they bored a hole in the wall through which they could talk privately. Stack did not try particularly to communicate with Ashe that night and Ashe may have been unaware he was on the committee, until Friday. Stack has asserted, and there appears no reason to doubt it, that Thomas Ashe was not a leader in organising the protest. In a matter so grave, thought Stack, responsibility ought to be divided between a group.

The evidence he gave at the inquest forms the basis of our narrative for the moment. He gave no orders to break anything in the cells. He did not approve of such action, considering it unwise with winter approaching and the prospect of being kept indefinitely in jail. Certainly he kicked his cell door and shouted. So did a number of his colleagues and the noise could be heard far and near. If the authorities wished to call this pandemonium, then pandemonium there was. When everything was removed from his cell and his boots were forcibly taken away he broke the glass in his cell door to communicate with the others. He advised them that, if forcibly fed, they were not to endanger their lives by resisting after being placed, as he thought they would be, on the 'operating table'. He also advised them not to walk of their free will to the operating room but to insist on being carried. At no time did he tell them to resist the actual feeding operation. The disturbance in the prison continued all day on Thursday and nearly all that night; it continued all next day and night although he thought the men were getting very tired and hoarse on Friday night. But, said Stack, 'we made as much noise as we could'. Such is his picture of the prison scene.

The floor of a Mountjoy cell was no comfortable resting place and in the small hours of the September morning the feel of it must have been misery. Thomas Ashe lay on it, unsustained by food and thinly protected by his overcoat, absorbing its chills into his body. The arctic air searched to his marrow, sapped his vitality and slowed the blood in his veins. No use to toss or turn as if sleep might be cajoled to come, for on the cold bed of that floor sleep was fitful and unrefreshing and left only a numbing tiredness.

What thoughts occupied his mind we can surmise. Prayers for his comrades who died in Kilmainham the year before, for victory and blessing on the Irish cause, for Edward O'Dwyer, Bishop of Limerick, recently dead, who had thrown his republican defiance in the teeth of black Maxwell. Thomas Ashe, who could be determined and fierce in the role of athlete or soldier, was very much a man of thought. In the grey solitude of prison he had much time to think, of music, poetry, airs old and new, songs and ballads of the Kerry fairs. Not long after his arrest he wrote from Mountjoy to Kathleen, younger sister of Mary Monks, who as a little girl used to go on walks with him to 'the Arches' down by the sea near Lusk. To her he said: 'I may not be among you for years – I'll be gray, gray from hoping and thinking.'

Thinking long's the weary work and I must spin and spin,
To drive the fearful fancies out and keep the hopeful in.

He talked about writing songs and composing new airs and finished his letter by quoting:

'Let me carry your cross for Ireland Lord,' that's my prayer – join with me that I may carry it with honour. It's a great delight to me that I should be selected as one of its bearers.

During those grey, icy hours there must have been times when the conflict was intense between fancies hopeful and fearful.

On Saturday morning an unforeseen and dramatic intervention caught the authorities of Mountjoy off guard. The prisoners had, by their own secret means, got in touch with the outside world. Word reached Alderman Laurence O'Neill, lord mayor of Dublin, that there was trouble in Mountjoy and he considered it his duty to go and investigate it. In the company of Sir John Irwin he visited the prison about twelve noon. During his visit he interviewed six prisoners and described what he saw with his own eyes as 'something alarming'.

It certainly was.

Amongst the prisoners they saw was Thomas Ashe. They were accompanied on their tour of inspection by Deputy Governor Boland, Chief Warden Ryan and two other warders. Ashe's cell door was open and he was lying on the bare boards, without bedding, seating, support or furniture of any kind. The lord mayor explained that he had come to investigate what complaints the prisoners had to make. Ashe pointed out that his bed and bedding had been taken away and that four warders had, by force, removed the boots off his feet. Could he give any reason as to why he was treated in this way, asked the lord mayor. Ashe could give none. He had in no way interfered with the cell furniture and the glass of his cell window was intact. 'You can see it for yourself.' Ashe stated further that owing to the airless condition of his cell he might presently have to break some panes of glass to get air. Alderman O'Neill asked him had he any complaints to make about the officials immediately dealing with him. Ashe said he had not. The lord mayor saw no furniture or sanitary accommodation in the cell. Ashe made his mind perfectly clear to the lord mayor. The hunger strike on which he was engaged since Thursday was in protest against being designated a criminal. Along with his colleagues he stood on the principle that they were not criminals, and that they were not in fact particular about how they were treated as long as they were not classed as such. During this interview Deputy Governor Boland was standing by. Not one word did he volunteer of explanation, comment or reply. That was the time for him to talk, if he had a mind to.

The visitors left. The cell furniture, mattresses and bedding were restored at once to Ashe and his fellow prisoners. The deputy governor had been caught red-handed. Publicity is a mighty lever.

The lord mayor and Sir John Irwin were disturbed at what they had seen. They were aware that in the small hours the cells would be ice-cold and that grave damage to the prisoners' health would result from lying without covering or protection on the floor. They went at once to Dublin Castle where they asked to see the chief secretary, Duke. They told him the position. The chief secretary was sympathetic and evidently anxious to do something. Sir John Irwin said the impression left on his mind was that Duke seemed disposed to make some concessions to the prisoners. He pointed out that there were certain legal difficulties in the way. He sent for Max Green, chairman of the Prisons Board, so that they could discuss the matter with him. Green arrived. The lord mayor related what he had seen in Mountjoy. He did not specifically mention Thomas Ashe. He mentioned Joseph MacDonagh, who he thought was the worst affected by his treatment, and gave the gist of his conversation with the prisoners, which was that they did not want any compliments from the government but objected to being classed as criminals. He also referred to the forcible feeding which it was proposed to carry out.

The chief secretary's sympathy was not shared by Green. These men, he said, were handed over to him as criminals and must be treated as such. He had no other alternative. The Prisons Board had no power to relax the rules or change the status of prisoners. He had no discretion in the matter except to insist on the rules laid down by Parliament. The forcible feeding could do no harm if properly administered.

The lord mayor realised that his errand was futile. He told the chief secretary and Max Green that they were taking on a dreadful responsibility and that, if any ill should befall, the responsibility would be theirs. Duke said he would confer with the law advisers. If he did, and if they said anything that mattered, no record of it has come to light. Sir John Irwin was sorely worried. When he saw that the mission of the lord mayor and himself to the chief secretary had produced nothing except sympathy from Duke and a dedicated loyalty to the rules on the part of Max Green, he went on Monday afternoon to see Sir Bryan Mahon, commander-in-chief of the British military forces in Ireland. By virtue of his office Mahon was lord justice and charged with the governing of Ireland in the absence of the viceroy. Sir John explained the situation to him and told him the prisoners would resist to the end in pursuing their claim for political status.

Sir Bryan Mahon, too, was sympathetic and sorry for the condition of things. That was the net result.

26

THE ORDEAL
OF THE STOMACH PUMP

In the medical officer's book, Mountjoy prison, under date 20 September, there is the entry:

> A number of prisoners undergoing sentence in this prison have today commenced hunger-striking. I propose to feed these prisoners to-morrow artificially.

On the following day there is this further entry:

> With reference to my general entry of yesterday regarding the prisoners on hunger-strike, I find these men, 40 in number, refused to partake of their dinner or supper yesterday, and have taken no breakfast this morning. I have no doubt that the hunger-strike will be continued, and I am of opinion that artificial feeding should commence tomorrow morning.

On Saturday 22 September there is the significant entry:

> All the prisoners on hunger-strike are to be given their beds.

That was the morning of the lord mayor's unexpected visit. Whether the beds would have been returned if he had not come is a matter of speculation. For Sunday 23rd there is written:

Artificially fed prisoners on hunger-strike.

It is interesting to compare what happened on previous occasions when hunger strikes were threatened in Mountjoy prison. Some years before this a number of suffragettes jailed in Mountjoy determined on such a course when they were classed with common criminals. Sir John Irwin was at that time, too, chairman of the Visiting Justices and Dr Dowdall was medical officer. Two distinguished medical men were called in by the prison authorities to consider the question of forcibly feeding the suffragettes and advised against it. Sir John went to interview the viceroy, Lord Aberdeen. The result was that by an authority within the discretion of the viceroy the suffragettes were treated as first-class misdemeanants, a wise concession to the honour of their cause. Sir John Irwin's intervention was timely, too, in the case of Francis Sheehy Skeffington in 1915, when a decision to feed him forcibly was prudently not pursued. James Connolly in 1913 was released after a few days' hunger strike. No similar course of wisdom was resolved on by the authorities who held within their power Thomas Ashe and his comrades.

The lord mayor telephoned Mountjoy on Sunday to see how matters stood and was told by the deputy governor that all the prisoners were well, especially MacDonagh, whose condition had caused the lord mayor concern. That morning Phil MacMahon spoke with Ashe before and after Mass. MacMahon, who was confined in a basement punishment cell, had been forcibly fed earlier. Ashe talked of the unpleasant prospect of being forcibly fed and asked him what it was like. MacMahon related his own ordeal, which was virtually torture. Ashe said the prison authorities had gone beyond all bounds. He said he felt very weak and that he felt the cold very badly in his cell on Thursday and Friday nights. He added: 'I don't mind so much about myself, but I could not help thinking all the night about those poor young boys who hadn't even as much as an overcoat.' Ashe compared their treatment in Mountjoy with the more humane behaviour of the Lewes authorities and blamed Dublin Castle for the present victimisation of Irish political prisoners.

That morning he had his first experience of forcible feeding. He was put in a chair, his hands strapped to its arms and his feet bound. He told Dr Dowdall he was sorry to see a doctor reducing a noble profession to the level of an executioner's trade. The doctor did not answer but asked him whether he would like to be artificially fed. It would be easier on him, Dr Dowdall said, to have the feeding tube through the mouth than the nose. Ashe said he would rather have it through the mouth. A warder stood on each side of him while he was being fed. On the way back to his cell Ashe said to Warder Watters: 'This is a horrible ordeal.' Later in the day he discussed with Stack whether they ought to ask that an outside doctor be permitted to be present during the forcible feeding. Ashe favoured the idea strongly. He said the doctor had the greatest difficulty in feeding him. Ashe advised all the men to pray for strength to carry on the fight.

When the archaeologia of Irish penology come to be studied, the stomach pump and its accoutrements will form an interesting, if hardly attractive, exhibit. The National Museum does not possess one but social historians will probably locate some examples in good time to instruct posterity. From published descriptions we gather that it was a pump with India-rubber tubes fixed to it. A report says: 'The tube was put on to the end of the stomach pump. The end of the pump was put into the vessel containing food, and the food then pumped into the stomach.'

Fionán Lynch had unpleasant recollections of it. 'Each man,' he said, 'was strapped legs and hands to a high chair, mouth forced open with a wooden spoon and then the stomach pump pushed in by a doctor and the food poured in through it.' To remain down or not, said Stack. The tube was passed into the patient's stomach through the mouth or nose and the operation of pumping was carried out by a certain number of hand-operated strokes. The length of the operation varied from five to ten minutes. The insertion of the tube into the patient's stomach was a delicate and painful process. There were four pumps in the prison with which to operate on forty prisoners, one to every ten. According to Warder Bernard Watters's account (which differs from Dr Dowdall's) seven or eight men were artificially fed on Sunday before Ashe. The same pump and the same tube were used in all these operations. There was no sterilising. Hot water was passed through the pump and tube and rinsed out again. Dr Dowdall had an assistant in the prison but in order to mechanically feed forty prisoners he considered further help necessary, so he called in Dr William Lowe. Dr Lowe, who had been in practice since his graduation in 1909, had no experience in mechanical feeding. The prisoners were forcibly fed twice a day. Thomas Ashe went through the experience five times in all.

Details of the prisoners' ordeal reached the outside world. From Fingal a group of Ashe's followers came to the city to be near him and join in the protest which republican Dublin organised. On Sunday 23 September a great meeting was held in Smithfield to voice its abhorrence of the treatment the prisoners were undergoing in Mountjoy. De Valera, Cathal Brugha and Countess Markievicz spoke. Then a large procession formed up four deep and, headed by the speakers in an outside car, marched to the vicinity of the prison, where another earnest protest was made by de Valera, after which the crowds quietly dispersed.

Ashe had already been forcibly fed three times when the lord mayor and Sir John Irwin came again to see him about 11.30 on Monday morning. With them were Deputy Governor Boland and two warders. On arriving at Thomas Ashe's cell they found him standing up. He was not in prison clothes but was very lightly clad. The lord mayor observed that his bed and bedding had been restored. Ashe said they had been restored on Saturday evening after the visit of himself and Sir John Irwin. Since then he had to break three or four panes of glass in his cell to get air, as he feared he would become exhausted. To the query of the lord mayor as to how he felt he replied that he was well, but said they had been putting him through the revolting operation of forcible feeding. He said an outside doctor advised him that his throat was delicate and if they persisted in feeding him as they had that morning he feared the end would be fatal. The lord mayor tried to persuade him out of the hunger strike. He pointed out that his protest had succeeded to the extent that the authorities had restored his bed and bedding, and would he not consider it best for his life to take his food? Thomas Ashe's resolve was unbreakable: 'No. They have branded me as a criminal. Even though I do die, I die in a good cause.' The lord mayor left in a saddened mood. He realised from his appearance that Ashe's strength was giving way.

Was Ashe at that stage contemplating the imminence of death? There is the clear suggestion that he suffered greatly that morning at the hands of his mechanical feeder, even to the extent that he could visualise his death as something not remote. Fionán Lynch suggested that Ashe had a premonition when the hunger strike began that he would not survive it. Yet he cannot have surmised how very close death was to him now.

The following morning, Tuesday 25 September, Sir John Irwin again called to Mountjoy prison and Thomas Ashe was one of the first prisoners he saw. Ashe was in his cell. Sir John asked him how he was. Ashe said he was feeling rather light in the head. Sir John asked did he have any complaint to make about his treatment at the hands of the officials. 'No,' said Ashe, 'they are acting as humanely as possible under the circumstances.' The interview took place before Ashe was forcibly fed that morning and that was the last time Sir John saw him alive. Each time he saw Ashe, said Sir John, he appeared cheerful and determined to continue the protest he was making, and on no occasion did he complain of any ill-treatment at the hands of the officials. For that picture of Thomas Ashe in the midst of his adversity we may record our gratitude to the chairman of the Visiting Justices. An hour later, when Sir John was seeing Joe MacDonagh in the prison hospital, he heard that Ashe had been brought over and placed in the ward. In that hour the beginning of tragedy was made.

Thomas Ashe was fed that Tuesday morning about 11.15 a.m. by Dr Lowe in the presence of Warders Watters, MacManus and Gilroy. We summarise here the evidence of Watters and Mac-Manus about that last forced and fatal meal.

Watters stated that Ashe protested against being forcibly fed.

The doctor said he was there to do his duty and if Ashe refused his food he had no option but to feed him. Ashe made no reply. A warder stood on each side of him. He opened his mouth when the doctor inserted the tube of the stomach pump. He seemed inclined to vomit. The doctor brought up the tube, put it down again and asked Ashe if he was all right. Ashe nodded his head. 'The food was then pumped into the stomach.' The operation lasted from five to eight minutes. 'When the contents had been pumped into the stomach the tube was withdrawn and Ashe then vomited about a wineglassful of food, which was a thing that often happened. As Ashe was a little weak the doctor told the warders to bring him out carefully …' Ashe was sent from the patient room to the hospital. Before being fed he seemed all right. Immediately after the forcible feeding the serious symptoms arose. To the question whether Ashe's throat was held by anyone, Watters said it was not. He could not account for the marks on his throat and chin. Warder MacManus stated that Ashe walked quietly to the operating room, sat on a chair and made no resistance when strapped around each arm and leg. The doctor had some trouble in putting down the tube. Ashe coughed violently when it was placed in his throat. He told the doctor the tube was put down the wrong passage. Dr Lowe replied, impossible, no such thing, and after he had stopped coughing put it down again. From the time Ashe left his cell to the time he was brought to hospital was no more than ten or twelve minutes. Dr Lowe administered about twenty or thirty strokes of the pump per minute. After the tube was withdrawn Ashe appeared to get weak. He collapsed in the chair and said he felt very weak. Dr Lowe heard him say so and ordered the warders to take him back to his cell and let him lie down. MacManus and Gilroy took him by the arms to help him and on the way they met Dr Dowdall, who told them to take Ashe to the hospital. 'What happened to Thomas Ashe in five minutes at the hands of Dr Lowe?' was a question asked of MacManus at the inquest, by Tim Healy, and to it he gave the extraordinary reply: 'I am not prepared to answer.' He did not see Ashe's lips getting blue but he saw him getting weak at the finish of the feeding. While in that condition the tube was not withdrawn before the operation was finished.

Here is Dr Lowe's own account of what happened to Ashe:

I remember speaking to him; there was no force used when he came into the room. I asked him how he felt, and he replied, 'I feel well, but a bit weak.' I then took his pulse, which was steady, regular, somewhat quick, and a little weak. I was satisfied as a result that he was fit for artificial feeding. He sat in the chair, and offered no resistance whatever; the warders had not to restrain him in any way; he voluntarily opened his mouth. I passed the tube gently into his mouth, and when it passed into his throat it caused him inconvenience, so I withdrew it. The nature of the inconvenience was that he coughed slightly, and I withdrew it to enable him to clear his throat, and after that I was enabled to put the tube in without any difficulty. When I got it in and down sufficiently I asked if he felt all right, and he said 'Yes.' The food, continued Dr Lowe, consisted of a pint of milk and two eggs. It took between five and ten minutes to put the food in. 'When the feed was over, after I had withdrawn the tube, he vomited slightly.' He asked Thomas Ashe how he felt and Ashe replied, 'I am all right, but a bit weak.' … I noticed his lips were somewhat blue just when he was going to get out of the chair, when the feed concluded, said the doctor. I then told the warders to take him away, and get him lying down as quickly as possible. That was the last I saw of him.

That is Dr Lowe's testimony. How much truth is there in it? What happened in that sinister room? We may never know exactly. Stack and Lynch gave evidence to the effect that Lowe virtually rammed the tube down their throats. Was no force then used against Thomas Ashe? If not, how are we to explain the evidence of Professor McWeeney? When in the presence of other distinguished medical men he examined Thomas Ashe, he found on him, on the right side of the face, at the angle of the jaw, twelve superficial scratches, averaging half an inch in length; smaller scratches extending from the angle of the jaw to the chin; nine superficial excoriations on the chin; on the left side of the chin, an inch below the lip, a triangular excoriation three-quarters of an inch long; six or seven other point-like excoriations; in the neck, near the Adam's apple, a number of small oval-shaped excoriations; on the prominence of the thyroid another small excoriation; on the left side an excoriation an inch and a quarter in length; beyond the thyroid cartilage a semilunar depression such as would be caused by pressure of a thumbnail; and other marks.

These marks and bruises were not inflicted by Thomas Ashe on himself. They could not possibly have been caused in shaving. Ashe grew a beard in prison and was shaved in the Mater Hospital. Gregory Ashe told me that John Ashe of Kinard went with a relative to the Mater Hospital to see his brother's body, that he drew down the clothes around Thomas Ashe's neck and saw it covered with bruises and marks. What caused them? I also heard from Nora Ághas how Thomas Ashe himself, describing in the Mater Hospital what had happened, said that the food was pumped into his lungs and that he could feel it going down into them. There are Ashe's words spoken to Fathers Albert and

Augustine who saw him in the Mater about 7.45 that evening. 'I was splendid this morning until I was forcibly fed. The forcible feeding upset me completely.' Those spare and tragic words tell the story.

With the fellow feeling for each other induced by common suffering, Ashe's colleagues watched as much of the drama as could be seen from the limited range of their cells, without knowing how deadly it really was. Peter Howley saw him being helped away in a collapsed condition and feared the bad work was done.

Fionán Lynch was back in his cell after forced feeding when he saw Ashe being brought to the operating room. He shouted: 'Stick it, Tom boy!' and Ashe answered: 'I'll stick it, Finn.' Lynch recalled:

> Four or five minutes later, I saw Tom brought back by the warders, and it was quite apparent that something had gone wrong for he was unconscious and his face was quite purple. I told Stack that Ashe appeared to me to be very ill indeed, but we heard no more about him until my cell was opened next morning.

Austin Stack, recalling his experiences, said the work of forcible feeding was unpleasant for many of the warders who were decent fellows, but they had no choice.[1] But with the young doctors who were brought in from outside it was not the same thing 'and it was one of those who caused Ashe's death'. Stack himself was fed immediately after Ashe and suffered a revolting experience. He did not then know that Ashe had been removed from the operating room in a collapsed condition. Soon after Stack was brought back to his cell he was visited by Sir John Irwin who told him Ashe wished to speak to him in the prison hospital, and Stack went there with Sir John. When Stack got there he had to wait while Irwin went away on some purpose. Sir John returned after a while and brought Stack back to his cell without letting him see Ashe. He gave no explanation and Stack asked for none. He had no apprehension that there was anything seriously wrong.

27

I DIE IN A GOOD CAUSE

It was twenty to twelve noon when Dr Dowdall met the two warders taking Ashe back to his cell from the forcible feeding room. The doctor asked Ashe how he was. Thomas said he felt weak and the doctor told the warders to remove him at once to the prison hospital. Dr Dowdall was obviously alarmed at the grim turn of things. In the hospital Ashe was placed in charge of Warder Fitzpatrick, who was kind and considerate. He put Ashe in bed, propped pillows around him to make him comfortable and placed a hot jar at his feet. Dr Dowdall came in to examine him.

> I found the heart weak [wrote Dr Dowdall], the extremities some-what cold, temperature subnormal, respiration laboured, rate 32 per minute. There were *râles* (crackling sounds) over the chest, the pulse weak, the face and hands slightly cyanosed (bluish) in appearance.[1]

Dr Dowdall evidently feared the worst. He told Ashe he was very seriously ill and that he would secure his release. He asked him to take some brandy and milk. Ashe agreed to take food on the understanding that Dr Dowdall would guarantee his release. This the doctor did. He told a warder stay with him and give him brandy, milk and beef-tea every fifteen minutes. On being asked where he would like to be sent on release, Ashe told him he wished to be sent to the Mater Hospital. Did he feel fit to undertake the journey? Ashe said he did. Dr Dowdall told Father Dargan, one of the chaplains, that Mr Ashe was bad and asked him to get a bed at the Mater Hospital. In the prison hospital Joe MacDonagh, recovering from the effects of his own ill-treatment, was told about two o'clock by Father Doyle that Ashe was very ill and he would give him Extreme Unction as he was sure he was going to die.

Dr Dowdall asked Ashe if there was anyone he should wish to be communicated with. 'He mentioned a name and this I handed to the Governor.'[2] The name was that of Mícheál Ó Foghludha. This request was not granted.

C. A. Munro, the governor of Mountjoy, had, it appears, returned the day before. There were forms to be signed by himself and the doctor. It is hardly to be expected that a prison form from the hands of Thomas Ashe's jailers would reveal any hint of their behaviour towards him over the previous few weeks. For all that Prison Form 52 makes a tragic piece of reading. Here it is:

(Copy)

Form 52
A.D.
15025
1902

FORM OF REPORT BY MEDICAL OFFICER OF PRISON UNDER STANDING ORDER NO. 1.
(RULES 138 and 172 [5])

H.M. Prison Mountjoy

THE GOVERNOR

In accordance with Rule 172 (5), I have to report that I am of opinion that *the illness of prisoner Thomas Ashe may terminate fatally within a brief period and before the termination of his sentence.*

I also forward replies to the queries attached hereto.

Signature
of Medical ⎫
Officer of Prison ⎭   (SD) R. G. DOWDALL M.D.

Date 25th. September 1917.

THE CHAIRMAN,
General Prisons Board,
The above is a copy of a Report forwarded this day to the Under Secretary.
The prisoner referred to is at present on hunger strike and being artificially fed. I have so noted on the covering report to the Under Secretary.

(SD) C. A. MUNRO
Date 25th. September 1917.

QUERIES TO BE ANSWERED BY GOVERNOR

A. CRIME	Attempting to cause disaffection among the civilian population 25th. July 1917. Contrary to Reg. 42 D.R.R.
B. SENTENCE	2 years H.L. from 3.9.17 (year rem'd)
C. DATE OF CONVICTION	3:9:1917
D. DATE FROM WHICH SENTENCE TAKES EFFECT	3:9:1917

E. DATE ON WHICH
   ELIGIBLE FOR
   RELEASE OR
   REMISSION OF
   SENTENCE   5.7.1918

F. BEFORE WHOM TRIED   District Court Martial Dublin

G. IF BEFORE CONVICTED,
   FOR WHAT OFFENCE   Armed rebellion.

H. PREVIOUS CHARACTER
   AND CIRCUMSTANCE   Has a previous conviction of P.S.
                            (commuted from Death) imposed at
                            a Field General Court Martial in
                            May 1916.

SIGNATURE OF GOVERNOR (SD) C. A. MUNRO
DATE 25th SEPTEMBER 1917.

QUERIES

1. Name of Prisoner   Thomas Ashe
2. Age   31 years
3. Nature of disease   Weak heart semi collapse
4. Has the disease been caused
   by confinement in Prison?   No.
5. Has it been aggravated by
   confinement in Prison?   No.
6. State in detail the ground   The prisoner's heart is very weak.
   upon which you have arrived The respiration rapid (32 per min.)
   at the conclusion recorded   and shallow & the hands and face
   in your report on first page somewhat cyanosed.
   of this form.

270

7. What benefit would the prisoner be likely to derive by being discharged?	The case is one requiring careful watching by qualified nurses.
8. Is the prisoner in a fit state of health to be at once discharged?	Yes: the case is urgent.
9. If not, when will the prisoner be likely to be fit for discharge?	–
10. Has the prisoner any friends who are willing and able to take care of him or her? If so, give names and addresses.	–
11. Is the prisoner anxious to be discharged? or Would he or she prefer to remain in the Prison Hospital under proper Medical Treatment?	Yes.
12. Where does the prisoner intend to go if discharged?	I propose having him transferred to the Mater Hospital.
Signature of Medical Officer of Prison	(SD) R. G. DOWDALL
DATE	25th September 1917.

It will be seen that Ashe would have been due for release on 5 July 1918. Also that news of Ashe's imminent death was sent to two people who were not unconcerned with the events that brought it about, the chairman of the General Prisons Board, Max Green, and the chief secretary, Duke. The replies written in answer to queries four and five, if meant to deny that Thomas Ashe received ill-treatment in prison, have no honest value.

On another prison form entitled SICK PRISONERS UNDER CONTINUOUS TREATMENT the particulars relating to Thomas Ashe under the heading DISEASE read:

> Hunger strike
> Heart weak
> Extremities Cold
> Temp. Subnormal
> Respirn. 32 per min
> Dyspnoea
> Pulse weak & irregular
> Face and hands cyanosed

Dyspnoea in layman's language means difficulty in breathing. His condition is described under STATE by the single word 'BAD'. Written across under several headings are the words 'Reported to Govt. life in danger S. O. No. 1. Released and sent to Mater with Wr. Fitzpatrick about 5.5 [*sic*] p.m.' The entry is initialled by the Governor.

Only a short distance separates the Mater Hospital from Mountjoy prison. A few minutes after 5 p.m. Ashe was removed to the hospital in an ambulance in charge of Warder Fitzpatrick. Dr Dowdall told the ambulance men to drive slowly. A crowd had collected outside, sensing tragedy. Someone shouted: 'They have murdered Tom.' The warder tried to allay their alarms, saying he had hope yet. In the Mater Ashe was placed in Saint Raphael's Ward. Sister Lucy (Higgins) went to call the house surgeon, Dr

Patrick McKenna, who was a native of Holy Ground, Dingle, and virtually a neighbour of Ashe's. She told him a patient named Ashe had been brought in by two policemen, as she took the warders to be, and wondered could he be a son of Gregory Ashe of Minard, with whom she was at school. 'He is very like him.' It was already known to Dr McKenna that Ashe was one of the prisoners on hunger strike. He told Sister Lucy it was in fact Gregory Ashe's son and that he knew him personally although he had not seen him since 1915 when he was leading a route march of the Lusk Volunteers. Dr McKenna found Ashe fully conscious but in a state of collapse. His breathing was very difficult, his heart action weak and he felt faint with thirst. Temperature was below normal and there were signs of marked congestion in his lungs. Dr McKenna asked him when did he become ill. Ashe told him he got a fit of coughing that morning after being forcibly fed and that he then collapsed. He said that for two nights of the previous week he had slept on the floor of his cell without any covering but the clothes he wore and that he suffered intensely from the cold. He also described to him the treatment given his fellow prisoners.

To Dr McKenna one conclusion was clear as day. The authorities of Mountjoy prison had sent Thomas Ashe out to die.

Dr Martin Dempsey, visiting physician to the Mater Hospital, saw Ashe about 5.45 p.m. and did everything medical skill could do. Ashe was quite conscious and had evidently rallied slightly from the time he was admitted. Dr Dempsey on checking his condition found his pulse rapid, about one hundred to the minute, also his breathing, thirty-six per minute. On the hospital chart pulse is given as one hundred and four and respiration thirty-two. His fingers were cold and blue and his lungs showed moderate bronchitis and congestion. The heart sounds were weak but Dr Dempsey did not think them dangerously so. Though he was nervous about Ashe's condition he did not despair of it.

But Ashe was beyond the aid of medical skill, and grew steadily worse.

Silent anxious crowds packed the road in front of the Mater and pressed round the main door. A few special friends were admitted, amongst whom were the Countess Markievicz and a young man unknown yet to the general public, by whose personality Dr McKenna was much impressed, brief though their meeting was. It was Ashe's colleague, Michael Collins, who had been in touch as far as possible with every turn of the tragic drama. Ashe's friends must already have feared the worst when at 6.35 p.m. Mícheál Ó Foghludha sent a telegram to Nora at Cappamore which she received at 7.15 p.m. The message read:

TOMAS IN MATER ADVISABLE YOU COME UP TO-MORROW

MICHEAL

About a quarter-to-eight Father Albert and Father Augustine of the Capuchin Order, Church Street, came to see Ashe. Few priests had endeared themselves more to Irish hearts than they. During the fighting of Easter 1916 they ministered to the republican soldiers and gave spiritual consolation to the leaders of the Rising in their last hours. They arrived now, as it happened, to say farewell to another. They sat by Ashe's bedside for about five minutes. He was then very weak and even breathing caused him extreme distress. They asked him how he was and he told them:

'I was splendid this morning until forcibly fed. The forcible feeding upset me completely.' There were agonising pains in his back. They could see that he was dying and for that reason they did not ask him any questions but gave him their blessing. Before they left Ashe said to them: 'We made a great fight.' Father Augustine spoke to him in Irish, words of comfort that have been uttered from time immemorial by the Irish hearthstone: 'God is good and He has a good Mother' and Ashe replied in Irish: 'Yes, indeed. Father.' That is about his last recorded utterance.

Outside the crowds waited. Amongst them was Ashe's comrade of the Dublin quaysides, Sean O'Casey, who caught the sense of the hour in memorable prose. The minutes ticked painfully by. St Raphael's Ward was hushed and quiet, but for the murmur of prayer. Ashe could hardly speak any more. A burning soreness scorched his throat. He could not swallow at all. His lungs filled with water, oedema the doctors called it. The final notation on the night nurse's chart is 9.50 p.m. After that there was no more to say. He died about half-past-ten. Father Murray was there to give him the last rites. His end was happy. His features settled calmly in the repose of death, and his friends saw no more his grave and beautiful smile.

Someone brought the news to the waiting crowds. They prayed and then melted quietly into Dublin's streets, with hearts full of grief and other thoughts.

It was only a short few weeks since Ashe had written to Kathleen Monks the letter in which he said: '"Let me carry Your Cross for Ireland, Lord", that's my prayer – join with me that I may carry it with honour.' He had no idea then how soon he would be called on to carry it to the consummation of the grave. He had borne his burden with fortitude and honour. It is suitable to give here the poem 'Let Me Carry Your Cross for Ireland, Lord,' which he wrote in the solitude of Lewes prison and is a statement of his patriotic credo, expressed with the stark and primal simplicity of the psalmist.

LET ME CARRY YOUR CROSS FOR IRELAND, LORD

Let me carry your Cross for Ireland, Lord!
The hour of her trial draws near,
And the pangs and the pains of the sacrifice
May be borne by comrades dear.
But, Lord, take me from the offering throng,
There are many far less prepared,
Though anxious and all as they are to die
That Ireland may be spared.

Let me carry your Cross for Ireland, Lord!
My cares in this world are few,
And few are the tears will fall for me
When I go on my way to You.
Spare, oh! spare to their loved ones dear
The brother and son and sire,
That the cause we love may never die
In the land of our heart's desire.

Let me carry your Cross for Ireland, Lord!
Let me suffer the pain and the shame,
I bow my head to their rage and hate,
And I take on myself the blame.
Let them do with my body whate'er they will,
My spirit I offer to You,
That the faithful few who heard her call
May be spared to Róisín Dubh.

Let me carry your Cross for Ireland, Lord!
For Ireland weak with tears,
For the aged man of the clouded brow,
And the child of the tender years;
For the empty homes of her golden plains;
For the hopes of her future, too!
Let me carry your Cross for Ireland, Lord,
For the cause of Róisín Dubh.

28

THE FUNERAL
OF THOMAS ASHE

Early the night Thomas Ashe died, his cousin, Sheila Devane (Mrs Sheila Gunning), who was his only relative within call, hurried at Dr McKenna's request to the Mater Hospital and was admitted to the ward to see him. This was a few hours before he died. She saw British soldiers all over the place. Ashe was still their prisoner. With his death they withdrew, leaving in the possession of his countrymen the dead body of Thomas Ashe. Almost imperceptibly, the Irish Volunteers took control. They posted guards at various points within the hospital and in its neighbourhood. His soldier comrades of Fingal, who had been summoned to the duty of guarding their dead leader, stood to attention, under arms, four at a time, to be changed at regular intervals. It is one of the sorrowful memories of Volunteer John Devine of Lusk that he was one of the last four to keep vigil over his leader's remains. Ashe was dressed in his Volunteer officer's uniform and laid out on a hospital bed. Sister Juliana recalls combing back his auburn hair. 'He was such a handsome young man, with lovely hair. He looked beautiful.'

It is not easy to describe in words the traumatic effect of Thomas Ashe's death. There was a sense of irreparable loss. It seemed as if a harrowing personal tragedy had occurred to each individual, so universally was it felt. Standing in O'Connell Street the day of Ashe's funeral, Douglas Goldring heard a woman near him say: 'Ah, they always kill the ones we love best,' and turned to see her face writhing with grief. She spoke for all. To Paddy Doyle of Lusk, who fought under him at Ashbourne, the loss was something that time has never healed, and today Paddy, now seventy-four years of age, asks, half to himself, half to the world: 'Why the hell did he go and die at all? We never knew how good a man we had till he went and died.' For him, as for many a man who admired Ashe, the blow remains unhealed and unsoftened.

Ashe's old colleague in De La Salle, Andrew Keaveney, who was teaching in Loughglynn, County Roscommon, remembers the day. He had not yet heard the news when he saw a neighbour, a farmer he was, coming towards him deeply agitated. He could hardly speak. At last he blurted out: 'Tom Ashe is dead.' He was overcome with emotion. Such sorrow was typical. Throughout Fingal, which had a closer bond with Ashe than any place in Ireland, grief was unrestrained. To talk to the people there who knew him and were moved by his death is to learn the fact that nothing could ever compensate for their loss, as with words and gesture they recall what he was like and what he meant to them, and with their vivid memories all but bring him to life again. The news filtered in to Mountjoy. Fionán Lynch and Peter Howley had seen Ashe being carried away on the Tuesday morning in a state of collapse. They heard no more until next morning. A friendly warder opened Lynch's cell door and whispered that Ashe had died in the Mater the night before. Lynch sent the tragic news to Austin Stack and they took counsel what to do:

We both then agreed that we should not give up our hunger-strike until our complete demands were granted, though the demands made by us were, for that time, revolutionary in the extreme, and were really intended as a basis for bargaining. During the day, the news of Ashe's death spread from cell to cell and the Brennans and all the other prisoners agreed that we should not surrender now until every demand was conceded. The effect of Tom Ashe's death on the prisoners was to harden their attitude against any compromise.[1]

The forcible feeding was actually continued for some days longer. Only on the night before the funeral did the authorities yield and then from no motives of altruism but from alarm at the rising tide of public anger.

Thomas Ashe's death changed the mood and mind of Ireland almost overnight. Sensitive to public opinion, the popular daily press now expressed itself in terms which a short time before would be unthought of. By no stretch of the imagination could it be said that *The Freeman's Journal* was other than hostile to the cause for which Ashe stood. Yet it could write like this the morning after he died:

> … his death will make a painful impression. It will greatly increase the flood of bitterness which was the legacy of the Maxwell regime to Ireland … The passions that it will rekindle and arouse needed no fresh fuel to keep them burning and the tragedy is a most deplorable climax to a long course of official obstinacy and callousness … The effect upon Irish and Irish-American feeling will be most serious and grave … There must be a hidden malignant and malevolent influence somewhere in the government of Ireland, whether in the War Cabinet or the Castle, determined that Ireland shall not have peace in freedom and that there shall be no reconciliation between the British and the Irish peoples. Intelligence might defeat such malignancy and

malevolence, but intelligence is the last thing one looks for to the present Government.

The comment quoted above represents fairly enough that major segment of the nationalist press which looked askance until then at republicans.

It is recorded by Stephen Gwynn that John Redmond had time and again appealed to Chief Secretary Duke to grant political status to the prisoners and predicted tragedy unless he did, but Duke, who might have been expected to listen to Redmond with some favour, was to be moved by nobody from carrying out his government's wishes and so the tragic prophecy went on to be fulfilled. How many of those who had followed Redmond now transferred their allegiance to the cause of the dead man is not easy to estimate, but that a massive transfer of support and sympathy did take place was indicated by the size of the funeral and the radically changing mood of the press and public bodies. People remembered that Sir Edward Carson had uttered rebel sentiments not unlike those of Thomas Ashe. So did people contrast the treatment which brought Sir Edward high into the councils of the British government and brought Thomas Ashe to his death. They drew the obvious moral, which was grim in its implications.

On his death the poets of Ireland rallied to the cause and praise of Thomas Ashe. Not the much anthologised and trumpeted poets, but the heirs of Blind Raftery and Owen Rua, the ballad and song makers who responded to the fervour of the hour in the Gaelic tradition and proclaimed the grief of Ireland over his bier. The surging emotions of the time were finely recorded by his comrade Sean O'Casey with ballad and with touching prose in 'Lament for Thomas Ashe' and *The Sacrifice of Thomas Ashe*, and long years later in the magnificent *Inishfallen Fare Thee Well*. The ballads written about Ashe would fill a volume. The country and regional newspapers of Ireland, innumerable broadsheets, magazines, leaflets and anonymous handbills carried verses in his memory. The ballads-men wrought into their lines the passion of their country's experience. The masses of people that crowded into Dublin to pay final tribute to the man that was Thomas Ashe bear testimony, thousands of times over, to the anguish that racked Ireland in her bereavement.

His body was removed for solemn requiem Mass to the Pro-Cathedral in Marlborough Street and from there to the City Hall to lie in state until the day of his funeral, which was appointed to be Sunday 30 September. An armed guard of uniformed Irish Volunteers kept vigil as thousands of his countrymen entered to pay their respects and say a prayer for his soul. The funeral arrangements were taken in charge by the Wolfe Tone Memorial Association under the presidency of Seán McGarry. Announcements were published at the weekend indicating to the country and city organisations expected to arrive where they were to assemble in order to take their places in the procession.

No special trains were run that weekend for the benefit of the great crowds expected to converge on Dublin. As on the occasion of Rossa's funeral, two years earlier, the railway companies were notoriously unhelpful. But no absence of transport could prevent the people coming in thousands from south, west and north when their hearts willed to be in Dublin to say farewell to Thomas Ashe. Soldiers and civilians, old men and young, girls and women, they came to throng the city streets, quietly and decorously. Two hundred Irish Volunteers travelled from Kerry on the Saturday. A contingent was said to have travelled on foot from Athlone. They came from the farthest glens and parishes.

To this day the occasion of Thomas Ashe's funeral is recalled in West Kerry as it is in Fingal. Families will mention with pride that one or more of their household journeyed to Dublin to take part in it, having risen in the small hours to walk, or cycle, or go by horse-cart to the nearest railway station. They gathered from early Sunday morning in the streets around the City Hall. Each organisation, trade union, public body and group had its appointed meeting place. Morning trains to the city were packed to the limit. The roads leading to Dublin were crowded with people, some of whom walked twenty or thirty miles to the city. All kinds of transport were called into use, cars, carriages, outside cars, brakes, bicycles, wagonettes, traps and gigs. Trade unions turned out in immense force. Eight thousand mustered under Tom Foran in Essex and Exchange Streets, six thousand more at Wood Quay, four thousand more in Werburgh and Bride Streets. Nine thousand Irish Volunteers assembled, marching with order and precision to their allotted places. There was much admiring comment on their smartness and discipline. Most were in full uniform.

Dublin City Hall is located on the rising terrain of Cork Hill, close to the heart of the old metropolis. On either side of it, a short distance away, there is a gateway giving access to Dublin Castle, which sprawled over many acres behind it and housed for centuries the central system of British administration in Ireland. A principal act in the process that made that administration powerless was now being carried out, quietly, on its doorstep and there was nothing on earth it dared do about it. Its officials cannot have looked with easy minds on the multitudes that were gathering without its gates. The previous night it had announced the concession of their full political rights to the comrades of the dead man in Mountjoy. But those crowds coming in from the country were alarming. Their restraint, quietness and discipline boded something. There can have been little comfort felt that weekend in the fortress at the rear of the City Hall.

Tens of thousands of people had come to see Thomas Ashe lying in state before the City Hall was closed to the public at noon on Sunday. Only relatives, clergy and close friends remained inside. They knelt beside the coffin and prayed. At ten minutes to two, six uniformed Volunteers, companions of the dead man in Lewes jail, brought the coffin out to the waiting hearse, while the dense crowd of people stood with bared heads. Masses of flowers and wreaths were placed in the hearse all around the coffin. Many more were heaped on a dray behind. The coffin was covered with the republican flag, made of Irish poplin, the gift of Countess Markievicz to the obsequies of Thomas Ashe. (On the fiftieth anniversary of the Easter Rising this flag was presented by Nora Ághas to Áras Thomáis Ághas, the central office of the Gaelic League at 6 Harcourt Street.) The close-packed crowds stood to reverent attention. Stewarding was carried out by Fianna and Volunteers. There were police on the streets but merely as onlookers. The funeral wound up through Lord Edward Street and Christ Church Place with a long line of carriages containing the mourners following the hearse. The lord mayor with his chaplain occupied one. Count Plunkett occupied another. Conspicuous in the procession was the motor car, with blinds drawn, of His Grace Most Rev. Dr Walsh, Archbishop of Dublin. He had written to the lord mayor:

I feel it a duty to take part in the public protest that will find expression in the funeral. Kindly say to what place I should send my car, so that it can most conveniently find its place in the procession.

Not since 1861 had an archbishop been publicly associated with a Fenian funeral and that was in distant New York where Archbishop Hughes delivered his famous panegyric over the remains of Terence Bellew MacManus, the 1848 rebel whose funeral to Ireland was organised by the IRB. Dr Walsh's secretary marched with the crowd. He was one of the two hundred priests who took part in the procession. Some had come long distances. Practically every religious order in the country was represented. Near three score years had gone by since the bleak November afternoon when the body of Terence MacManus was borne through Dublin's streets to Glasnevin. Three or four priests attended, conspicuous among them Father Patrick Lavelle from John MacHale's archdiocese, who followed his coffin to the graveside to bless his burial in Irish clay. A great and important part of modern Ireland's history is manifested in its republican funerals. The large body of priests who walked in the funeral of Thomas Ashe, chief of the IRB, showed the depth of the revolution that had taken place. His old friend Father Togher of Lusk was there, and so was Father Hoey. There, too, were the noted priests of the Capuchin Order, Fathers Augustine, Albert and Aloysius. Some twelve bands marched, of which the Raven Pipers occupied foremost place. The procession passed through Thomas Street and by the place in front of St Catherine's Church where Robert Emmet died, turned right into Bridgefoot Street, crossed Queen Street Bridge to the northern quays and proceeded to Bachelor's Walk and O'Connell Street.

The funerals of Rossa and MacManus had each gone by different routes to this, but once they reached O'Connell Street they all went the familiar way northward through O'Connell Street, North Frederick and Blessington Streets, North Circular Road, Phibsboro and Finglas Roads to the cemetery. Mountjoy prison, heavily guarded, was passed in death-like silence. Marching quickly, four deep, it took the procession an hour and a half, and at some places longer, to pass a given point, with the order of movement perfect and unbroken throughout. Republican flags, draped with mourning crepe, were displayed all along the route, while everyone in the procession wore the republican colours. Blinds were drawn in almost every window. Conspicuous in the funeral were the members of the Dublin fire brigade wearing uniform and displaying the rebel colours. Thousands of young women and girls, including a company of little school children, took part. Countess Markievicz, in full uniform, with revolver at belt, headed a detachment of the Citizen Army. Each group carried its own standard, the trade union organisations being particularly impressive with their picturesque banners and flags. Numbers of soldiers in khaki watched with interest, the puzzled expressions on their faces showing plainly that they did not understand.

On each side of the hearse, a uniformed firing party marched in single file, with rifles reversed, while an officer with drawn sword followed behind. This was an act in defiance of the government's laws. There was open drilling, military orders were given and obeyed, arms were carried, Volunteers and pipe-band uniforms were worn, republican flags, favours and banners were flourished throughout the city. The newspapers commented on the military splendour and precision of the funeral. All these things the law forbade. But that day no government dared interfere.

About four o'clock the hearse reached Glasnevin Cemetery where the remains were received by Father James Fitzgibbon and borne to the graveside by six ex-prisoners of Lewes. The grave was near those of the great pioneers of the IRB – O'Leary, Stephens and Rossa – near also to Ashe's valiant colleague of the Volunteers and Gaelic League, The O'Rahilly. The burial service was recited, the coffin lowered and the grave was filled in, amidst silence and profound emotion. The inscription on the coffin read:

Tomás Ághas
Ceannard, Co. Chiarraighe
Taoiseach ar Arm Phoblachta na hÉireann
d'fhulaing bás ar son a Thíre
An 25° lá de Mheadhón Fhóghmhair 1917
Ar aos a 32 bliana
I Ríoghacht na Naomh go raibh a anam.

There followed a brief silence. It was broken by a sharp word of command from a young Volunteer officer, in vice-commandant's uniform, who was seen to be Michael Collins. The firing party, which had been standing by with arms reversed, brought their rifles to the ready at a word from Captain Liam Clarke, and three volleys crashed into the stillness over Thomas Ashe's grave. Fianna Éireann buglers sounded the Last Post. Michael Collins stepped forward and spoke. He uttered a few words in Irish which nobody was alert enough to record. He said in English:

Nothing additional remains to be said. That volley which we have

287

just heard is the only speech which it is proper to make above the grave of a dead Fenian.

That brief speech over the freshly covered grave of Thomas Ashe carried a significant note of determination and challenge.

Slowly and with perfect orderliness and decorum the crowds dispersed into Dublin and thence gradually home to all parts of Ireland.

'Where the prince or chief may be found whose remains so many people would follow to burial is something I myself cannot tell,' wrote Father Patrick Dinneen, who appreciated Ashe's scholarship in the Irish language. 'He was a man that was earnest in his life.'[2] Father Dinneen went on to reflect with sorrow that the loss of great men suffered in Easter Week was renewed in the tragedy of Thomas Ashe.

The thoughts of the quiet and academic Father Dinneen were shared by his countrymen. That day the nation set the seal of its approval on the cause for which Ashe stood and for which he had died. This latest deed of the administration served by Maxwell aroused the most robust feelings of protest and resistance. The young men of Ireland who came to Dublin to march behind the coffin and saw their strength and sensed the meaning of that hushed September afternoon returned to their homes with minds steeled by their experience. The doing to death of Thomas Ashe was a major act of hostility to the Irish republican cause. The treatment which resulted in death for the victor of Ashbourne produced a temper which hardened into the national resistance of 1919–21. Signs of that hardship were clear enough in the challenge uttered by the leaders of republican Ireland.

Speaking in the City Hall the night after the funeral, William Cosgrave said:

> The last headline that he gave to humanity was the basis of his life-time: 'My Lord Mayor, if I die it is in a good cause.' The empire of his genius, his courage and his tenacity shall outlive the Empire of wealth and power and despotism which has deprived Ireland of one of her most valiant sons.[3]

The day of the funeral Éamon de Valera addressed a great meeting in O'Connell Square, Ennis, and his words have been reported as follows:

> Dreamers were they who asked them to be loyal to the Constitution which was responsible for Tom Ashe's death. But he would ask them to be loyal to Ireland, and to be true and honest to the flag that that day was unfortunately draped for Tom Ashe ... His death would tell the world the spirit that was left in Irishmen, and it would tell the world that nothing but freedom would satisfy the Irish people, and that they were ready to perish, one after the other, rather than submit to be conquered.[4]

Most of all was the temper of Young Ireland reflected and forecast in that speech, of classic pith and brevity, which was delivered at his graveside by his friend Michael Collins. It carried a message that boded no good for the government that had encompassed Thomas Ashe's death. There was confidence, warning and battle in it.

The occasion gave the republican movement an opportunity to appraise its potential support in the country. It is dealt with at length here, because in circumstances where a small nation is kept unfree against its will by a large and powerful one, the manner of its moral protest calls for more than ordinary attention. The funeral of Thomas Ashe was a moral protest of intense depth.

As a supplement to this chapter it may serve to give extracts here from three published utterances, out of a great number which show the feelings that pervaded Ireland on Thomas Ashe's death. The first two are taken from the leading articles of the two principal daily papers. The third appeared in a weekly review over the name of a distinguished man of letters.

The *Irish Independent* of 1 October 1917:

THE COUNTRY'S PROTEST

Dublin was yesterday a City of almost universal mourning for the late Mr Thomas Ashe. It is no exaggeration to say that as regards dimensions the funeral procession from the City Hall to Glasnevin has not been surpassed by any similar display for more than a generation. It was generally admitted that it was large and even more impressive than the funeral of Parnell ... Never has more heartfelt grief and sympathy been exhibited in the streets of the Capital.

The Freeman's Journal, 1 October 1917:

SURRENDER OR SANITY

... The unprecedented scenes at the funeral of Thomas Ashe yesterday conveyed a message and a warning which no Government, however blind, could misread. It was not only a tribute of sympathy with the victim of insensate methods of barbarism, but a direct challenge to the whole spirit of a latter-day English policy in Ireland.

That challenge was backed, not by Sinn Féiners alone, but by every Nationalist whose belief in Nationalism is a reality. If Great Britain has no other remedy for Irish ills than the ruthless application of the mailed fist, she must expect not meek submission, but uncompromising opposition. Irishmen who hold that Prussianism is the greatest danger that threatens civilisation are not to be tricked into agreeing that it can only be killed in Germany by establishing a new and worse variety of the monstrous phenomenon in this country ... the tragedy of Mountjoy proved to be the breaking point. The death of Thomas Ashe has ranged a united Ireland against the continuance of an impossible system, and already the defenders of the system are making signals of distress.

New Ireland, 6 October 1917:

HIS SOUL GOES MARCHING ON

... Today strong men weep in the streets when they talk of the suffering of Thomas Ashe. Today Dublin witnessed perhaps the greatest manifestation of public regret that Ireland has yet known. And because this is so we are sure that the future of Ireland is secure. The soul of Ireland is stirred as it has been many times before by a superb act of devotion to the national ideal. And Ireland will respond. Ireland will follow where Thomas Ashe has led. The tremendous potency of passive resistance to alien government has been demonstrated. The policy of passive resistance has had its first great victory and at the same time its first martyr. The great French historian, Michelet, says that the world does not brood very long on the myriads who fall by the sword in battle, but the spectacle of one man unjustly hunted down may establish a cause and herald a new order. The history of the world is full of such cases, the history of our own country affords us a long succession of sacrifices, and by each sacrifice has Ireland been spurred on to the attainment of that national freedom which is our goal and our ideal. 'If I die it will be in a good cause,' said Thomas Ashe before he died, and in practically the same words has every Irish patriot spoken throughout the centuries. The cause of human freedom is a good cause; there is none better; and in our case the cause of human freedom is the freedom of our country, the freedom of ourselves. We cannot afford to be generous before we are just, and justice demands the freedom of Ireland ... slowly, we are filing away our bars and fetters; it is a tiring work; many have died of it, and perhaps many more are fated to die at it, but on the work must go. In the great work we are fortified by the spirit of those that have gone. The completion of the work devolves upon us who live, so long as we live we must carry it on; it is our great heritage. With the death of Thomas Ashe we have marked another great milestone ... The spirit of Thomas Ashe, his enthusiasm, his devotion, his courage and his determination will certainly quicken the pace of his onwards march towards a decisive victory. What a spirit was his, what fidelity, what nobility! And each and every one of us must be prepared to do what he did. We may fail. Not to everyone is given such great qualities. But at least we must be prepared to try. By all and every means must the holy cause of Irish freedom be advanced; 'But righteous men must make our land a nation,' said Davis. A righteous man was Thomas Ashe in all conscience, and in following his footsteps we shall not go wrong ... May he rest in peace.

Andrew E. Malone.

29

THE VERDICT OF A JURY

An inquest into the death of Thomas Ashe was opened in the Mater Hospital on Thursday 27 September by the city coroner, Dr Louis A. Byrne. It was resumed on the following day at the Coroner's Court, where it continued until its conclusion. It developed into a long and dramatic inquiry, eleven days in all, which, owing to adjournments, did not end until 1 November.

It drew widespread public attention, because of the circumstances of Thomas Ashe's death, his eminence as a republican nationalist and the intense public grief manifested at his funeral. The Coroner's Court was packed every day. The factors and events relating to his death were brought into discussion, the circumstances were probed as thoroughly as possible and light was shed on some very dark doings of the prison authorities. Material evidence of primary importance was withheld, on the plea of privilege, by the Prison Board in a wholly unadmirable manner.

The legal personnel in the case were, for the next of kin, Tim Healy, KC, MP, and Joseph Dixon (instructed by R. J. Duggan), and, for the prison authorities, Henry Hanna, KC (instructed by Chief Crown Solicitor H. A. Wynne). Mr Wynne also appeared for S. H. Douglas, secretary of the Prison Board.

A word is necessary about the chief legal personalities. Henry Hanna was a lawyer of distinction who later became a High Court judge of Saorstát Éireann.

Timothy Michael Healy was an experienced politician. Elected in 1880 to the House of Commons as a member of Parnell's nationalist party, he had given valuable service in that capacity. He could speak with special authority on land law. His patriotism, at times controversial, always had a salty and individualist flavour. Not uncritical of his chief, he became estranged from him at the split and in the heat of difference he uttered some unfortunate and hurtful rhetoric. A skilled parliamentarian, he earned the admiration of O'Donovan Rossa for his scorching assaults in the Commons on members of British governments and no endearment from the rueful occupants of Saxon benches. He was a critic now and for many a long year of John Redmond's Irish Party. His learning in the law was formidable. His skill at cross-examination could be terrifying. There is a cartoon by Grace Plunkett showing him with an unfortunate witness, shrunk to pygmy size, impaled by him on a fork. Such could be the effect of his unfriendly cross-examination.

He was no supporter of the British government. When Thomas Ashe's friends looked round for a man who could probe the circumstances of his death without fear or favour they considered Tim Healy would be a suitable choice. Batt O'Connor was one of the republican group who went to ask him take up the case. At first Healy pleaded pressure of business. To his query whether Batt O'Connor's group represented the IRB the answer was 'Yes.' This answer appeared to influence Tim Healy's decision at once. Since the land wars, he can hardly have been unconversant with the power of the IRB. He agreed. The result was that he performed one of the most striking services of his career in his exposure of the conditions under which Thomas Ashe died. It may well have been one of the factors which later made him acceptable to the Irish Free State government for the post of governor-general.

The jury consisted of a foreman and sixteen men chosen by the police, on the instructions of the coroner, from the neighbourhood in which the tragedy happened. The coroner decided that owing to the importance of the case a specialist should be called in to perform the post-mortem examination. Accordingly Professor McWeeney, pathologist at the National University and the Mater Hospital, was sent for. The attorney-general, for his part, sent instructions to Sir Thomas Myles and Sir Arthur Chance to be present on behalf of the crown. Professor McWeeney carried out the post-mortem in the Mater on the morning of 26 September and stated in his evidence that the cause of death was heart failure and congestion of the lungs. Sir Arthur Chance and Sir Thomas Myles agreed. Thus three of the most distinguished men in the medical profession formed one and the same opinion. In the course of the inquiry Dr Dowdall alone contested it, putting forward the view that death was due to a weak heart and starvation.

Tim Healy asked Sir Arthur Chance during cross-examination:

Do you approve of the action of the Medical Officer for Mountjoy prison in administering forcible feeding to Mr Thomas Ashe with the knowledge that he had been left in the body of the jail for 48 hours without bed, bedding, without clothes, without a seat to sit on, and standing in a cold cell?

Sir Arthur replied:

I don't approve of the treatment meted out to Mr Thomas Ashe. I do not like apportioning responsibility as between one officer and another. I do not approve of this treatment.

Brief as it was, that statement, from a specialist representing the attorney-general, created a profound impression. It was, however, only one item in the mass of evidence that mounted up against the prison authorities as the inquiry proceeded. The prison authorities tried to defend, even to justify, their conduct. Their efforts were in vain. The incisive thrusts of Healy's cross-examination cut their defence to ribbons. Their façade of self-justification crumbled as fact after fact accumulated against them. Healy wrote to his brother Maurice on 13 October:

> Without having a scrap of information when we began, I have driven the prison authorities from pillar to post.

Six days later he wrote again:

> At the Ashe inquest we have twisted the Jail officials into a black knot.

So they had.

Vital testimony was given by the lord mayor. Following a legal request by Healy, four of Ashe's prison colleagues were admitted to attend court to give evidence: Austin Stack, Fionán Lynch, Joseph MacDonagh and Philip MacMahon. What they had to say added materially to the factual picture that was placed before the inquiry.

There were certain official documents bearing on the treatment of Thomas Ashe which might have shed an important light on the circumstances of his death. The crown, on behalf of the prison authorities, pleaded that they were privileged documents and refused to let the court see them. Mr H. A. Wynne showed a letter from the chairman of the Prisons Board stating that the production of certain measures, letters and minutes of the Board would be 'prejudicial and injurious to the public service of his Majesty' and they would not be given to the court.

The chairman of the Prisons Board was Max S. Green. As the son-in-law of the parliamentary leader John Redmond he was projected into special prominence. He was called on to give evidence and was cross-examined by Healy. To all questions he pleaded privilege and declined to give information. Healy asked whether he gave the governor of Mountjoy directions, contrary to the prison rules, to remove the bed, bedding, bedclothes, sheets and boots of the deceased Thomas Ashe. By reason of privilege he did not have to answer. The effect thus created by the Prisons Board in withholding evidence was very bad. The jury reacted dramatically. They handed the coroner a statement, signed by the foreman and all sixteen members, expressing their surprise that members of the Board seemed to have the power to prevent vital evidence being given. They stated that they would like to hear from the Board's members, from S. H. Douglas, likewise from Chief Secretary Duke and the under-secretary.

It is through no desire on our part that we were summoned on this jury [the document went on], and we are as anxious as anybody can be to get back to our business; but, being concerned to ascertain the cause of Mr Ashe's death, we think it extraordinary that the

Government, having brought us jurors here for this purpose, should now prevent us getting the information necessary to enable us to discharge our duty properly.

The jury's request was made on 18 October. The court sent it on to the Chief Secretary and adjourned the inquest until 29 October. By that time Duke's reply, dated at London, 26 October, was available. It stated that there were no documents under his control which ought in the public interest to be produced. It was a blank refusal. The inquiry proceeded.

It should be said that Thomas Ashe's death was still under the court's consideration when, on 23 October in the House of Commons, the chief secretary, who refused to show documents pertaining to it, took it upon himself to give his own version of events, quite different from the facts, and his own verdict, in contempt of coroner, court and jury:

These prisoners [he stated, meaning the republican prisoners at Mountjoy] had made application for special treatment, and before it had been dealt with they organised a prison mutiny and resorted again ... to violence of the same kind which was used in Lewes jail. Events occurred of most sinister and melancholy omen with regard to the situation in Dublin. A hunger strike took place, and an athletic young fellow reduced himself to a condition in which he died from failure of the heart and trouble in the lungs after forcible feeding.

The behaviour of the chief secretary was brought to the jury's attention by Joe Dixon, deputising for Tim Healy, on the last day of the inquiry, 1 November. Dr Byrne, the coroner, reviewed the evidence and told the jury he required from them a verdict as to the cause of death. They might add a rider if they wished. The jury, which had sat there day after day, observing the witnesses, listening to statement, question and answer, noting everything, retired to consider their verdict. This they brought in after an absence of some sixty minutes. It was unanimous.

It is unlikely that the jury included a republican; it is probable enough that some of its members were not nationalist at all. What their private political convictions were we do not know. But they recorded a verdict in accordance with what they had seen and heard. Nationalist or not, unionist or not, the verdict they returned was one of the most significant moral acts ever performed in the unlevering of British control over Ireland. Let it be noted once again that it was the police who selected the members of the jury. In the annals of jurydom their verdict stands as a signal victory of conscience. For the circumstances and importance of that verdict the men who composed the jury deserve to have their identities placed in this study of Thomas Ashe. They will be found in an appendix. This is their verdict:

We find that the deceased, Thomas Ashe, according to the medical evidence of Professor McWeeney, Sir Arthur Chance, and Sir Thomas Myles, died of heart failure and congestion of the lungs on September 25 and that his death was caused by the punishment of taking away from his cell his bed, bedding and boots, and being left to lie on the cold floor for fifty hours, and then being subjected to forcible feeding in his weak condition, after a hunger-strike of five or six days. We censure the Castle authorities for not having acted promptly, especially when the grave condition of the deceased and other prisoners was brought under their notice on the previous Saturday by the Lord Mayor and Sir John Irwin; and find that the hunger-strike was adopted against the inhuman punishment inflicted, and as a protest against their being treated as criminals after they demanded to be treated as political prisoners in the first division. We condemn forcible or mechanical feeding as an inhuman and dangerous operation, and say it should be discontinued. We find that the assistant doctor that was called in, having had no previous practice in such operations, administered forcible feeding unskilfully; and that the taking away of the deceased's bed, bedding and boots was an unfeeling and barbarous act. And we censure the Deputy Governor for violating the prison rules and inflicting punishment which he had no power to do. We infer that he was acting under instructions from the Prisons Board at the Castle, which refused to give evidence and documents asked for. We tender our sympathy to the relatives of the deceased in this sad and tragic occurrence.

The press of 8 October announced that concessions, amounting to full political or prisoner-of-war treatment, had been granted to the prisoners in Mountjoy. The victory had cost a young and brilliant life.

30

THOMAS ASHE:
MAN AND HERITAGE

Thomas Ashe's portrait holds pride of place in the headquarters of the Gaelic League, 6 Harcourt Street, and the splendidly proportioned main room within the building is named in his honour Áras Thomáis Ághas. The identification thereby acknowledged of Thomas Ashe with one of Ireland's primary ideals is the most natural thing in the world. Immediately after his death, when steps were taken by his friends to perpetuate his memory, there was no question as to the most fitting way in which it might be done. An announcement published and signed by Eoin MacNeill, president of the Gaelic League, and other leaders of the organisation, stated that Thomas Ashe, whose loyalty to Ireland had brought him to the grave, would be commemorated by a monument worthy of his ideals:

> The Coiste Gnótha of the Gaelic League, that claims the honour of having originally called forth the exercise of his great powers for good, has decided to erect in the National Capital a hall, to be called Áras Thomáis Ághas, where the Irish ideals that were his will be promoted, the Irish language and Irish music will resound, Irish social life will be restored unfettered and unspoilt, and where visitors in sympathy with his principles, whether they come from the provinces or the lands beyond the wave, will be ever assured of an Irish welcome …

It is for us who have survived him to lose no time in raising a Memorial worthy of his fame and worthy of the Ireland for which he lived and died.

The result was that 14 Parnell Square was acquired by the Gaelic League, named in his honour, and served as headquarters of the organisation until about the middle of the last decade. Then, in 1966, by a generous inspiration, the government presented the fine building at 6 Harcourt Street to the Gaelic League for its headquarters. Once the residence of Cardinal Newman, again the centre of intellectual and resurgent Sinn Féin, the building now has the name of Thomas Ashe added to its other historic associations. It is, however, a monument of brick and stone, like many such that are named after him across the face of Ireland. His real monument is of the mind and spirit. The name of Thomas Ashe has become synonymous with what is elevated in Irish tradition, its chivalry, scholarship and endeavour. Representing the Gaelic ideal, his name is a powerful and pervasive influence throughout Ireland. Sean O'Casey, who knew him well, wrote of Thomas Ashe: 'The Irish language opened to him the inner secret and enchanted recesses of the Irish nature, and he understood Ireland as none but the Irish speaker can understand her.'[1]

We quote another passage that speaks finely for Ashe's ideals from the leading article of Arthur Griffith's weekly *Nationality*, 6 October 1917, written when his death was recent and the perception of his ideal was urgent:

Let Ireland build a memorial to him which will ensure the ideals that possessed him. Long we knew Thomas Ashe as a pioneer of

Irish-Ireland. No month passed for years in which he did not come to discuss and try to plan ways and means with us for reviving that language which was his own, and he kept, which is our own, and we have lost. In Lewes Prison, his comrades tell us, he kept up the same enthusiasm, and spent the recreation hours instructing fellow-prisoners in their own tongue. Here is a monument Ireland – Young Ireland – can raise him ... Let them learn the Irish language – the language in which Ashe was cradled, which he loved, and which is the surest bulwark of our nationality. If when the spring comes again to the earth a quarter of a million men and women who today speak none but the language of Ashe's destroyers speak, however indifferently, the language of the gallant Irishman whose death has moved every heart, then they will have raised a memorial to Thomas Ashe the noblest he could desire, making him in death triumphant – potent in the grave. Between us and national annihilation stands the Irish language. Thomas Ashe realised this, and worked to secure its permanence. Let the life and death of Ashe inspire today those whose hearts are sore with indignation to vow that each one individually will raise to his memory the living monument of the Irish language.[2]

He has been called Ashe the romantic and it is true to say that he was fully sensitive to the music and splendour of life. To this side of his make-up may be traced to some degree his fine strain of idealism. The kilted pipers marching to a North County Dublin hosting with the great Viking banner streaming in the air, their leader striding in front, was an outward expression of the poetry and pageantry that Ashe would wish to see flourish as a normal part of the Irish pattern. But there was nothing imprecise or unrealistic about his romanticism. It was balanced by an awareness that would prompt him to comment on certain spurious aspects of Irish life in ways that were, as recorded, acid and pungent enough.

In a letter from prison, Ashe wondered whether Ireland would ever see against the skyline any factories of industry other than brewing and distilling. It was a thought born of his wish for a thriving and busy country. He put his trust in hard work and self-reliance. He believed no country ever won its prosperity without the sweat of toil. A hard worker himself, he used to send soil samples from the Kinard farm for testing to the Agricultural College, Glasnevin, to find out its qualities and deficiencies and the types of crop it suited best. So he would urge his own family, as they were industrious workers, to seek for progress and improvement at every opportunity. He was no theorist but a practical man, close to the land, aware of its problems as well as its resources.

If Thomas Ashe's spiritual character has been emphasised in this book it is because it was of such paramount influence in his life. It gave him his strong soul and indomitable will. His poems and correspondence throw into relief this primary quality of his mind. But it was part of his interior life and not for display. It is possible that by stressing it to the exclusion of his other human qualities the real man might be lost to view. For Thomas Ashe was very much a man's man. He liked a drink and a smoke. He enjoyed dancing and the gaiety of social life. He liked mixing with people, yarns, the exchange of chat and banter. He could flash into anger. He did when occasion required use robust language.

The question occurs: was he in love with Nellie McAllister? In his first letter from Dartmoor (24 May 1916) to his sister his references to her would suggest that he was. 'Give my love to Nellie … I would have given a lot to see her before I left but it was impossible.' But the relationship does not appear to have developed. I base this view on a study of later correspondence. It may be that prison separation brought about a change. In this view, however, I may be mistaken. I have been told, in reply to inquiries, that Nellie McAllister, who survived Thomas Ashe by some years, was so affected by his death that she died of a broken heart. I have also been told that the real love of Thomas Ashe's life was Elizabeth Dempsey of Grace Dieu, described to me by a friend of Ashe as 'a very superior girl', who died some years before the Rising. Closer research, which I have not had leisure to undertake, may be more conclusive. Enough to say that, in his human relationships, Thomas Ashe's human qualities stand out. They serve to increase our feeling and regard for the man who met his death in a good cause.

APPENDIX I

ORATION DELIVERED BY COMMANDANT THOMAS
ASHE AT CASEMENT'S FORT, ARDFERT, COUNTY KERRY,
ON SUNDAY 5 AUGUST 1917.

THE ORATION

Men and women of Kerry, it is a great honour to me to be asked to speak here today – to speak to the great gathering of the men and women of Kerry, of my native county, who have come to this fort in order to show by their presence, and to show to the world that is watching us, that we stand by the same principles that Sir Roger Casement stood by when he mounted that strand (loud applause). There are other men more fitted to speak to you on this great subject than I am. There are men standing on this fort today who co-operated with Casement (applause) – men against whom one of the charges preferred was their knowledge and their friendship and their co-operation and assistance to Casement. I do not know why it was I was selected to speak here. (Voices – 'You are welcome.') Other men were sentenced to death. Men who have worked the County Kerry up to its present attitude should speak here and not I; but being invited, and not being in any way 'Duholough,' I will try to do my little best to put before you some of the ideals and some of the principles that Roger Casement stood for; and I will also try and tell you some of the work he did for Ireland, both in this country and in countries beyond the sea. Since my very childhood on the side of the hill or the shores of Dingle Bay, I heard old native speakers of Corcaguiney [sic] tell us of the prophecy by St Columbcille. That prophecy stated an O'Donnell would land on the strand at Corcaguiney; that he would land on the sands of his native land, and that he would bring liberty to the shores of Ireland, which we are sighing after for centuries (loud cheers). Old people in Corcaguiney looked forward to this mystical O'Donnell to land on the strand of Corcaguiney with a powerful army and powerful armaments. Back in the years of history many an eye similar to the eyes of the old Irish speakers in numerous other countries outside of Ireland, looked on many occasions for the mystical liberator of their country to come with the sword and bayonet for their deliverance; and it's no wonder that the people of Kerry thought that the deliverer would come with an army and armaments, and he did come. The mystical man of Columbcille's prophecy came; he came unknown, but I tell you he is not unknown today. He is not unknown today, nor will he be unknown tomorrow. He did not bring with him that great army; he brought no great powers in his train to back up his work for Irish liberty; but he brought with him a loving heart and an undaunted spirit that will live in Ireland as long as any man will live who believes in the Irish ideals of an Irish republic. In looking back at the history of Ireland we can see clearly before our views many a landmark, many a stepping-stone that leads us in our ideals and in our desires, and that screws up our courage in order that we might try to attain for Ireland what the men in the past failed to attain for our country; we look away in the distant ages of the past to the figure of the king who died in the battle of Clontarf, and we think of the Ireland over which he ruled; and the Ireland of our ideals is a similar one. We go down the paths of history from the days of the great Brian, and we meet with the O'Neills of Ulster; we meet with the chieftains of Munster; we go on through the period of Shane O'Neill down to the days of the sacrifices of Wolfe Tone and of Robert Emmet (loud applause). All the stepping-stones of our history are stepping-stones of sacrifice – if I may use such words – and in our own age of sacrifice of life for Irish nationality it is not completed. We had an honour from God – it was a Godly honour, and could not be called by any other name. We have got the honour from God to live in the years that are at present, and to see men lay down their lives in the spirit our forefathers laid theirs down (loud applause). It is an honour only a few generations, and only choice generations of the people of Ireland, have got; and we should thank God that we have lived in the years of Irish nationality, so militant and so self-sacrificing, and the last stepping-stone to Irish liberty was laid down last year – the martyrs of Easter Week and the martyrdom of the beautiful and honourable Casement. Previous landmarks of our history are dimmed through the passing of many long years; but, the one that is close by, the one that you and I know of, that will be the last stepping-stone to the complete and absolute independence of our country (loud applause). Men would ask some years ago who was Roger Casement? Roger Casement was born on 1 September in the year 1864. In his early manhood he went into the service of England, where many a good Irishman, through economic reasons, has often to go. For twenty-one years of his life he served England and, during these twenty-one years of his life, he felt himself as much in bondage and in chains as he did during his stay in Pentonville prison last year (a voice – 'His mind was in Ireland then'). I will be able to read for you an extract from one of his letters – one of his letters written in 1914 to a friend of his. He speaks of his work for England in one of the republics of South America as a consul-general. He said, regarding his work in those far-away districts in the southern world: 'All that I ever did that was unselfish and chivalrous in public life, and I have striven to do both in all my public service, has been done with the image of Ireland before me.' There was Casement wandering over the prairies of South America, wandering over the free republics of the southern world, with a vision of Ireland, bound in chains, always before his gaze. Imagine how he felt as he went amongst free peoples, and lived his life in countries while his brain rang with the thought of Dark Rosaleen on the western verge of the Atlantic; when he thought of her bound in chains, with no hopes – no visible hopes of ever breaking through, no wonder that his solicitude and exile in those countries swept away his strength and wore away his health, and forced him into retirement in the prime of life. We can understand the noble and chivalrous heart of Casement bursting with the desire to come back to his native land – for there was now a young Ireland that has been reborn in the previous dozen years – to come back and throw his weight in with men who were working and striving to place Irish nationality on a strong foundation. 'All,' he says, 'I have striven for during all my public life has been done with the image of Ireland before me. I looked to the Ireland of my ideals when I went to find Leopold on the Congo, and the rubber contractors, and, please God,' he says, 'before I die I will do something for Ireland' – and we have it from God's own Son that no man can do a greater thing for his friends than lay down his life. And you will see that God has honoured Casement when he called on him to shed his blood for Ireland; to shed his blood in charity and love for the liberty of his people. During my stay in America in 1914, I had the honour of meeting Casement on a few occasions. At the time he was weak and he was frail in health, but his weakness did not prevent him from touring the States in order to raise funds to arm the Volunteers of Ireland. I was present at the convention of the Ancient Order of Hibernians of Norfolk City, Virginia, when Casement spoke before 4,000 delegates from all parts of the States. He appealed at this time for funds to arm and equip the Volunteers in Ireland, and a resolution was passed by the delegates in answer to his appeal, pledging themselves to raise in America 400,000 dollars for the purpose of arming and equipping the Volunteers. The Irish in America clearly saw that Casement's and the Volunteers' leaders only hope of saving the soul of Ireland – to save Ireland from sinking into slavery, and to save the young men of Ireland from being murdered on the plains of Flanders, in order that England might live – they saw that the only guarantee to save the honour of Ireland before the nations of the world was to arm the young men of Ireland. And the answer to his appeal at the time, showed that the Irish in America, understanding what freedom means, and understanding that the only means of acquiring and protecting liberty and freedom [*sic*], shovelled out their dollars to Casement in order that Ireland might be preserved from the tyranny of the Jews and money-lenders of London who are at present running the world war. After his visit to America, Casement, as you all know, departed for Germany, that he might get the assistance of the Central Powers to help Ireland to gain the liberty that we have been yearning over for years. We know a good deal about the work of Casement in Germany. We know one fact that will stand for ever; one fact that Casement is more responsible for than any other Irishman, and that is, the Central Powers, publicly, are pledged to see, that, before peace is declared, and the peace conference is settled, in the new world that will exist after the present war, that [sic] Ireland will be one of the free nations of Europe. Ireland's enemies were Casement's enemies, and we know how he was brought up before a bench of London judges. England believed, and I believe she had a good right for that belief, that a judge and jury could not be found in Ireland to convict Casement of high treason to his own country. Therefore, they took him to England to convict him of high treason to England. And they found him guilty, and I think we, today, should ring out our voices and let them be heard from one corner of Ireland to the other, we should shout to the judges of London that Casement was guilty of high treason to England. There are many things I would like to say to you, but I will read for you a few remarks on Casement's death that were written in one of the leading newspapers in America. I will show you clearly what these American people thought of the sacrifice of Casement's life for Ireland. The remarks appeared in a leading paragraph, and they recorded that the English government's dealing with the Irish people for 300 years has been one long story of tyranny and incredible stupidity; and we believe that the sober judgement of history will rank the hanging of Roger Casement amongst the chief governmental crimes and blunders. That is what the Irish-Americans thought of the sacrifice of Casement's life for Ireland. But the ministry, when it had Roger Casement in its grip, resolved to put him to death and the hangman performed his loathsome function; and listen to what the American journal says – 'and that day the brutal empire lost Ireland for ever.' This article finishes up and says: 'That a country that can provide patriots to die gladly and cheerfully for the cause of liberty and the common good proves to mankind its right to freedom and the government of its own country by its own people.'

The voice of each succeeding patriot and martyr ringing from the scaffold is but another call – a trumpet call to the generations that are to come. The attempt which is meant to strike terror into the hearts of patriots reveals only a fierce resolve to be ever more determined to resist all that tyranny can do to crush the spirit of liberty. Roger Casement, it says, is not dead. Sir Roger Casement still lives. The English gaolers can bury his body – but his soul lives. He has escaped, and is now where no one can reach him. He lives in Irish hearts a hero. No Scotland Yard man can lay hands on him there. His sacrifice reiterated and renewed the old desire for freedom, and the old spirit of nationality that was left latent in the minds of the Irish Race.

I will finish by telling you that, coupled with the sacrifice of Casement's life, we must not forget the many sacrifices of the men who were murdered in Kilmainham gaol. A few minutes ago when Captain Lynch recited the Rosary here before us, I was glad that our meeting took place on Sunday that you might merge your prayers in his. He read out the five Glorious Mysteries of the Rosary; the Mystery of the Resurrection and the Ascension, and it was meet and fitting that these should be the Mysteries of the Rosary that we prayed before Heaven today, because you will agree, and everyone will agree, that the Resurrection has taken place in the life of Ireland; and let us pray that the Resurrection that has taken place in Ireland will never die; will never cease to live until the liberty and freedom we have fought and striven for will be ours. Some men here, I am sure, know more about Fionn McCual than I do. On one occasion the enemies of Fionn McCual held him in slavery, and there was but one way of cutting his chains, and that was by sprinkling them in blood. I believe that the sprinkling of the blood of the martyrs of Easter Week is wearing away the chains that have bound Ireland. Our opponents tell us we are criminal idealists. You can see that the men of Easter Week were the most practical Nationalists that ever lived in Ireland for the last 100 years. There was no dreaming about them or idealism but the dreams and ideals of absolute Irish liberty, and they worked for it and placed it on a foundation that it will never again be taken down from. I had the pleasure during Easter Week – in fact I think it was on Wednesday of Easter Week – of receiving a despatch from Jim Connolly, who commanded in Dublin (loud applause). His despatch said, amongst other things: 'The Republican Flag still flies triumphantly over Dublin city. There will be glorious days for Ireland yet.'

Will you mark these words, my friends? Will you mark the words of Connolly; take them to your heart and think of the mind of the man who saw clearly from behind the barricades of Dublin streets that there would be glorious days for Ireland yet (applause). Pearse and McDermott told me that the Republican flag flies triumphantly over Dublin, and that they never withdrew those words. The Republican flag still today flies over Dublin city, and still flies over every county in Ireland, and any forces of Great Britain, and any army of England, will not drive the tricolour flag from the hills and fields of Ireland. It is there, and not only can we see it with our eyes, but we can feel it with our minds, because I have seen since I was liberated that there is a tricolour in the mind of every young man and every young woman from north to south, and from east to west, and though they may tear them down from the house-tops, they can never obliterate the tricolour nor the blood of Easter Week from the minds of the young men of Ireland (loud applause). The last words, practically, the last words to his comrades, were told to half-a-dozen of our boys in Kilmainham by P. H. Pearse on the night before his execution. He told them in Kilmainham gaol that 'the insurrection was a success. We have gained what we were out for. The Irish question is no longer a British imperial question. It is now an international one.' Ireland, since Easter Week, has made the Irish question an international one, and you are to keep it an international one here today, and do the same tomorrow, so that no measure of liberty for

Ireland will be accepted by the Irish people unless it is guaranteed by the nations of Europe. Don't take the pledge of any one nation as a guarantee of your liberty. The nations of Europe will guarantee whatever liberty will be accepted by the people of Ireland. If you do that you will be following the path laid down for you by Casement in his work in the United States of America, and in his work in Germany and Austria, and if you accept any half measure you will be working absolutely in opposition to the law and rules laid down by Casement and laid down by Pearse for the people of Ireland. Those martyrs who laid down their lives for Ireland, as the American newspaper stated, are not dead. They are living with us today more than they ever did before. It is only fitting that we should honour their memories, and there is only one way of honouring their memories, and that is to help to forward the policy and principles that these men died for in 1916 (loud applause). They knew it was an honour to lay down their lives for Ireland, and many of their friends knew likewise. I cannot finish my advice to you today without telling you of the words of a mother of one of the boys who died at Ashbourne, on Easter Week of last year. On our side there were two men killed; one patriot from Lusk, a fine manly fellow, who ran from his work to take up his rifle when we sent out the call. His body was taken to a house in Ashbourne, and the women of Meath, who had heard the rifles ringing the whole long day, were in the house with the body of young Rafferty. They stepped aside when his mother entered, trembling in fear and sorrow for the young fellow who lost his life, and for the mother, an old woman. She entered and looked at the dead body of her son, and moved the long locks, and, looking up towards Heaven, she said: 'Thank God it is for Ireland you died.' Now, say Rosaries for Casement, for the dead men of Easter Week; echo out the prayer of this woman of Lusk; cry out to Heaven: 'Thank God it is for Ireland they died.'

APPENDIX II

IN THE HIGH COURT OF JUSTICE IRELAND
KING'S BENCH DIVISION
CROWN SIDE

AFFIDAVIT OF EDMUND J. DUGGAN

I, EDMUND J. DUGGAN of 12 College Green in the City of Dublin, Solicitor, aged 21 years and upwards make Oath and say as follows:

1. I am the Solicitor for the next-of-kin of the late Thomas Ashe who died in the Mater Misericordiae Hospital Dublin on Tuesday the 25th September 1917 within five hours after his discharge from Mountjoy Prison where he was serving a sentence of one year's imprisonment with hard labour for a speech alleged to have been delivered by him at Ballinalee in the County of Longford in July last. He was convicted and sentenced by a Courtmartial the sentence to take effect from 3rd September 1917 and during the currency of his sentence there were incarcerated with deceased about forty other prisoners under the Defence of the Realm Act under order of similar tribunals with one exception, Mr Joseph MacDonagh, who was sentenced by order of a Dublin Police Magistrate.

2. In consequence of the death of the said prisoner the Coroner of the City of Dublin Dr Louis Byrne held an inquest on the deceased in the Mater Misericordiae Hospital on the 27th day of September 1917 which was continued in the City Morgue on the 28th ultimo and is still proceeding there. Counsel for the Prison Authorities has examined the following witnesses: Sir Thomas Myles, Sir Arthur Chance, Warder

Watters, Dr Lowe, Dr Dowdall, Medical Officer Mountjoy Prison, Dr Kinsella, Medical Officer Maryborough Prison, and the Deputy Governor of Mountjoy Prison, who in the absence of the Governor had the prisoners in custody. The Coroner directed a post-mortem examination, which was conducted by Professor McWeeney, who proved that the deceased died of syncope partly owing to the failure of a weak and slightly dilated heart and partly owing to the intense passive congestion and oedema of both lungs.

3. The Lord Mayor of Dublin and Sir John Irwin, who is Chairman of the Visiting Justices of Mountjoy Prison were examined by the Coroner and proved that on Saturday 22nd September ultimo they found deceased in his cell where he had been since the previous Thursday morning deprived of his bed, bedding, boots and cell furniture. It was afterwards admitted by the Deputy Governor that for over 50 hours the deceased had been left in this condition with nothing to sit or sleep upon save the bare floor and that this deprivation had been inflicted upon him and the other prisoners without any inquiry or sentence of punishment.

4. I say that the excuse offered for this ill-treatment was that the deceased in combination with other Defence of the Realm Act prisoners was at the time of the removal of his boots, bedding, etc. engaged in a hunger-strike and in pursuance of a common design contemplated the destruction of his said bed, bed clothes and prison furniture whereupon the Deputy Governor did the acts complained of.

5. I have had access to several of the prisoners subjected by the said Deputy Governor to similar treatment and they have informed me and I believe that such allegations, which had previously been made by Mr Hanna, K.C. on behalf of the Prison Authorities, are totally without foundation. I refer to the opening address of the said learned Counsel and the evidence of the various Prison Officials as published in the 'Irish Times' 'Independent' and 'Freeman's Journal' which are substantially correct, as I have been present at the inquest during the entire course of

the proceedings from day to day. It appears from the Prison records put in evidence that several of the said prisoners were subjected to forcible or artificial feeding on Saturday the 22nd ultimo and while suffering from the deprivations aforesaid, it was admitted they were sent back to their cells to lie on the bare floor without bed or bedding, and I am informed and believe that one of them, James Griffey, was then bleeding profusely from the treatment he had received and has since been sent to the Mater Misericordiae Hospital, where he now lies.

6. As Solicitor for the next-of-kin I propose to show that the case made on behalf of the Prison Authorities that deceased died partly from starvation and partly from a weak heart caused thereby is unfounded and it is put forward to screen the illegality to which the deceased was subjected. I say that the Deputy Governor admitted that the deceased and the other prisoners partook of their breakfast as usual on Thursday morning the 20th September and that it was only after they were assaulted by warders about 10 a.m. on that day and their boots, bed, bedding and cell furniture taken away, that they refused food at dinner time on that day and began a hunger-strike as a protest against the illegal treatment to which they were subjected. I say that said prisoners informed me and I believe that no attempt at hunger-strike was made by them until after the assaults and deprivations aforesaid and that it was not because of any apprehension of such hunger-strike or destruction of property as sworn to by the Deputy Governor that they and the said deceased were subjected to the barbarities which led to the death of the deceased. I say that the Prison Doctor in his evidence stated that he was wholly unaware of the deprivations by the Prison Governor of the prisoners' bed, bedding and boots, until after a number of them had been forcibly fed on Saturday the 22nd ultimo. As to this, he was contradicted by the Deputy Governor who deposed that the Doctor was throughout aware of said deprivations. I say that it is vital in the interests of justice and in order that a right verdict may be arrived at that the jury should be able to apportion the responsibility as between the various officials.

7. That the next-of-kin are being greatly embarrassed by the disobedience of the Prison Rules by the Deputy Governor in various respects including his failure to enter the punishment of the deceased and other prisoners in the Governor's Punishment Book or any note of his orders to his subordinates in the Governor's Order Book or to enter any note of the cause of his neglect under Rule 131 of the Statutory Prison Rules for Ireland 1904 to which I refer. The deprivations inflicted on the said prisoners were not inflicted under any Rule of the Prisons Rules for Ireland aforesaid or under any sentence of the Governor or of the Visiting Justices, and it was admitted by the Deputy Governor that in the history of the Prison Service, no precedent existed for same.

8. I say that the Jury have been strongly appealed to for a verdict in favour of the Prison Authorities on the ground that the deceased wilfully committed suicide in order to secure special treatment in prison, and hunger-struck to gain same but the witnesses whom I propose to examine will prove that there is no foundation for these allegations and that the hunger-strike was subsequent to the said trespass upon them and was resorted to as the only protest deceased could make against the illegality. My clients have also been concerned about allegations that deceased wantonly committed suicide in the effort to obtain such special treatment as aforesaid and I refer to a newspaper called 'The Impartial Reporter and Farmers Journal' in which the allegation is made that deceased committed suicide by starvation.

9. I say that I am advised and believe that the evidence of the following witnesses, who are at present undergoing sentence in Mountjoy Prison and who are amongst the said Defence of the Realm Act prisoners, should be presented at the said Inquest, in view of the allegations made by the learned Counsel and witnesses for the Prison Authorities, namely: The said Joseph MacDonagh, Austin Stack, Finian Lynch and Philip McMahon [*sic*]. These prisoners will be able to prove that the allegations of the Deputy Governor against the said Thomas Ashe are

entirely unfounded, and more than one of them will be able to show that the forcible feeding applied by the doctor under whose hands the deceased collapsed immediately after being fed, was incompetently and brutally administered.

10. I say that this application is made bona fide in the interests of justice, and not from any indirect motive but solely to secure legal evidence upon which the Coroner's Jury may arrive at a just and impartial verdict.

Sworn before me this 11th day of October 1917 at 16 Fleet Street in the City of Dublin and I know deponent.

EDMUND J. DUGGAN

JOSEPH McDERMOTT, A Commissioner to administer Oaths for the Supreme Court of Judicature in Ireland.

Filed this 11th day of October, 1917.

APPENDIX III

NATIONAL MUSEUM
ROLL OF HONOUR 1916 – ASHBOURNE

Signatures:

Peadar Ceallaigh

Colm Lawless

Christopher Nugent

Bartle Weston

James Masterson

Patrick Belton

Patrick Brogan

Thomas Weston

William Norton

Patrick Joseph Ryan

Charles Weston

Thomas Seaver

Caitlín Nic Alastair

Séamus Mac Domhnaill

Christopher Moran

Bennie McAllister

William Doyle

Patrick J. Early

Christopher Taylor

Matthias Derham

John Devine

Thomas McArdle

James Gough

Máire Ní Driain

Thomas Doyle

Peter Moran

Thomas Maxwell

James Connor

Monica Lawless

(née Fleming)

Seosamh Ua Droighneáin

Margaret McNally

Matthew Kelly

M. Julia Weston

Éamon Ua Murchadha

Séamas Ó Ceallaigh

Thomas Reilly

Joseph V. Lawless

Patrick Doyle

Joseph P. Kelly

Richard Aungier

James Rickard

John Rafferty	Jerry Golden
Patrick Birney	Thomasina Lynders
	(née Weston)

List of deceased members:

Jack Crenigan	Edward Stafford
William Dempsey	Joseph Taylor
Frank Lawless	Thomas Ashe
John McGowan	Richard Kelly
Thomas Rafferty	John McCann
Thomas Kelly	John Sherlock
John McAllister	

The above list was compiled about 1933–34. Deceased members' names were as a rule written down by the senior surviving officer of the garrison. Captain Richard Coleman's detachment is not listed with the above. The list does not include the names of Richard Mulcahy, Michael McAllister, Martin Walsh, Patrick Holohan.

The National Museum has another list, catalogue number EW 3180, supplied by Ailbhe Ó Monacháin.

APPENDIX IV

MEMBERS OF THE JURY

Owen McIntyre (foreman), 40 St Patrick's Road. Clerk.

John Robinson, 1 Lindsay Terrace. Provision merchant.

Benjamin S. Allshire, 3 Botanic Road. Gentleman.

George S. Woods, 108 Phibsboro Road. Chandler.

E. McGuinness, 89 Phibsboro Road. Provision merchant.

Thomas Smith, 100 Primrose Street. Provision merchant.

John Coyne, 48 Upper Dorset Street. Provision merchant.

James Casey, 8 Upper Dorset Street. Newsagent.

William S. Graham, 318 North Circular Road. Builder and contractor.

James McEntee, 21 St Anne's Road. Provision merchant.

Samuel Walton, 12 Lindsay Road. Gentleman.

Alex. Cochrane, 383 and 435 North Circular Road. Builder and contractor.

William H. Turley, 80 Upper Dorset Street. Publican.

Thomas Walsh, 93 Upper Dorset Street. Provision merchant.

Michael McGuire, 18 Phibsboro Road. Publican.

Michael Bolger, 99 Phibsboro Road. Provision merchant.

Patrick McGuinness, 114 Phibsboro Road. Publican.

APPENDIX V

THOMAS ASHE

I

The children of Éireann are listening again
To Death's sullen, sad, sombre beat of the drum;
Oppression has seized on a man amongst men,
And an eloquent life's stricken senseless and dumb,
While we, left behind, wait the life from your death that shall come!

II

In your fight to unfetter Humanity's soul,
Your body was blazoned with scars,
To oppression you fearlessly tendered the toll,
Removing for progress the Bolts and the Bars,
With your hand to the Plough and your eyes on the stars.

III

On the cold seat of death now your body's enthroned.
And your warm heart is silent and still,
For our life that is Death, your great life has atoned,
And we feel in our hearts a swift answering thrill,
To take up your work, all hard fallow nature to till.

IV

Here hope and Endeavour with energy braid
Leaves of honour to garland the Dead,
Here Liberty rests with calm Courage arrayed,
By the side of the Kingly but now passive head,
Anointed with blood that this Hero has shed.

V

Huge Labour looks down on your battle-scarred face,
Ignoble and noble with sweat on his brow,
Unable to fathom this soul of his race,
Half-conscious that soon, when he springs from the Slough,
He shall understand then, if he can't do it now!

VI

To your soul, for awhile, we all murmur, Farewell!
And we take the Dear Gift that you gave,
For your great Life stamped out in the cold prison cell
Shall be potent our own slavish nature to save,
Tho' your body we leave in the drear hidden gloom of the grave.

Seán Ó Cathasaigh

THOMAS ASHE

Another hero's knell to toll,
Another prayer for a parted soul,
Another name on the patriot's roll –
Brave Thomas Ashe;
Back with our tears! – 'twas a soldier fell,
Who laughed as he starved in his prison cell
At the thought of the troops he trounced so well –
Brave Thomas Ashe!

He held his life as light as dross,
He wrote that few would mourn his loss,
And for Ireland's sake he asked the Cross –
Brave Thomas Ashe,
And the Lord received His servant's prayer,
And chose, for him, the rest to spare,

But gave him the heavy Cross to bear,
Brave Thomas Ashe!

He carried the Cross till death drew nigh,
And little dreamed when he came to die
How he like a king in state should lie,
Brave Thomas Ashe,
While the flag of Dublin hung half-mast,
And tens of thousands of people passed,
In mourning files to look their last
On brave Tom Ashe!

Few to mourn? Half Ireland's here
To honour the fallen Volunteer,
And marching follow his soldier's bier,
Brave Thomas Ashe,
And the men in jail whom his death will save
Hear the measured tramp of his comrades brave
As they bear his corpse to its hero's grave,
Brave Thomas Ashe!

They lay him low in his narrow bed,
They plant the Cross at the martyr's head
They fire three volleys above the dead,
Brave Thomas Ashe –
God welcome you on the other side!
God comfort us that in Ireland bide!
God bless the cause for which you died,
Brave Thomas Ashe!

Elizabeth Healy

THOMAS ASHE

(Letter to *The Irish Times,* from Mrs Marie Johnson, widow of Thomas Johnson, parliamentary Labour leader, published 29 September 1967.)

Sir, – May I crave a small space in your paper re the commemoration of the death of Thomas Ashe, as depicted in *The Irish Times* (25 September). There are very few of that period left who would remember the horror of that hunger-strike and sequel if I may call it so, of his untimely death. Seeing the picture of his sister, Miss Nora Ashe, in your paper, I was reminded of the fact that my husband, Thomas Johnson, and I, with William O'Brien of the ITGWU were present at the funeral. As William was incapacitated by a leg injury, he was obliged to travel in a carriage, and he asked us to accompany him, but he was able to walk through the cemetery with help. His sister, Mary F., known as 'Cissy,' marched with the Franchise League contingent of women whose secretary, Mrs M. Connery, carried our banner to Glasnevin.

I wonder if there are any other members still alive to share in the honour of that tribute to the noble pioneer of freedom, Thomas Ashe, the first hunger-striker of modern Ireland; or if the Fianna boys of 1917, now in their sixties and seventies, look back with pride to have been associated as they were by their service on that day when their youthful imaginations were fired by his sacrifice.

Yours, etc.,
Marie Johnson

Ralahine,
49 Mount Prospect Avenue,
Clontarf.

I gCUIMHNE THOMÁIS ÁGHAS

Do sceinn an faoileán go hard os Ceann Sibéal,
Múnla a sciathán mar aingeal ag snámh ins an aer,
Ag treabhadh an ísleáin, is ag gabháil do chúraimí an lae
Bhí ainm Thomáis Ághas sa chomhrá i bhfarradh Mac Dé.

Cé chreideann Fionn agus an Fhiann
Ná stair imchian Chúchulainn áigh?
Cad iad ach scáile as meisce mearaí na seanúdar?
Siúd thall an tigh inar rugadh Tomás Ághas.

Fuil dár bhfuil. Meon dár meon. Chuir sé áille nua sa chuntas,
Tháinig dúthracht úr sa lá.
An cailín óg i mbéal a pósta móide binneas a hamhrán
Is an ghrian bhuí ag luí san Iarthar is órga a maise ag dul fé scáth.

Shiúlaíos anuraidh bóithre agus bánta Fhine Gall
Ag lorg a thásc, is ag labhairt le fuíoll aosta an áir.
Am naofa an Cháisc. Dúirt liom a gclann:
'Tá a dhúchas inár gcuisle; linne a chroí, a ghrá agus a ghreann;
Tomás Ághas ó Chinn Aird deartháir dlúth ár gcine
Agus beidh a chlú i mbéal ár gclainne luath is mall.'

Feasta, Iúil 1968

ENDNOTES

3 In De La Salle
1 Minard National School. The first school was opened in 1864 and a new one in 1873. See John Ashe, PP, *Annascaul Revisited and Reviewed*, p. 31.

4 The Teacher
1 *An Cosantóir*, November 1946.

8 The Gaelic League
1 *Sinn Féin*, 25 November 1911.
2 *Ibid.*, 25 May 1912.
3 *The Freeman's Journal*, 4 July 1913.
4 *Sinn Féin*, 26 July 1913.
5 *Ibid.*, 12 July 1913.
6 *Ibid.*, 15 February 1913.
7 *The Freeman's Journal*, 14 July 1913.
8 *Ibid.*, 12 July 1913.
9 *Sinn Féin*, 12 July 1913.
10 Leading article, *Sinn Féin*, 26 July 1913.
11 'Dr Hyde and Sinn Féin', *Sinn Féin*, 26 July 1913.
12 *Devoy's Post Bag*, Vol. II, p. 427.
13 *Sinn Féin*, 19 July 1913.
14 Béaslaí, P., 'A Veteran Remembers', *Irish Independent*, 14 May 1957.
15 Béaslaí, P., *Irish Independent*, 16 May 1957.
16 *Imeachta na hArd-Fheise*, 1915.

9 A Journey to America
1 *Devoy's Post Bag*, Vol. II, pp. 427–8.
2 Ashe, Thomas, *Oration delivered by Commandant Thomas Ashe at Casement's Fort on 5th August 1917*, p. 7.
3 Letter to Pádraig Ó Dálaigh, 2 July 1914.

4 Gwynn, Denis, *Life of John Redmond,* pp. 391–2.

5 *Evening Press,* 15 September 1961.

10 The Irish Volunteers

1 There is a striking acknowledgement of the stimulus given to Irish republicanism by Sir Edward Carson in the article 'The New Liberator' by 'Seághan Ultach', in the issue of *Irish Freedom* (August 1914) which followed the landing of arms at Howth. This is an extract:

> Things have changed so swiftly and so completely of late that the full significance of the new situation is as yet but half realised. Less than a year ago the man who looked for an armed Ireland was regarded as a fool. Many good Nationalists at that time thought and said that physical force was quite impracticable and most of the remainder of the nation was too dispirited to dream of arming ... For the great change that has come to Ireland we have to thank one man. Ever since Mitchel there have been men of his brave breed urging Ireland to strike for her rights – telling her clearly and persistently to realise her strength, to take heart, to dare to be free. And they urged in vain. It was not until the Liberator rose that Ireland heard and understood. He was the man for whom we have waited so long, who by swift decisive action speaking louder than words called to Irishmen to rise as men and claim the rights of man. He, while all the men in England who hated him mocked, and all the little men in Ireland who feared him protested, shook an Irish province free of foreign politics and bade it choose its own fate. It was he – Carson the Liberator – who shook Ulster from the English grasp and wakened in the rest of Ireland the courage and the hope of freedom that had slumbered long. He smashed English authority in this country for ever, so that the future of the nation is now in her own hands if she will only choose aright. He has done more to shake the Empire from its arrogant supremacy than every soldier of freedom who ever fired a shot at an English uniform. He it was – the Liberator – who snapped his fingers at the whole British navy and made the British Admiralty the laughing stock of the world. He drove – not the proverbial coach and horses – but a score of rifle-laden motors through a British Royal Proclamation; he laughed

at English law and marched his forces armed through their city, and the impotent English Government could only hold up its finger at the naughty men. Without a shot fired, the Liberator has taken his province out of the sphere of English authority. Men of Ireland, learn the lesson. England fears your guns.

Accounts vary as to the exact time Thomas Ashe was appointed commandant. Pádraig Ashe, in notes he gave me, writes:

Tomás was in Liberty Hall on the Saturday or Sunday night before the Rising and was appointed Commandant on that occasion. Previously he had been captain.

Colonel Joseph Lawless has written:

Some weeks before the Rising, the command of the battalion was assumed by Commandant Thomas Ashe, in succession to Dr R. Hayes, who became battalion adjutant. ['Fight at Ashbourne' in *Capuchin Annual*, 1966, p. 307.]

Jack Devine, 5th Battalion, told me:

Dr Hayes was Commandant at first. He was not a fighting man and he resigned in favour of Tom Ashe.

Christopher (Kit) Moran, 5th Battalion, told me that Thomas Ashe was elected commandant at the Second Annual Convention of Irish Volunteers, Dublin, 31 October 1915.

2 O'Brien, William, *Labour News*, 1 May 1931.
3 'A Nation in Revolt,' *Irish Independent*, 14 January 1953.
4 *Ibid.*, 15 January 1953.
5 *Intelligence Notes, 1913–16*, p. 176.

11 'There Will Be Glorious Days for Ireland Yet'

1 Ashe, Thomas, *Oration at Casement's Fort, 5th August 1917*, p. 5.
2 It is stated in p. 33 of the *Ashbourne Memorial Book*:

Joe O'Reilly, subsequently Michael Collins's aide-de-camp, arrived about ten o'clock on Monday morning with the message from Pearse calling for action at one o'clock.

3 Note in Dr Hayes's copy of Béaslaí, P., *Michael Collins and the Making of a New Ireland*, Vol. I, p. 87. Information courtesy of Thomas P. O'Neill.

4 Ashe, Thomas, *Oration at Casement's Fort, 5th August 1917*, pp. 9–10.

12 Ashbourne

1 Golden's narrative, O'Connell Schools' library.

2 In the following books there are errors, which may derive from official reports, about the numbers engaged at Ashbourne:

McKenzie, F. A., *The Irish Rebellion* (London, 1916), pp. 100–1.

IO: [C. J. C. Street] *The Administration of Ireland, 1920* (London, 1921), p. 30.

Phillips, W. Alison, The *Revolution in Ireland 1906–1923* (London, 1923), p. 103. Also in 1926 edition.

The number of Irish Volunteers is exaggerated in Wells, W.B. and Marlowe, N., *A History of the Irish Rebellion of 1916* (Dublin, 1917), pp. 180–3.

3 *Intelligence Notes, 1913–16*, p. 233.

4 Ashe, Thomas, *Oration at Casement's Fort, 5th August 1917*, p. 11.

13 The Echoes of Kilmainham

1 *Sinn Féin Rebellion Handbook*, 1917, p. 62.

2 The president, Mr de Valera, interviewed on his eightieth birthday, said: 'I was tried on the same day as Seán MacDermott and Tom Ashe …', *The Kerryman*, 9 April 1966. In the communiqué from British Army headquarters, Parkgate Street, on 12 May 1916, announcing the execution of Connolly and MacDermott, it is stated that their trial took place on 9 May.

3 *Sinn Féin Rebellion Handbook*, 1917, p. 224.

4 *The Kerryman*, 9 April 1966.

5   Cab/37/150 PRO [now National Archives], London.

6   Early in May, John Redmond appealed to Campbell to use his influence to restrain further vindictive measures, and received from him a letter dated 4 May, saying he would do all he could though he had absolutely no control in the matter, an assurance in direct contrast to the extract quoted above. At no time was John Dillon under any illusions about Campbell and the burden of his references to him can be summed up in a phrase from one of his letters: 'Campbell must go.' See Gwynn, Denis, *The Life of John Redmond*, pp. 485–6.

7   The following words are crossed out here: 'and ask to call to see me, as I have got permission'.

14 Dartmoor

1   *Kerry Champion*, 29 September 1928.

2   *Catholic Bulletin*, Vol. VII, p. 454.

3   Original in Dingle Library.

15 Lewes Jail

1   *Kilkenny Journal*, 6 October 1917.

2   From photostat copy in National Library.

16 After the Rising

1   *Mar Mhaireas É*, Vol. I, p. 27.

2   Gavan Duffy Correspondence NLI: quoted in *Art Ó Gríofa*, p. 268.

3   See *The Irishman*, 4 November 1916 for Sweetman's letter; for Martyn's, 11 November 1916.

4   *Irish Opinion*, 3 February 1917.

5   *Ibid.*, 10 March 1917.

17 Ashe and Collins

1   *An tÓglach*, Christmas 1962.

18 Strike and Release

1   Joint statement of Ashe and Stack, *The Kerryman*, 30 July 1917.

2   *Ibid.*

3   *Nationality*, 7 June 1917.

4   Statement of Ashe and Stack, *The Kerryman*, 30 June 1917.

19 Return to Kinard
1 Fionán Lynch to the writer.
2 *Evening Press*, 19 July 1968.
3 Quoted by Edward MacLysaght, 'The East Clare By-Election,' *The Irish Times*, 29 November 1966.

20 At Casement's Fort
1 MacLysaght, 'The East Clare By-Election,' *The Irish Times*, 29 November 1966.
2 Lynch, D., *The IRB and the 1916 Insurrection*, ed. O'Donoghue, p. 32.
3 O'Donoghue, Florence, 'Re-Organisation of the Irish Volunteers, 1916–17,' *Capuchin Annual* 1967, p. 384.
4 *Tréithe Thomáis Ághas*, pp. 32–33.
5 Fionán Lynch to the writer.

21 A Prisoner Again
1 *Kerry Champion*, 29 September 1928.
2 *An tÓglach*, Summer 1964.

22 Court Martial
1 *The Kerryman* of 8 September states it was 'of moderate length'.
2 Original in Dingle Library.

24 The Assault on the Prisoners
1 *Kerry Champion*, 29 September 1928.

26 The Ordeal of the Stomach Pump
1 *Kerry Champion*, 29 September 1928.

27 I Die in a Good Cause
1 Deposition in National Library, MS 13734.
2 *Ibid.*

28 The Funeral of Thomas Ashe
1 Fionán Lynch to the writer.
2 *The Leader*, 6 October 1917.
3 *The Freeman's Journal*, 2 October 1917.

4   *Ibid.*, 1 October 1917.

30 Thomas Ashe: Man and Heritage

1   O'Casey, S., *The Sacrifice of Thomas Ashe*, p. 3.

2   The first portion of this leading article was evidently written by John Chartres. An undated press-cutting in my possession, entitled 'Memories of Griffith', states that on Ashe's death Griffith used an article by Chartres as the leading article in his newspaper *Nationality*. The passage quoted, which forms the latter part of the leading article, was hardly the work of Chartres, however. It is more likely to be Griffith's.

SOURCES

Manuscripts:

Thomas Ashe's personal papers and correspondence in possession of Nora Ághas; these include his American correspondence, detailed letter to his brother Gregory in the USA, prison correspondence, draft of novel, poems, memoranda, documents relating to his court martial (1917), prison treatment, etc., and other miscellaneous material [note: much of this material is now in Kerry County Library]

American diary (mainly addresses, etc.)

Poems, which are included in Vol. I of two foolscap-size notebooks used by Thomas Ashe in Lewes prison and containing mainly the draft of his novel. The poems are:

    (i) 'To Whisper a Word or Two' (with music)

    (ii) 'I Came to You'

    (iii) 'Caitlín Ní hUalacháin'

    (iv) 'Young Mollie was a Milkmaid'

    (v) 'Oulart Hill – A '98 Ballad' (with music)

    (vi) 'My Colleen by the Lee'

    (vii) 'Let Me Carry Your Cross' (with music)

    (viii) 'Ireland Came Between You and Me' – music to 'Brennan's Farewell'

Dingle Library collection of Ashe material

National Library MSS: 11,123; 11,128; 13,734 (deposition of Raymond Dowdall, MD, MO Mountjoy prison); 3,903 (two letters – photostat – to Pádraig Ághas from prison)

National Museum 1916 Section: List of participants in the Battle of Ashbourne; some letters and photographs

Notebook of personal recollections from Pádraig Ághas

O'Connell Schools' library, North Richmond Street, Dublin: *The Story of the Fight at Rath Cross Roads* or *The Battle of Ashbourne* by Jerry

Golden; prison notebook of Éamon de Valera; Ashe inquest papers and miscellaneous

O'Curry Library, University College Dublin: Ó Lochlainn MS 15. *Forus Feasa ar Éirinn, An Leabhar Muimhneach*, etc., transcribed by Séamus Ás, Dingle, 1762–3

Public Record Office [now National Archives of Ireland]: M5249 (1) Census return of Ashe family of Aughills, County Kerry, 1851

Recollections from Miss Mary Monks, Dublin

Recollections from Miss Annie McAllister, Donabate, County Dublin

Recollections from S. Bean Mhic Thalbóid, Tralee

Recollections from Fionán Lynch, Dublin

Personal Recollections:

Ághas, Nora, Baile Átha Cliath

Ashe, Gregory, County Dublin

Ashe, Thomas, Ballsbridge, Dublin

Ashe, Matthew, Clondalkin, County Dublin

Gunning, Mrs Sheila (Sheila Devane), Clontarf, Dublin

Ashe, Pádraig, Straffan, County Kildare

Béaslaí, Piaras, Baile Átha Cliath

Boland, Father Maurice, Waterville, Maine, USA

Brangan, Thomas J., Gormanstown, County Meath

Brunton, John, Rath Cross, Ashbourne

Carton, Joe, Hanna's Avenue, Corduff, County Dublin

Casey, Con, Tralee

Coleman, Anna and family, Dublin

de Blaghd, Earnán, Baile Átha Cliath

Devine, Jack, Lusk, County Dublin

Doyle, Paddy, Lusk, County Dublin

Howley, Peter, Ardrahan, County Galway

Kavanagh, Michael, Lispole, County Kerry

Keaveney, Andrew, Clontarf, Dublin

Kelly, Joe, Lusk, County Dublin

Kelly, Miss Katie, Corduff, County Dublin

Kelly, Richard, Rogerstown, Lusk, County Dublin
MacGallogly, John, Dublin
McArdle, Thomas, Lusk, County Dublin
McKenna, Dr Patrick, Cahirciveen, County Kerry
Moran, Christopher (Kit), Swords, County Dublin
Mullins, William, Tralee
Ní Chonchobhair, Eibhlín, Dublin
Ní Fhoghludha, Bríd (Mrs Bríd S. Martin), Cork
Ó Briain, An tOllamh Liam, Baile Átha Cliath
O'Brien, William, Donabate, County Dublin
Ó Conaire, Pádraic Óg, Baile Átha Cliath
Peppard, Thomas, Rush, County Dublin
Sheehan, Michael, Mount Merrion, County Dublin
Sheridan, James, Corduff, County Dublin
Sheridan, Mrs James, Corduff, County Dublin
Ward, Mrs Kathleen, Dublin

Printed Writings of Thomas Ashe:

'Creideamh agus Grádh', *An Lóchrann*, Meán Fómhair, Deireadh
Fómhair, 1918

'De La Salle agus Éire Ghaodhalach', *Irisleabhar De La Salle*, Leabhar I,
Uimhir 1, 1911

*Oration delivered by Commandant Thomas Ashe at Casement's Fort on 5th
August 1917* [?Dublin, 1917]

Printed Accounts of Battle of Ashbourne:

Account of Battle of Ashbourne by Major J. V. Lawless, in *An
Cosantóir*, No. 6, 13 June 1941; also in *Dublin's Fighting Story*, pp.
60–66; *Capuchin Annual*, 1966; *Ashbourne Memorial Book*, pp. 11–21.
Sunday Press, 10 January 1960, by Michael O'Halloran, with letter
of comment 24 January from Col. J. V. Lawless and reply thereto
31 January 1960 by Nora Ághas. John Austin contributes a brief
eyewitness account in *Ashbourne Memorial Book*, pp. 39–42

Gaelic American, 23 September 1916. Writer not named but identified as Vol. Patrick Holohan. See photostat copy, with introductory typewritten letter from Gen. Mulcahy to Dr Richard Hayes, in National Library

'The Work of Thomas Ashe' by General Richard Mulcahy, in *An tÓglach*, Christmas 1962, includes a description of the battle

Reports:

The Death of Thomas Ashe: Full Report of the Inquest. Published by J. M. Butler, 41 Amiens Street, Dublin, 1917

Newspapers, Periodicals, etc.:

An Claidheamh Soluis
An Cosantóir
An tÓglach (Dublin, 1961–), ed. Major-General Piaras Béaslaí
Catholic Bulletin, 1917
The Cork Examiner
Éire–Ireland
Evening Press
The Freeman's Journal
The Gaelic American
Irish Freedom
Irish Independent
Irish Opinion, 1916–17 (Dublin)
Irish Press
The Irish Times
Irish Volunteer
The Irishman, 1916–17 (Dublin)
The Kerry Annual, 1963, ed. Michael Glazier
The Kerryman, 1916–17
Kilkenny Journal, 1917
Limerick Leader, 1917
Nationality, 1917
New Ireland, 1917
Sunday Press

Special Articles, Series, etc., in Newspapers and Periodicals:

The Leader, 6 October 1917: 'Tasc Thomáis Ághas' le Pádraig Ó Duinnín

An Claidheamh Soluis, 13 Deireadh Fómhair, 1917: 'Tomás Ághas' le Pádraig Ó Siochfhradha; 20 Deireadh Fómhair 1917: 'Óige Thomáis Ághas' le Duine dá Chomrádaí

The Kerryman, 11 August 1917: 'Casement Anniversary'; 28 December 1917: Article on Thomas Ashe by Bryan O'Hara (i.e. Gerald Leahy)

Kerry Champion, 29 September 1928: 'Tomás Ághas, the story of a noble life' told by Austin Stack

Labour News, 1, 8 May 1937: Series by William O'Brien with references to Ashe

An Cosantóir, November 1946: 'Thomas Ashe' by Col. J. V. Lawless

Irish Weekly Independent, 31 December 1953, 7 January 1954: 'The 1916 Rising: Events Outside Dublin' by Liam Skinner

Irish Independent, two series by Piaras Béaslaí: 'A Nation in Revolt,' commencing 5 January 1954; 'A Veteran Remembers,' commencing 13 May 1957

Feasta, Meán Fómhair 1961: 'Tomás Ághas' le Seán Ó Lúing

An tÓglach, Christmas 1962: 'The Work of Thomas Ashe' by General Richard Mulcahy

The Kerryman, 13 June 1964: 'The Forgotten Poet' by Seán Fitzgerald; 29 August 1964: 'The Black Ravens also Returning'

ESB Journal, April 1966: 'Colmán ó Sord Cholmcille' by Risteard Ó Colmáin

The Kerryman, 9 April 1966: 1916-66 Golden Jubilee Commemoration Supplement

Deirdre, Samhradh 1966: 'Ag Trácht thar Ua Rathaille' le Eibhlín Ní Mhurchú

The Kerryman, 11 June 1966: Career of Fionán Lynch

Capuchin Annual, 1967: 'Re-Organisation of the Irish Volunteers 1916–17' by Maj. Florence O'Donoghue; 'Thomas Ashe' by Seán Ó Lúing

Irish Press, 17 January 1967: 'Secrets of the British Cabinet, 1917–22. Reprieve of Ashe Opposed.'

Sunday Independent, 30 April 1967: Article on surrender of Fifth Battalion after Ashbourne by General Richard Mulcahy

Inniu, 9 Meitheamh, 29 Meán Fómhair 1967

The Irish Times, 21 August, 25 September 1967

Irish Press, 25 September 1967

Evening Press, 29 September 1967: Article by Cathal O'Shannon

The Kerryman, 30 September 1967

Feasta, Samhain 1967: 'Tomás Ághas', léacht chuimhneacháin le Seán Ó Lúing

The Kerryman, 28 September 1968: Ashe ancestry of Hollywood actor Gregory Peck

Other Printed Sources:

Ashbourne Memorial Book (Cumann Cabhartha Sean-Óglach Fhine Gall, n.d.)

Ashe, John, PP, *Annascaul Revisited and Reviewed* (Renown Press, Carnegie, n.d.)

Béaslaí, Piaras, *Michael Collins and the Making of a New Ireland*, 2 vols (Phoenix, Dublin, 1926)

Brennan, Robert, *Allegiance* (Browne & Nolan, Dublin, 1950)

Bromage, Mary C., *De Valera and the March of a Nation* (Hutchinson, London, 1956)

Devoy's Post Bag, 1871–1928, edited by William O'Brien and Desmond Ryan, 2 vols (C. J. Fallon, Dublin, 1948, 1953)

Foley, Patrick: *History of County Kerry* (Sealy, Bryers & Walker, Dublin, 1907)

Genealogists' Magazine, Vol. 6, No. 8, December 1933: 'Ashe Families of Ireland'

Goldring, Douglas, *Odd Man Out* (Chapman and Hall, London, 1935) – Chapter Three: 'The Funeral of Thomas Ashe' reprinted from *The Stranger in Ireland*, Dublin, 1918

Gwynn, Denis, *The Life of John Redmond* (G. G. Harrap and Co., London, 1932)

Gwynn, Stephen, *John Redmond's Last Years* (Arnold, London, 1919)

Healy, T. H., *Letters and Leaders of My Day*, 2 vols (Thornton Butterworth, London, 1928)

Intelligence Notes, 1913–16, edited by Breandán Mac Giolla Choille (Oifig an tSoláthair, Baile Átha Cliath, 1966)

King, Jeremiah, *History of County Kerry,* 3rd edn (London, n.d.)

Lynch, Diarmuid, *The IRB and the 1916 Insurrection,* edited by Florence O'Donoghue (Mercier Press, Cork, 1957)

Ó hAnnracháin, Peadar, *Fé Bhrat an Chonnartha* (Oifig an tSoláthair, Baile Átha Cliath, 1944)

Ó hAnnracháin, Peadar, *Mar Mhaireas É,* 2 iml., 1953, 1955

Ó Broin, León, *Dublin Castle and the 1916 Rising* (Helicon, Dublin, 1966)

O'Casey, Sean, *The Sacrifice of Thomas Ashe* (Fergus O'Connor, Dublin, 1918)

O'Casey, Sean, *Inishfallen Fare Thee Well* (Macmillan, London and New York, 1949)

O'Casey, Sean, 'Lament for Thomas Ashe', *The Kerry Annual,* 1953

Ó Lúing, Seán, *Art Ó Gríofa* (Sáirséal & Dill, Baile Átha Cliath, 1953)

Ó Muirthile, An tAth. Seosamh, *Tréithe Thomáis Ághas* (Clódhanna Teo, Baile Átha Cliath, 1967) – the best study in Irish of Thomas Ashe

Ó Snodaigh, Pádraig: *Comhghuaillithe na Réabhlóide 1913–16* (Clóchomhar, Baile Átha Cliath, 1966)

O'Sullivan, Thomas F., *Romantic Hidden Kerry* (The Kerryman, Tralee, 1931) – includes 'The Martyrdom of Tom Ashe', pp. 339–46

Phillips, W. Alison, *The Revolution in Ireland 1906–23* (Longmans, London, 1923)

Sinn Féin Rebellion Handbook, Easter 1916 (Weekly Irish Times, Dublin, 1917)

Reference Books, Directories, etc.:

Burke, John, *History of the Commoners of Great Britain and Ireland,* Vol. II (London, 1836)

Burke, John Bernard, *The General Armory of England, Scotland, Ireland and Wales* (London, 1884)

Burke, John and Burke, John Bernard, *The General Armory of England, Scotland and Ireland* (London, 1844)

De Hae, Risteárd, LL.D., *Clár Litridheacht na Nua-Ghaedhilge 1850–1936*, 3 iml. (Oifig an tSoláthair, Baile Átha Cliath, 1938–40)

Dictionary of National Biography

Hayes, Dr Richard J., *Manuscript Sources for the History of Irish Civilisation* (G. K. Hall & Co., Boston, 1965)

Irish National Teachers' Organisation, Annual Directory of: 1916, Thomas Ashe's membership of Dublin Central Association, p. 201

Imeachta na hArd-Fheise, 1910, 1911, 1912, 1913, 1914, 1915: Indicate Thomas Ashe's membership of Coiste Gnótha, attendance on committees, votes received, etc. See Nat. Library Catalogue s.v. Gaelic League, Annual Report 1894–1916. Ref. No. Ir 49162 g 1

MacLysaght, Edward, *Irish Families* (Hodges Figgis, Dublin, 1957)

O'Hart, John, *Irish Pedigrees*, 2 vols, 5th edn (Duffy, Dublin, 1892)

Thom's Irish Who's Who 1923 (Dublin, 1923)

Miscellaneous:

Special collections, exhibitions, etc.:

Ballads, broadsheets, etc., relating to Thomas Ashe

Correspondence with London re court martial of Thomas Ashe

Mater Hospital Chart re Thomas Ashe, 25 September 1917

Sketch plan of Battle of Ashbourne, by Thomas Ashe. Original in possession of Claire Bean Uí Éigeartaigh, Dublin

The Ashe exhibition in St Canice's School, Finglas, organised by Eoghan Mac Cárthaigh, NT, includes photostat of entry by Thomas Ashe in autograph book of J. J. Quilty, Kilrush; *Daily Mirror* photographs of funeral: photograph, with names, of Black Raven Band; two large plans of 5th Battalion's Easter Week campaign; instructions to Capt. R. Ua Colmáin from T. Ághas; photographs and articles of related interest

ACKNOWLEDGEMENTS

For assistance in the writing of this biography of Thomas Ashe, my gratitude goes first and foremost to his sister Nora Ághas. Not only did she allow me full access to Thomas Ashe's correspondence and other writings but she gave liberally of her time and attention to answer my queries and, in the course of many conversations, supplied me with much valuable information about her brother and family. Without her help it is only the plain truth to say that this book could not have been written. (As this book was in its final stages, Nora Ághas died. *Aoibhneas na bhFlaitheas dá hanam dílis Gaelach.*)

To Thomas Ashe's brother Gregory my thanks are no less due, as well for his store of recollections, inimitably told, as for his cheerful company on many journeys throughout North County Dublin to cover again, at first hand, his brother's familiar terrain, and meet surviving associates.

I am indebted to Thomas Ashe's nephews, Thomas Ashe of Ballsbridge, Dublin, and Pádraig Ashe of Straffan, County Kildare, for information and many helpful suggestions; while the patriot's cousin, Matthew Ashe, of Monastery Road, Clondalkin, readily placed at my service his extensive knowledge of the Ashe family history and genealogy.

It is with a special sense of gratitude that I place on record my debt to the late Pádraig Ághas, formerly of Dunbeg, County Clare, one-time member of Seanad Éireann, a cousin and boyhood companion of Thomas Ashe. I have drawn considerably on the detailed notes which he compiled for me and most of all I appreciated his friendly encouragement. *Ar dheis Dé go raibh a anam lách uasal.*

In Fingal, where Thomas Ashe spent his most active and creative years, his name is talismanic. I can testify to this. Among my happiest recollections are the hospitality and kindness with which I was received everywhere I went in that friendly region in quest of the tradition and personality of Thomas Ashe. Meantime three men of Lusk who helped me generously have passed to their reward – Joe Kelly, Paddy Doyle and Jack Devine. Peace to their gentle, courteous souls.

I should like to place on record my thanks to Richard Kelly, Tommy McArdle, Thomas Peppard, Christopher (Kit) Moran, James and Mrs Sheridan, Joe Carton, Thomas J. Brangan, Miss Katie Kelly, Miss Mary Monks, Mrs Kathleen Ward, Michael Sheehan (RIP), William O'Brien of Donabate, Anna Coleman and family, Andrew Keaveney, Bríd Ní Fhoghludha (Mrs Bríd S. Martin), Eibhlín Ní Chonchobhair, Piaras Béaslaí (RIP), an tOllamh Liam Ó Briain, Earnán de Blaghd, John Brunton, John McGallogly, General Richard Mulcahy, Pádraic Óg Ó Conaire, Dr Patrick McKenna, Peter Howley, Mrs Sheila Gunning (RIP), Father Maurice Boland, William Mullins, Con Casey, Senator Seán Brosnahan, Michael Kavanagh, Mrs Annie Finnegan; Pádraig Ó Snodaigh of the National Museum, who located letters and photographs for me; Tomás P. Ó Néill, Rev. Bro. Bernardine, FSC, formerly president of De La Salle College, Waterford, who copied for me the entries relating to Thomas Ashe in the college register and loaned me useful documents; Claire Bean Uí Éigeartaigh, Pádraig Ó Lúing, Captain Tadhg Mac Loinsigh, Frank Sloane, Rev. Bro. Brendan, FSC; Mrs Eileen O'Casey, for permission to reproduce her husband's poem; Bro. Allen of O'Connell Schools for generous help and full access to his splendid library; and Bro. Treacy of O'Connell Schools. To the National Library staff, for unfailing courtesy and attention, a special word of acknowledgement and praise is due. The Department of Education kindly supplied me with the dates of Thomas Ashe's teaching service, for which I am grateful. My best thanks are due to Finian Cuddihy, who read the manuscript and made many useful suggestions.

If any name or acknowledgement has been omitted it is due to inadvertence. Responsibility for any errors that may be found is solely mine.

For introducing a brief personal note may I ask the reader's indulgence. Growing up in West Kerry not many miles from Thomas Ashe's native place, I could not help but become sensible, not alone to the reverence and affection in which his memory was held, but to the impact, greater than words can convey, created in people's minds by his character, personality and sacrifice. The experience was lived silently but profoundly in the lives of those all around me. I can only say that the writing of this book, with all its imperfections, has been a task of tribute and dedication to one of life's noblest spirits.

Seán Ó Lúing

Teach Lorcain

Co. Átha Cliath

Eanáir 1970

INDEX